Early Spanish Lyric Poetry:
Essays and Selections

Dorothy Clotelle Clarke
UNIVERSITY OF CALIFORNIA, BERKELEY

Early Spanish Lyric Poetry:
Essays and Selections

1967

LAS AMERICAS PUBLISHING COMPANY

To

Professor S. Griswold Morley

INDICE:

"Yo, poseído a mi vez por la convicción de que la más poderosa creación individual va arrastrada por mil corrientes colectivas . . . " —R. Menéndez Pidal (ed. *Historia Troyana en prosa y verso*, pp. XIX-XX)

LYRIC POETRY AS A LITERARY GENRE

Mester de juglaría — mester de clerecía

Lyric poetry is one of the most complex forms of literature. It deals almost invariably with the abstract, even though its materials may ostensibly represent the concrete. It is essentially subjective though on the surface it may appear to be purely objective. It is a complexity of subtleties—there is more written *between* the lines than *on* the lines. It has constant appeal to the aesthetic sensibilities of the reader, who must be co-creator of the poem.

The term *lyric* is derived from *lyre,* the name of an ancient Greek stringed instrument of the harp class used especially in accompanying song and recitation. Webster's definition of *lyric* gives, in part, the following information: "1. Of or pertaining to a lyre or harp. 2. Suited to be sung to the lyre; appropriate for song; as, *lyric* poetry. *Lyric poetry,* whether actually sung or not, is generally composed in stanzas, and, as distinguished from *epic* and *dramatic poetry,* is expressive of the poet's feeling rather than of outward incident or events, and may take a special form, as ode, sonnet, hymn, roundel, or any of numerous verse schemes. 3. Musical; singing. 4. Characterized by

ardent, tender, or joyous emotion." All this information
is essential to the understanding of the nature of lyric
poetry. Other definitions and variations of the term *lyric*
may be given, but the above will serve the purpose of
introduction to the subject at hand.

It is well to keep in mind this basic idea of the word-
less (instrumental) *musical background* originally asso-
ciated with *lyric* poetry, for all good lyric poetry produces
in the sensitive reader the sensation of music. Musicality
is one of the basic elements of a lyric poem. The musical
effect is produced by the skilful use of such essential in-
gredients as sounds and silences and rhythm, by way of
synesthesia often through imagery or color symbolism, and
by a large variety of rhetorical devices, such as rime,
alliteration, onomatopoeia.

Spanish poetry, both lyric and epic, grew at least in
part directly from the song and the chant. The apparent
and so-called "irregularity" of the metrics of much of the
early Castilian poetry stems from the fact that the words,
often the only extant part of the song, carried the burden
of the melody, while serving as the major vehicle in convey-
ing the thought, against a harmonizing background of instrumental music that for the most part supplied the time
measure and some of the rhythm. When the instrumental
music accompaniment was discontinued, substitutions for
it had to be made by transferring the function of instrument
to the words of the composition. For the substitution Mediaeval poets generally chose either syllable count or marked
stress beat. Since the words of the composition were intimately and inseparably linked with the melody, they gradually assumed the function of the melody as the latter was
dropped formally from the recitation of the poem. Time
measure, rhythm, and melody thus all became dependent

on the words alone, and all are still clearly discernible in any good poem.

Music, then, is an essential ingredient of lyric poetry, and, in the dual nature imposed on it by circumstances, the poetry must furnish both instrumental and vocal harmonies and melodies. Like music, poetry is a temporal art, an art ruled by time, that is, and not by space.

Another important bit of historical information that should always be borne in mind when lyric poetry is being studied also may be traced to the ancient Greeks: that is, the concept of the close relationship between lyric poetry and the other arts and sciences. The following succinct definition of *Muses* from *The International Encyclopaedic Dictionary* will clarify this point: *"Greek and Roman Mythology:* One of nine nymphs or inferior divinities, distinguished as the peculiar protectresses of poetry, painting, rhetoric, music, and generally of the *belles lettres* and liberal arts. They were the daughters of Zeus and Mnemosyne (Memory). Originally there appear to have been only three of these divinities, and their names—Mneme, Melete, and Aoede, or Memory, Reflection, and Song—sufficiently show the nature of the faculties over which they were supposed to preside. According as the fine and liberal arts were cultivated and expanded, the province of each muse seems to have been more restricted; and additions were made to their number, which ultimately was fixed at nine, their names and respective functions being: Clio, the muse of History; Euterpe, of Lyric Poetry; Thalia, of Comedy and Idyllic Poetry; Melpomene, of Tragedy; Terpsichore, of Music and Dancing; Erato, of Erotic Poetry; Calliope, of Epic Poetry; Urania, of Astronomy; and Polyhymnia (or Polymnia), of singing and harmony. Helicon and the region round Parnassus was the favorite seat of the muses, where they were supposed under the presidency of Apollo, to be perpetually engaged in song and dance, and in elevating the style and conceptions of their favored votaries. Apollo, as patron and conductor of the muses, was named Musagetes, 'Leader of the Muses;' the same surname was also given to Hercules. They were generally represented as young, beautiful, and modest virgins, usually appareled in different attire, according to the arts and sciences over which they presided, and sometimes as dancing in a chorus, to intimate the near and indissoluble connection between the liberal arts and sciences. Their worship was universally established particularly in Greece, Thessaly, and Italy. No sacrifices were offered to them; but the poets invariably prefaced their compositions with a solemn invocation for the aid and inspiration of the muses." Note that the muses *served*, the poets *honored*.

This inter-relationship of the arts and sciences (bodies of knowledge) has been noted in more modern times also: to wit, Cervantes' statement in his commentary on the sagacious Licenciado Vidriera in the story whose title bears the name of its protagonist: "que admiraba y reverenciaba la ciencia de la poesía, porque encerraba en sí todas las demás ciencias: porque de todas se sirve, de todas se adorna, y pule y saca a luz sus maravillosas obras, con que llena el mundo de provecho, de deleite y de maravilla."

The point that must be made here is that there is no clear, or even subtle, line of demarkation setting lyric poetry off from other expressions of man's thoughts and emotions, for, in spite of recent efforts to write "pure poetry" (Valéry, Guillén), rhythm leads to dance or to mathematics (or stems from them); melodic words lead to song (or stem from it) or other form of music; language is a form of communication, which necessarily involves the sciences of psychology and of social and intellectual inter-course; the subject matter may have to do with philosophy, religion, history, geography, or any other conceivable body of knowledge—indeed, *must* be concerned with one or more of them.

Although lyric poetry generally preserves its identity sufficiently to be distinguished readily from any of its in-gredients, it does tend at times to merge almost indistin-guishably with other literary forms to produce what almost could be termed a hybrid—and so we hear of the lyric drama, the lyric novel, or lyric prose, and we think of such works as *Amadís de Gaula, La Diana, La vida es sueño,* Rubén Darío's prose poems, Azorín's or Valle-Inclán's novels or Agudiez's *Las tardes de Thérèze Lamarck.* In such works the fusion of two or more genres is complete and there is no way of separating the lyric element from the other elements of the work, and a piece can be categor-ized only by the predominance of one characteristic or an-other—or it may be impossible to tip the balance in favor of either, and we are left with a compromise term, such as *prose poem.* Some, like *La Vida es sueño* or *Las tardes de Thérèze Lamarck,* are so thoroughly permeated with lyricism that one hesitates to say merely *drama* or *novel.*

There are other works, however, of various genres, in which lyricism also appears, but rather sporadically and as a discrete element merely interspersed and at best grace-fully blending with surrounding non-lyric materials or smoothly introduced into and dismissed from them. A short passage in an epic poem or in the narrative of a saint's life or in a tale of adventure may suddenly give us a moment of lyric pleasure in the midst of an account of a military campaign, or relieve for us the suspense of a dra-matic incident. The passage may be the wife's prayer for the safety of her hero-husband, or the expression of the poet's joy or fervor as he undertakes the recounting of the Virgin's miracles, or the voicing of the adventurer's sudden nostalgia for the familiar sights of home and family. Whatever the subject, it and its treatment differ noticeably from the central subject and its treatment in mood and in stylistic artifice.

It is for such passages as those just mentioned, buried in long poetic works, usually narrative or expository, that one must search in order to be able to piece together the history of the early lyric tradition of Castilian literature. It is, indeed, not until the latter part of the fourteenth century that Castilian lyric poetry begins to appear as an independent genre and to show cohesiveness as a separate body, to have an observable independent development, and to give convincing evidence of an uninterrupted existence. The usual explanation offered for this circumstance, apparent or real, and the lack of early "school," is the simple one given in the Marqués de Santillana's *Prohemio e Carta al Condestable de Portugal* (1448 or 1449): "E después fallaron esta arte que mayor se llama, e el arte común, creo, en los reynos de Galiçia e Portugal, donde non es de dubdar que el exerçiçio destas sçiençias más que en ningunas otras regiones e provinçias de España se acostumbró, en tanto grado, que non ha mucho tiempo qualesquier dezidores e trovadores destas partes, agora fuessen castellanos, andaluçes o de la Extremadura, todas sus obras componían en lengua gallega o portuguesa. E aun destos es çierto resçebimos los nombres del arte asy como maestría mayor e menor, encadenados, lexaprén e mansobre." In other words, in lyric poetry in independent form the literary fad for two or three centuries had been to write not in one's native dialect, but in Galician-Portuguese and in the manner prescribed by the troubadours, many of whom had come on pilgrimage into the peninsula in order to visit Santiago de Compostela and thence had traveled into Galicia and Portugal, it seems, and there had become the masters of local poets, whose work attracted poets from other regions. Some troubadour influence on the Spanish poets came directly, of course, through the prolonged visits of certain Provençal poets to the various Spanish courts. As evidence of the influence of the Galician-Portuguese fad we have the voluminous collection of Alfonso X's *Cantigas de Santa María*, composed in the western dialect, though the Learned King's prose works are in Castilian. The influence of the Galician-Portuguese *cancioneiro* type of poetry on the Castilian is most pronounced in the works of the late fourteenth and fifteenth centuries, when Castilian lyric poetry finally became freed from its dependence on the longer, usually didactic, historic, or novelistic works. In these long works, fortunately, there has been preserved enough material to allow us to trace the development of the learned Castilian lyric in its earliest stages.

Although recent investigation has unearthed the *jarchas* (theme-germs, mostly on love, in Spanish written in Arabic or Hebrew characters, used as refrains to Arabic or Hebrew poems, and dating back as far as mid-eleventh century), these stray bits of lyric expression as yet merely indicate the early existence of a lyric tradition, particularly a popular one, but shed only faint light on the history of the development of early formal lyric expression, especially of the learned types. Except for their sporadic appearance, usually in longer works, they seem to have remained in the popular tradition waiting for artists of later periods to adapt them to learned use.

The major source of material for piecing together the

early history of Castilian lyric poetry is the long *mester de clerecía* (scholarly craft) type of poem in vogue in the Mediaeval period. To a lesser extent, the poems of the *mester de juglaría* (minstrels' craft) furnish some examples of poetic types important in the development of the lyric. Although in some poems the two crafts are merged, either deliberately or unintentionally, a general distinction between the two may be drawn in that the relatively simple *juglaría* poem, composed for popular entertainment, is usually narration and description concerned with epic subjects and is often though not always composed in chant form, the meter for which (described below, in the discussion on the *Poema de Mío Cid)* allows the poet some freedom in word-phrase length and riming, and places no restriction on sectioning; and the complex *clerecía* poem, written to be enjoyed and admired as *literature,* treats of almost innumerable topics and is highly restricted in metric form. No really clear line of demarkation exists between the two. The distinction lies primarily in the level of artistry and complexity, since the two crafts were fundamentally the same or at least similar, though Berceo, in claiming to be the *juglar* of Santo Domingo de Silos but the *trobador* of Saint Mary, would seem to differentiate by other means. The difference in literary refinement was apparently par-alleled by difference even in the quality of the instruments used by *juglares* and *escolares:*

Todos los estrumentos que usan los ioglares,
otros de maor preçio que usan escolares,
de todos auía hi tres o cuatro pares,
todos bien temprados por formar sus cantares. (*st.* 1971)
—*Libro de Alexandre*

That the *clerecía* mode was considered artistically superior to the *juglaría* is evident in an occasional humble or condescending remark:

> Sennores, hevos servido con poca sabidoría,
> por vos dar solás a todos fablévos en juglería (*st.* 1607)
> —Juan Ruiz, *Libro de buen amor*

or one perhaps intended as explanatory:

ca ovi grant taliento de seer tu ioglar (*st.* 775)
ca diçen que bien sueles pensar de tus ioglares (*st.* 776)
> —Berceo, *Vida de Santo Domingo de Silos*

or one of pride in accomplishment:

> Mester trago fermoso, non es de ioglaría,
> mester es sen peccado, ca es de clerezía,
> fablar curso rimado per la quaderna uía
> a sillauas cuntadas, ca es grant maestría. (*st.* 2)
> —*Libro de Alexandre*

The *mester de clerecía* poem is a multiple-genre, multiple-device discursive composition in which the poet moves rapidly from theme to theme to form a sort of pastiche or mosaic—or perhaps the term *medley* would more aptly describe the composition. Richness of texture resulting from variation of style, mood, topic, and genre, along with homogenization of the heterogeneous, was the mark of fine craftsmanship. Some poets, like Berceo, excelled in the concatenation method of structuring and in thematic interweaving, and so cultivated especially the art of digression and the art of modulation; some, like the poet of *El libro de Alexandre*, pressed the individual pieces mosaic-fashion against a general background, such as a biography; others, most notably Juan Ruiz, perfected the lamination process, which required skill in pattern matching and superimposition. The over-all pattern of a *mester de clerecía* poem perhaps was a reflection of the universe as envisioned by the Mediaeval contemplator: unity in diversity, harmony in miscellaneity.

Although such diverse types as prayer, debate, song, landscape or cityscape, dream or vision, allegory, confession, sermonet, apologue, aphorism, epigram, article of encyclopedic information, biography, compendium of Christian doctrine, historical narrative, to mention only a few, are clearly individualized in a *clerecía* poem, they are related and held together by logical transition or juxtaposition or by various other means, and each seems to fit into place in the whole as naturally as trees, rocks, water, and sky together fit into a landscape.

One of the obvious characteristics of the *mester de clerecía,* and one of its great innovations, is the versification. Syllable-count is the rule in verse measure, consonance in rime, and strict pattern in strophe structure. By far the most common form during the thirteenth and fourteenth centuries is the *cuaderna vía,* though other types are also employed, sometimes alone and sometimes in combination with the *cuaderna vía. Cuaderna vía* designates the metric pattern of a poem consisting of monorimed quatrains of *alejandrino* verse. The *alejandrino* (Alexandrine) is a line of two equivalent hemistichs of seven syllables each—that is, it is a line of seven-plus-seven syllables. The caesura between the two hemistichs is clearly marked in the rhythm of the verse. Syllables for each hemistich are counted as in any Spanish verse, that is, from the beginning to one (and one only) beyond the last stressed syllable whether or not a syllable actually is present after that stress. Two syllables following the final stress count as only one. The only modifications of the strict syllable-count rule in early verse were those allowed through limited use of elision and apocope and a very few other minor exceptions. Some stiffness resulted from the frequent hiatus and the rather extensive use of dieresis. Synaloepha and synaeresis were not in generally accepted use in the *cuaderna vía*, though they had begun creeping into it by the end of the fourteenth century, by which time the originally strict rules for verse measuring had been considerably modified.

Although most of the available texts for the period are not entirely reliable, it seems safe to say that syllable count was the rule in all *mester de clerecía* poetry until the *cuaderna vía* was replaced by the *copla de arte mayor*, and even there was generally employed though the counting system was slightly altered. In this respect the *mester de clerecía* had a tremendous influence on practically all subsequent Spanish poetry, since, with the exception of modern free verse and a very few minor forms, Spanish verse has been measured by the number of syllables it contains.

Verse-measure system was by no means the only contribution the *mester de clerecía* made to Spanish poetry. The *mester de clerecía* certainly did not, as is too often stated, cease to exist after the time of Pero López de Ayala and his *Rimado de Palacio*. Only the use of the *cuaderna vía* was discontinued after that time. The *mester de clerecía* as a mode still flourished and developed, though *coplas* of *arte mayor* or octosyllabic verse were substituted for the *cuaderna vía*. The *Decir a las siete virtudes*, Juan de Mena's *Laberinto de Fortuna*, and Jorge Manrique's *Coplas por la muerte de su padre* are only a few of the outstanding examples of *mester de clerecía* work in new verse form, but still characterized by the indispensable metabasis and metastasis. Gradually modified, of course, by new influences, it eventually lost much of its original identity, but traces of it can be found even after the *copla de arte mayor* is replaced by the Italianate hendecasyllable. It may well be said, in fine, that the *mester de clerecía* is the foundation —and certainly a solid one—of Spanish poetry.

Lyric poems of both the song and the recitative type are an integral part of the *mester de clerecía* amalgamation. Like the prayer or the confession or any of the other forms, each lyric poem (not including, of course, stray bits of lyric expression) is a completion in itself and follows specific rules of composition and style. Elaborate rhetorical embellishment, highly prized among the better *mester de clerecía* poets, shows direct influence of both ancient and contemporary rhetoricians, and especially of the style-conscious troubadours. Steady progression in the early development of Castilian lyric poetry can be observed in a study of the selections that can be made from the long poems, few and imperfectly preserved though they be, that have been left to us.

POEMA DE MIO CID

In order to find a passage of a length sufficient for the poet to develop a theme and to show his ability to sustain a mood, we will have to turn to what is considered Spain's earliest literary monument, the anonymous poem called the *Poema de Mío Cid* or *Cantar de Mío Cid,* written supposedly about 1140, but concerning exploits of some sixty years earlier. From this poem, generally classified as epic though it is not entirely epic in content, scholars have selected a somewhat independent passage that has sometimes been considered Spain's first lyric poem: the prayer offered by Jimena, wife of the hero, for her husband's safety, when he is about to depart for the frontier and certain battle:

Oración de Jimena

Passando ua la noch, viniendo la mannana.
Ellos mediados gallos pienssan de caualgar.
Tannen a matines a vna priessa tan grand. (*l.* 325)
Myo Cid e su mugier a la eglesia uan.
Echós' donna Ximena en los grados delant el altar,

rogando al Criador quanto ella meior sabe,
que a Mio Cid el Campeador que Dios le curiás' de mal:
   "Ya, sennor glorioso, padre que en çielo estás, (*l.* 330)
"ffezist çielo e tierra, el terçero el mar;
"ffezist estrelas e luna e el sol pora escalentar;
"prisist encarnaçión en sancta madre;
"en Belleém apareçist, commo fue tu voluntad.
"Pastores te glorifficaron, ouieron de alaudare. (*l.* 335)
"Tres reyes de Arabia te vinieron adorar:
"Melchor e Gaspar e Baltasar oro e tus e mirra
"te offreçieron, commo fue tu voluntad.
"Saluest a Jonás cuando cayó en la mar;
"saluest a Daniel con los leones en la mala cárcel; (*l.* 340)
"saluest dentro en Roma al sennor San Sabastián;
"saluest a Sancta Susanna del falso criminal.
"Por tierra andidiste XXXII annos, sennor spirital,
"mostrando los miraclos, por en auemos qué fablar;
"del agua fezist vino e de la piedra pan; (*l.* 345)
"resuçitest a Lázaro, ca fue tu voluntad.
"A los iudíos te dexeste prender do dizen monte Caluari.
"Pusiéronte en cruz por nombre en Golgotá,
"dos ladrones contigo, estos de sennas partes:
"el vno es en Parayso, ca el otro non entró alá. (*l.* 350)
"Estando en la cruz vertud fezist muy grant:
"Longinos era çiego que nunquas vio alguandre;
"diot' con la lança en el costado dont yxió la sangre;
"corrió la sangre por el astil ayuso, las manos se ouo de
                                    [vntar;

"alçólas arriba, lególas a la faz; (*l.* 355)
"abrió sos oios, cató a todas partes;
"en ti crouo al ora, por end es saluo de mal.
"En el monumento resuçitest e fust a los ynfiernos
"commo fue tu voluntad;
"quebranteste las puertas e saqueste los Padres Sanctos.
(*l.* 360)
"Tú eres Rey de los Reyes e de tod' el mundo Padre.
"A ti adoro e creo de toda voluntad,
"e ruego a San Peydro que me aiude a rogar
"por Myo Cid el Campeador, que Dios le curie de mal,
"quando oy nos partimos en vida nos faz iuntar." (*l.* 365)
    La oración fecha, la missa acabada la an.
Salieron de la eglesia, ya quieren caualgar.
El Cid a donna Ximena yuala abraçar.
Donna Ximena al Cid la mano l' va besar,
lorando de los oios que non sabe qué se far; (*l.* 370)
e él a las ninnas tornólas a catar:
"A Dios uos acomiendo, fijas, e al padre spirital.
"Agora nos partimos, Dios sabe el aiuntar."
Lorando de los oios que non viestes atal,
así s' parten vnos d' otros commo la vnna de la carne.
(*l.* 375)

Poetic prayers similar to this one in structure and style were common in the Middle Ages. Prayers of the same type are found, for example, in the eleventh-century Old French *Chanson de Roland.*

If we analyze this selection even summarily, we may

hesitate to agree with those who would consider it lyric, for it is hardly more than an enumeration of accounts and stories from religious sources, and yet it does express, in rhythmic language, the tremendous emotion felt by Jimena at a dramatic moment in her life. She attempts to compress all her religious instruction into one offering of prayer on behalf of her husband. Chronological sequence cannot be expected of her because she undoubtedly was not taught these things in chronological order, since she probably learned the stories as independent lessons or stories, and because her emotional state is not conducive to logic, to chronological or any other logical sequence. If we search deeper into the poem we will find much of Jimena's character tacitly revealed: her complete selflessness in riveting her whole attention on God and on the safety of her husband, her generosity and gentleness in her attitude toward what is usually considered evil: "two thieves with you, one on each side; one is in paradise, *for the other did not enter there*," her deep faith, her sincerity and earnestness, her humility, her attempt to talk to God about things that concern *Him*, that is, matters of mutual understanding, though she is so lacking in presumptuousness that she calls upon Saint Peter to plead her cause for her. As he depicts her here before the altar, the poet undoubtedly is vicariously experiencing Jimena's anxieties and sharing her attitudes.

In general structure this selection is clearly a fore-runner in Spanish literature not only of the poetic prayer popular throughout the Mediaeval period but also of a common late Mediaeval *cancionero* type of poem based on the theme-with-variations technique, the variations being presented in apparently random order—a famous example is fifteenth-century Jorge Manrique's *Coplas por la muerte de su padre*—and in a way, perhaps, even foreshadows the sonnet technique. It exemplifies, of course, in simple fashion, the basic form of lyric poems in general: thematic development via variation. The central theme in our selection is the omnipotence of God.

As for the general characteristics of the style of the *Poema de Mío Cid* as a whole, some of the most readily noticeable are: extreme directness, simplicity and consequent lack of artificiality, concentration on character portrayal through expression of natural emotions, realism. The work is largely a series of simple statements of fact generally enumerated in chronological order and rarely adorned, and only occasionally accompanied by a statement of opinion. The poet had not learned the devices of amplification and circumlocution, and so moved constantly on without dallying. The poem has two characteristics common to all great works of literature: forward movement and significant detail. The poet's technique is largely a pictorial and a cinematographic one, since the content of the work could be almost entirely depicted in a series of drawings or tableaux—there is a complete scene often in each hemistich, almost invariably at least in each line or at most two lines. The figures within each scene are clear and well balanced. The drawings are usually two-dimensional and unframed. This unique structure of line after line and line upon line reminds one of bricks stacked against bricks, without mortar and in such a way that the structure is held together by pressure. There is general and almost conspicuous lack of the use of graduated perspective, and even the panorama is so rare that its appearance is striking:

A tan grand ondra ellas a Valençia entrauan,
adelinó Myo Cid con ellas al alcáçar:
alá las subié en el más alto logar.

Oios velidos catan a todas partes,
miran Valençia, cómmo iaze la çibdad,
e del otra parte a oio han el mar.
Miran la huerta, espessa es e grand;
alçan las manos pora Dios rogar. (*ll.* 1610-1617)

The neutral color one must suppose as predominating is seldom relieved by colors chosen from the spectrum or even by pure white, though gold and silver do hold some importance both practical and aesthetic. The poet has an unusually fine sense of motion and direction. He would have been an excellent candid-camera photographer, and had he been a movie camera-man he could well have specialized in dramatic poses and situations, in pageantry, and especially in close-ups. Typical passages are:

Myo Cid Ruy Díaz por Burgos entraua.
En su conpanna LX pendones leuaua.
Exienlo ver mugieres e uarones:
burgeses e burgesas por las finiestras son puestos,
plorando de los oios, tanto auyén el dolor.
De las sus bocas todos dizían una razón:
"¡Dios, qué buen vassalo si ouiesse buen sennor!" (*ll.* 15-20)

D' ella part e d' ella pora las vistas se adobauan.
¿Quién vio por Castiella tanta mula preçiada,
e tanto palafré que bien anda,
cauallos gruessos e corredores sin falla,
tanto buen pendón meter en buenas astas,
escudos boclados con oro e con plata,
Mantos e pielles e buenos çendales d' Adria? (*ll.* 1966-1972)

In the following selection note particularly the "slow-motion" detailed poses in preparation for a pageant-like scene:

No s' detiene por nada el que en buen ora naçió. (*l.* 3085)
Calças de buen panno en sus camas metió,
sobr' ellas vnos çapatos que a grant huebra son.
Vistió camisa de rançal tan blanca commo el sol,
con oro e con plata todas las presas son,
al puno bien están ca él se lo mandó; (*l.* 3090)
sobr' ella vn brial primo de çiclatón,
obrado es con oro, pareçen por o son;
sobr' esto vna piel vermeia, las bandas d' oro son;
siempre la viste Myo Cid el Campeador.
Vna cofia sobre los pelos d' un escarín de pro, (*l.* 3095)
con oro es obrada, fecha por razón
que non le contalassen los pelos al buen Cid Canpeador.
La barba avié luenga, e prísola con el cordón:
por tal lo faze esto que recabdar quiere todo lo suyo.
Desuso cubrió vn manto que es de grant valor, (*l.* 3100)
en él abríen que ver quantos que y son.

The poet keeps the reader within touching distance of every character, group, or situation. He is a master in his manipulation of single-plane space. His battle scenes seem life-size although they are compressed into scene space not commensurately larger than the canvas on which we see Jimena kneeling on the gradins before the altar, or the area in which we see the nail against the flesh.

Although in sense-appeal in the *Cantar de Mío Cid* the

visual clearly predominates, the auditory and the tactile are by no means neglected (note the oft-repeated *cavalgar* and *aguijar*, riding and spurring, for example), and even the olfactory and the gustatory contribute realistic effects at times (example below).

The poet has a somewhat dramatic sense in handling both time and space. We feel, for example, the urging of time against the obstacle of distance in the early part of the poem when the Cid's term of grace within Alfonso's domain is about to expire, and time continues to be of importance in battle and in court, while space to be traversed, or to be contained in one picture, is carefully measured. The poet is conscious, too, of time of day, and he skilfully controls tempo, and with it emotion, by employing several means of reining in the onward plunge of the narrative: within the line he generally uses one of the hemistichs as either complement or supplement of the other, so that there is a general alternation of stress and relaxation; within the *laisse* he sometimes places series of nouns, or moves the attention from a dramatic situation to a concrete object; within the *cantar* he varies the length of the *laisses* and the subject from *laisse* to *laisse;* and of course he frequently centers attention on character instead of action, and alternates narrative and dialogue. For the most part, however, the poet merely equates time with chronological order, and space with itinerary. Chronology for the poem as a whole keeps the events in logical order and at the same time acts as a time-background upon which characters with their events and their motions and directions are superimposed, as if chronology as well as space were the canvas on which the figures were drawn—much in the same manner as time measure in the metric structure acts as a background for rhythm.

Attention to stylistic detail is one of the poet's assets. Enumeration, series, and accumulation are among his favourite devices, and with them, of course, doublets and parallelism, the latter occasionally marked by anaphora (*e.g.*, *Saluest . . . saluest . . . saluest . . .* , in Jimena's prayer):

Tanta gruessa mula e tanto palafré de sazón,
tanta buena arma, e tanto buen cauallo coredor,
tanta buena capa e mantos e pelliçones (*ll.* 1988-1990)

Repeated strict parallelism sometimes, though rarely, gives way to chiasmus:

Tú eres Rey de los Reyes e de tod' el mundo Padre. (*l.* 361)
Es' día es passado, e entrada es la noch. (*l.* 2062)

The remarkable economy of words that so enriches the style of the poem can contribute poignancy to similes and metaphors in the compression of expression of emotion:

así s' parten vnos d' otros commo la vnna de la carne (*l.* 375)
Cuemo la vnna de la carne ellos partidos son (*l.* 2643)
Partiéronsele las tellas de dentro de los coraçones (*l.* 2786)
"¿A quém descubriestes las telas del coraçon?" (*l.* 3261)

or produce a sudden thrill at a flash of beauty:

Sacaron las espadas Colada e Tizón,
pusiéronlas en mano del rey so sennor;
saca las espadas e relumbra toda la cort,
las maçanas e los arriazes todo d' oro son;

marauíllanse d' ellas todos los omnes buenos de la cort.
(*ll.* 3176-3180)
Martín Antolínez mano metió al espada,
relumbra tod' el campo, tanto es limpia e clara.
(*ll.* 3649-3650)

Although dawn breaks and night falls briefly, and primarily for practical purposes only, not aesthetic, and the
poet is interested mainly in time value, the periodic change
of light furnishes a slight poetic atmosphere to the realistic
scenes and events, while at the same time it expresses the
poet's preoccupation with the urging of time:

Antes seré connusco que el sol quiera rayar. (*l.* 231)

Apriessa cantan los gallos e quieren quebrar albores
quando legó a San Pero el buen Campeador.
El abbat don Sancho, christiano del Criador,
rezaua los matines a buelta de los albores. (*ll.* 235-238)

Passando ua la noch, viniendo la mannana (*l.* 323)

Avn era de día, non era puesto el sol (*l.* 416)

Ya quiebran los albores e vinié la mannana;
ixié el sol, ¡Dios, qué fermoso apuntaua! (*ll.* 456-457)

Otro día mannana el sol querié apuntar (*l.* 682)

Passada es la noche, venida es la mannana (*l.* 1541)

Ffincadas son las tiendas e pareçen los aluores;
a vna grand priessa tanién los atamores. (*ll.* 1658-1659)

El día salido e la noch entrada es. (*l.* 1700)

Es' día es passado, e entrada es la noch.
Otro día mannana claro salié el sol. (*ll*. 2062-2063)

De noche belaron las armas e rogaron al Criador.
Troçida es la noche, ya quiebran los albores. (*ll*. 3545-3546)

On the whole, however, these stray traces of lyricism are embryonic and fleeting. The poet has not acquired the technical means or the desire of expanding on a detail or of sustaining a mood. In this respect, except for Jimena's prayer, he has hardly reached the equivalent of the *jarcha* stage of lyric development. During the moments that he does stray slightly from the telling of his tale, he touches upon themes that later lyric poets will develop: religious devotion, space, time, light and shadow, dream, landscape. It is interesting to note in this matter that he even has the beginning of a description of a royal tent, the subject of a well-known lengthy description in the *Libro de Alexandre*. Here the Cid's poet gives us the miniature:

¡Tanta tienda preçiada e tanto tendal obrado
que a ganado Myo Cid con todos sus vassallos! (*l*. 1785)
La tienda del rey de Marruecos, que de las otras es cabo,
dos tendales la sufren, con oro son labrados.
Mandó Myo Cid Ruy Díaz que fita sovisse la tienda,
e non la tolliesse d' ent christiano:
"Tal tienda commo ésta, que de Maruecos es passada,
                                        (*l*. 1790)
"enbiarla quiero a Alfonsso el Castellano,
"que crouiesse sos nueuas de Myo Cid que auié algo."

Although the *Poema de Mío Cid* is largely epic and

novelistic in nature and belongs to the *mester de juglaría,* it shows the beginnings of a tendency to fuse poetic genres, and thus indicates a relationship with the *mester de clerecía,* which was introduced into Spanish literature at the beginning of the thirteenth century. Jimena's prayer, for example, is similar in both content and stylistic pattern to the many, many prayers scattered through the poetry of the next two centuries or more. The Cid's vision of the Angel Gabriel, during the hero's last night in Castile, is a foreglimpse of the "dream" and "vision" poetry to become popular throughout the Mediaeval period and even into modern times:

> Vn suenno prisso dulçe, tan bien se adurmió. (*l.* 405)
> El ángel Gabriel a él vino en suenno:
> "Caualgad, Cid el buen Campeador, ca nunqua
> "en tan buen punto caualgó varón;
> "mientra que visquiériedes bien se fará lo to."
> Quando despertó el Cid la cara se sanctigó; (*l.* 410)
> Sinaua la cara, a Dios se acomendó.
> Mucho era pagado del suenno que a sonnado.

The poetic debate, which will figure as a major poetic genre in the following centuries is already well developed in the court and the challenge scenes (*ll.* 3251-3392) of the third *cantar.* The sequence ends thus:

> Destos amos la razón fincó.
> Azur Gonçález entraua por el palaçio,
> manto armiño e vn brial rastrando; (*l.* 3375)
> vermeio viene, ca era almorzado.

En lo que fabló avié poco recabdo:
"¡Hya varones! ¿quién vio nunca tal mal?
"¿Quién nos daríe nueuas de Myo Cid el de Biuar?
"¡Ffuesse a Río d' Ouirna los molinos picar, (*l.* 3380)
"e prender maquilas commo lo suele far!
"¿Qui l' daríe con los de Carrión a casar?"
Essora Muno Gustioz en pie se leuantó:
"¡Cala, aleuoso, malo e traydor!
"Antes almuerzas que vayas a oración; (*l.* 3385
"A los que das paz, fártaslos aderredor.
"Non dizes verdad amigo ni ha sennor,
"ffalso a todos e más al Criador.
"En tu amistad non quiero aver ración.
"Ffazértelo dezir que tal eres qual digo yo." (*l.* 3390)
Dixo el rey Alfonsso: "¡Calle ya esta razón;
"los que an rebtado lidiarán, sin salue Dios!"

The *Poema de Mío Cid* is, in fine, the earliest known Spanish antecedent of the *mester de clerecía,* the works of which will be our richest source of lyric poetry of the following two centuries and more. Although the *clerecía* aspects of the *Poema del Cid* decidedly are minor and embryonic in comparison with the *juglaría* aspects, they are the most important evidence we have of interest in the so-called "learned" poetry that constitutes the foundation for practically all subsequent Spanish poetry.

In consideration of such factors in the *Poema de Mío Cid* as the general design, the monorimed *laisses,* the line roughly resembling the French Alexandrine, we may conclude that the poet undoubtedly was influenced by foreign models, particularly the French epic. Undoubtedly, as far as Castilian is concerned, he was relatively unhampered by force of poetic convention in his own tongue and therefore was free to shape his own lines, which he freely did, even though he was restricted by the scarcity of materials, including vocabulary, in his own language. This circumstance helps to explain why, aside from hardly more than the minimum of particles, his vocabulary consists largely of nouns and verbs.

Although several theories have been advanced in an attempt to explain the metric structure of the *Poema del Cid,* which seems to have been a perennial puzzle to scholars, it seems logical that, given the time of its writing, the lack of stylistic complexities in other phases of its composition, and especially the fact that this poem was written or in some way composed to be recited to an unsophisticated and generally illiterate audience, and almost certainly was intended for either chanting or singing and therefore probably was accompanied by instrumental music of some sort, however primitive, we should seek the simplest possible explanation of the verse pattern. With a little imagination we can hear and keep time to the rhythmic strumming of some stringed instrument in the background while we read and listen to the words of the poem. It is by no means necessary to fall into a sing-song rhythm while reading the lines aloud, but (and this is the important point) it is entirely possible to do so. Not only is it possible, but, if one scholar's experience in reading approximately half the poem aloud and with no preconceived notion of what the meter should be can be used as a criterion, it can be said that a certain definite and set pattern emerges, predominates, and finally imposes itself on all the lines. The verse pattern is simplicity itself. It has three constants: equivalence of time per line, hemistich pause, and four obligatory heavy-stress beats spaced with approximate regularity and varying in intensity according to relative position in the line. Its principal variables are the number of non-obligatory beats and pauses (either silences or prolongations of vowels) and the number of syllables per line. It is, in short, a four-stress-beat mid-divided line in which the rhythmic beat pattern has been superimposed on a time measure. The term *equivalence* in the measure of the line means *not necessarily exactly equal,* since the line, like any line of poetry, may be in actuality lengthened or shortened for *rhetorical* (but not for *metric)* reasons: for instance, the tempo of a passage may be quickened at a dramatic point, or slackened in a purely descriptive or expository passage, and so change the length of time normally devoted to the recitation of a verse, but the metric pattern remains the same.

Almost invariably in the *Poema de Mío Cid* one complete phrase is found in each hemistich—that is, one rhetorical unit coincides with one time unit—and each phrase ends with an important word—that is, a word containing both rhetorical stress on the last word and a marked rhythmic stress on either the last or the next-to-the last syllable, rarely on the second-to-the-last. (The terms for these types of endings are, respectively, oxytonic *(agudo,a-),* paroxytonic *(llano,-a* or *grave),* proparoxytonic *(esdrújulo-a).*

Theoretically the two hemistichs are alike. For rhetorical and purely phychological reasons, however, they cannot so be, for the weight of the narrative, or whatever content, normally is expected to be on the second hemistich. The most forceful word *position* in the line is the rime word position because the final stress beat is the rhythmic climax and because the reader is listening forward to the rime and anticipating a major pause, the pause between lines, which is usually called verse-end pause. No poet is obliged to observe the weight-position rule, or any other rule, slavishly, and in the *Poema de Mío Cid* we find frequently that the weight is shifted to the first hemistich.

A glance at any passage will reveal that the rime employed in the *Poema de Mío Cid* is assonance. Assonance *(asonancia)* is the riming of vowels without regard for the consonants. The riming of both vowels and consonants, as in most English rime, may conveniently be called consonance *(consonancia)*. In assonance the stressed vowels in the final or riming words must be identical, and last vowels of riming paroxytones or proparoxytones must likewise be identical with each other. Paragogic *e* may be added. The assonance remains unchanged throughout a *laisse*. A *laisse*, roughly equivalent to a paragraph in prose, is a section consisting of any number of lines; it may have only a very few lines or may continue for pages. The length of the *laisses* fluctuates within the poem.

The effect of the meter of the *Poema de Mío Cid* is one of ease, of a certain informality and relative freedom, and of strength of movement. The sturdy long-stride rhythm and the widely spaced and easily attained rimes allow the poet to move on with his tale without the hampering that a more restrictive measure system would cause. It is a heavy-duty meter appropriate for the recounting of rough and massive physical action.

RAZON DE AMOR

Qui triste tiene su coraçon
benga oyr esta razón.
Odrá razón acabada,
feyta d' amor e bien rymada.
Vn escolar la rrimó (*l.* 5)
que siempre duenas amó;
mas siempre ouo tryança
en Alemania y en Françia,
moró mucho en Lombardía
pora prender cortesía. (*l.* 10)
En el mes d' abril, después yantar,
estaua so un oliuar.
Entre çimas d' un mançanar
un uaso de plata ui estar.
Pleno era d' un claro uino (*l.* 15)
que era uermejo e fino.
Cubierto era de tal mesura
no lo tocás' la calentura.
Vna duena lo y eua puesto,

que era senora del uerto, (*l.* 20)
que quan su amigo uiniese,
d' aquel uino a beuer le diesse.
Quı de tal uino ouiesse
en la mana quan comiesse,
e dello ouiesse cada día, (*l.* 25)
nuncas más enfermarya.
Arriba del mançanar
otro uaso ui estar.
Pleno era d' un agua fryda
que en el mançanar se naçía. (*l.* 30)
Beuiera d' ela de grado,
mas oui miedo que era encantado.
Sobre un prado pus' mi tiesta
que no m' fiziese mal la siesta.
Partí de mí las uistiduras (*l.* 35)
que no m' fiziés' mal la calentura.
Plegém' a una fuente perenal,
nunca fue omne que uies' tall.
Tan grant uirtud en sí auía
que de la frydor que d' í yxía, (*l.* 40)
.C. pasadas a derredor
non sintryades la calor.
Todas yeruas que bien olién
la fuent çerca sí las tenié:
y es la saluia, y sson as rrosas, (*l.* 45)
y el liryo e las uiolas.
Otras tantas yeruas y auía,

que sol' nombra no las sabría;
mas ell olor que d' í yxía
a omne muerto rressuçitarya. (*l.* 50)
Prys' del agua un bocado
e fuy todo esfryado.
En mi mano prys' una flor,
sabet, non toda la peyor,
e quis' cantar de fin amor; (*l.* 55)
mas ui uenir una doncela,
pues naçí non ui tan bella:
blanca era e bermeia,
cabelos cortos sobr' ell oreia,
fruente blanca e loçana, (*l.* 60)
cara fresca como maçana,
naryz egual e dreyta,
nunca uiestes tan bien feyta,
oios negros e rridientes,
boca a rrazón e blancos dientes, (*l.* 65)
labros uermeios, non muy delgados,
por uerdat bien mesurados,
por la çentura delgada,
bien estant e mesurada;
el manto e su brial (*l.* 70)
de xamet era, que non d' al;
vn sombrero tien' en la tiesta
que no la fiziese mal la siesta;
vnas luuas tien' en la mano,
sabet, non ie las dio uilano. (*l.* 75)

D' las flores uiene tomando,
en alta uoz d' amor cantando,
e deçía: "¡Ay, meu amigo,
"si me ueré yamás contigo!
"Amét' sempre e amaré (*l.* 80)
"quanto que biua seré.
"Porque eres escolar,
"quis quiere te deuría más amar.
"Nunqua odí de homne deçir
"que tanta bona manera ouo en sí. (*l.* 85)
"Más amaría contigo estar
"que toda Espana mandar.
"Mas d' una cosa so cuitada:
"é miedo de seder enganada,
"que dizen que otra dona, (*l.* 90)
"cortesa e bela e bona,
"te quiere tan gran ben,
"por ti pierde su sen,
"e por eso é pauor
"que a ésa quieras meior; (*l.* 95)
"mas s' io te uies' una uegada,
"a plan me queryés por amada."
Quant la mía senor esto dizía,
sabet, a mí non uidía,
pero sé que no me conoçía, (*l.* 100)
que de mí non foyrya.
Yo non fiz aquí como uilano;
leuém' e prisla por la mano.

Junniemos amos en par
e posamos so ell oliuar. (*l.* 105)
Dixle yo: "Dezit, la mía senor,
"si ssupiestes nunca d' amor."
Diz ella: "A plan, con grant amor ando,
"mas non connozco mi amado;
"pero dizem' un su mesaiero (*l.* 110)
"qu' es clérygo e non caualero,
"sabe muio de trobar,
"de leyer e de cantar;
"dizem' que es de buenas yentes,
"mancebo barua punnientes." (*l.* 115)
—"Por Dios, que digades, la mía senor,
"¿qué donas tenedes por la su amor?"
—"Estas luuas y es' capiello,
"est' oral y est' aniello
"enbió a mí es' meu amigo, (*l.* 120)
"que por la su amor trayo conmigo."
Yo connoçí luego las alfayas
que yo ie las auía enbiadas.
Ela connoçió una mi cinta man a mano,
qu' ela la fiziera con la su mano. (*l.* 125)
Toliós' el manto de los onbros,
besóme la boca e por los oios;
tan gran sabor de mí auía,
sol' fablar non me podía.
"¡Dios Senor, a ti loado (*l.* 130)
"quant conozco meu amado!

"Agora e tod' bien comigo
"quant conozco meo amigo!"
Vna grant pieça alí estando,
de nuestro amor ementando, (*l.* 135)
ela m' dixo: "El mío senor,
"ora m' serya de tornar,
"si a uos non fuese en pesar."
Yo l' dix': "Yt, la mía senor,
"pues que yr queredes, (*l.* 140)
"mas de mi amor pensat, fe que deuedes."
Ela m' dixo: "Bien seguro seyt de mi amor:
"no uos camiaré por un enperador."
La mía senor se ua priuado;
dexa a mí desconortado. (*l.* 145)
Que que la ui fuera del uerto,
por poco non fuy muerto.
Por uerdat quisieram' adormir,
mas una palomela ui,
tan blanca era como la nieu del puerto, (*l.* 150)
uolando uiene por medio del uerto.
Un cascauielo dorado
tray al pie atado.
En la fuent quiso entrar;
quando a mí uido estar (*l.* 155)
entrós' en el malgranar
Quando en el uaso fue entrada,
e fue toda bien esfryada,
ela que quiso exir festino,

uertiós' el agua sobr' el vino. (*l.* 160)
Aquís' copiença a denostar
el uino, y el agua a malinar.

The second part of the modern editors' title of the poem, which bears no title in the extant manuscript, is *con los denuestos del agua y del vino,* reminiscent of the Provençal *debate.* The wine is angry because the water has spoiled it. The water reminds the wine that he, the latter, muddles man's mind. The wine reminds water that he has given her a beautiful red color. Water retorts that she has nourished the vine on which he grew. Wine answers that he fortifies men and animates the table. Water responds that wine does nothing but inebriate. Wine pontificates that he is used in holy communion. Water states that she is used for baptism. The humor is lively:

Ell agua iaze muerta rridiendo
de lo qu' el uino está diziendo

"En una blanca paret V kandelas ponet,
"e si el beudo non dixiere que son .c.
"de cuanto digo de todo miento."

Even a bit of sarcasm foreshadowing the satires of the following century is present: to wine are assigned powers similar to those later attributed by Juan Ruiz to money: to make the blind see, the lame run, the mute speak, and the sick sing. The piece is one of the best examples of the *debate,* a poetic form that was popular for some three centuries or more.

The early thirteenth-century *Razón de amor* introduces to Castilian literature the theme of courtly love. Courtly love is a literary convention resembling a religious cult. It seems to have originated in Provence late in the eleventh or early in the twelfth century under the influence of certain Hispano-Arabic poetry. Formal and elaborate rules governing love were codified by Andreas Capellanus in his treatise *De arte honeste amandi,* written at the request of Eleanor of Aquitaine (1122?-1204). Some of the important and most interesting aspects of the code were the idealization of the lady, who was the object of the lover's constant devotion, the absolute faithfulness of the lover, his veneration of his lady, his gallantry toward her at all times, and the ennobling power of idealistic love *(fin' amors).* The troubadour-lover expressed his devotion in poetry set to music, and the poetry itself followed specific patterns. The lady ordinarily remained somewhat aloof, since she was frequently married to someone other than her troubadour-lover. Her aloofness or disdain or her absence necessarily caused her lover grief, pain, and even spells of fainting. A glance or a smile from her, or even her mere presence, gives him unbounded joy. Otis H. Green, in the chapter on courtly love in Spanish literature, in his *Spain and the Western Tradition,* lists other aspects of courtly love, including that of suffering for its own sake, that of the lady's superiority to her lover because she is "desired and not desiring," that of desire's being the essence of love, that of the lover's longing for perfection.

The lady may be someone with whom the troubadour is acquainted—prosaically enough, she was not infrequently the wife of his overlord, who, it would seem, in order to increase his wife's and therefore his own prestige, subsidized the troubadour for writing his love lyrics in her praise and honor. On the other hand, the troubadour's love (and lyrics) may be devoted to a lady whom he has never seen, but whose fame for beauty and gentleness has reached him. The worship of the lady of his dreams seems sometimes to have fused with the worship of the Virgin Mary, so that occasionally, when a poet speaks of a "distant love," it is difficult to determine whether he has in mind a living and earthly being or the Virgin Mary, especially since one of the rules of courtly love was to conceal the real name of the beloved, bestowing upon her a poetic name *(senhal)* of his own invention. Courtly love and mysticism thus inspire identical expression.

All the above discussion applies to the ideal troubadour —that is, to the one who follows the rules. The coin has another side, however, a back side, which is somewhat different from the face, and so we may have occasion to find that some devoted lovers become disgruntled with their ladies and sing a different song altogether.

An excellent summary of the rules and practices of troubadour love is that found in H. J. Chaytor's *The Troubadours:*

"Thus there was a service of love as there was a service of vassalage, and the lover stood to his lady in a position analogous to that of the vassal to his overlord. He attained this position only by stages; 'there are four stages in love: the first is that of aspirant *(fegnedor)*, the second that of suppliant *(precador)*, the third that of recognised suitor *(entendedor)* and the fourth that of accepted lover *(drut)*.' The lover was formally installed as such by the lady, took an oath of fidelity to her and received a kiss to seal it, a ring or some other personal possession. For practical purposes the contract merely implied that the lady was prepared to receive the troubadour's homage in poetry and to be the subject of his song. As secrecy was a

duty incumbent upon the troubadour, he usually referred
to the lady by a pseudonym *(senhal);* naturally, the lady's
reputation was increased if her attraction for a famous
troubadour was known, and the *senhal* was no doubt an
open secret at times. How far or how often the bounds of
his formal and conventional relationship were transgressed
is impossible to say; 'en somme, assez immoral' is the judgment of Gaston Paris upon the society of the age, and is
confirmed by expressions of desire occurring from time to
time in various troubadours, which cannot be interpreted
as the outcome of a merely conventional or 'platonic' devotion. In the troubadour biographies the substratum of historical truth is so overlaid by fiction, that little reliable
evidence upon the point can be drawn from this source.

"However, transgression was probably exceptional.
The idea of troubadour love was intellectual rather than
emotional; love was an art, restricted, like poetry, by formal rules; the terms 'love' and 'poetry' were identified, and
the fourteenth century treatise which summarises the prin-
ciples of grammar and metre bore the title *Leys d'Amors,*
the Laws of Love. The pathology of the emotion was studied; it was treated from a psychological standpoint and a
technical vocabulary came into use, for which it is often
impossible to find English equivalents. The first effect of
love is to produce a mental exaltation, a desire to live a
life worthy of the beloved lady and redounding to her
praise, an inspiring stimulus known as *joi* or *joi d'amor*
(amor in Provençal is usually feminine). Other virtues are
produced by the influence of this affection: the lover must
have *valor,* that is, he must be worthy of his lady; this
worth implies the possession of *cortesia,* pleasure in the
pleasure of another and the desire to please; this quality

is acquired by the observance of *mesura,* wisdom and self-restraint in word and deed.

"The poetry which expresses such a state of mind is usually idealised and pictures the relationship rather as it might have been than as it was. The troubadour who knew his business would begin with praises of his beloved; she is physically and morally perfect, her beauty illuminates the night, her presence heals the sick, cheers the sad, makes the boor courteous and so forth. For her the singer's love and devotion is infinite: separation from her would be worse than death; her death would leave the world cheerless, and to her he owes any thoughts of good or beauty that he may have. It is only because he loves her that he can sing. Hence he would rather suffer any pain or punishment at her hands than receive the highest favours from another. The effects of this love are obvious in his person. His voice quavers with supreme delight or breaks in dark despair; he sighs and weeps and wakes at night to think of the one subject of contemplation. Waves of heat and cold pass over him, and even when he prays, her image is before his eyes. This passion has transformed his nature: he is a better and stronger man than ever before, ready to forgive his enemies and to undergo any physical privations; winter is to him as the cheerful spring, ice and snow as soft lawns and flowery meads. Yet, if unrequited, his passion may destroy him; he loses his self-control, does not hear when he is addressed, cannot eat or sleep, grows thin and feeble, and is sinking slowly to an early tomb. Even so, he does not regret his love, though it lead to suffering and death; his passion grows ever stronger, for it is ever supported by hope. But if his hopes are realised, he will owe everything to the gracious favour of his lady, for his own merits can avail nothing. Sometimes he is not prepared for such complete self-renunciation; he reproaches his lady for her coldness, complains that she has led him on by a show of kindness, has deceived him and will be the cause of his death; or his patience is at an end, he will live in spite of her and try his fortune elsewhere.

"Such, in very general terms, is the course that might be followed in developing a well-worn theme, on which many variations are possible. The most common form of introduction is a reference to the spring or winter, and to the influence of the seasons upon the poet's frame of mind or the desire of the lady or of his patron for a song. In song the poet seeks consolation for his miseries or hopes to increase the renown of his lady. As will be seen in the following chapter, manner was even more important than matter in troubadour lyrics, and commonplaces were revivified by intricate rime-schemes and stanza construction accompanied by new melodies. The conventional nature of the whole business may be partly attested by the fact that no undoubted instance of death or suicide for love has been handed down to us." [pp. 15-19]

The anonymous *Razón de amor* is the earliest extant example of the "courtly" lyric in Spain. It not only deals with the theme of courtly love, but contains other troubadour materials as well, and a number of techniques drawn from troubadour compositions but perhaps loosely interpreted. It has, moreover, borrowings from the Galician-Portuguese *cantiga de amigo*, that is, a "plaint sung by a maiden whose lover is absent." Metrically the poem is far removed from the elaborate and sometimes highly complex forms developed by the Provençal poets, and is much more nearly akin to the Spanish ballad form. It differs radically, too, from the Spanish epic, though the metric arrangement is still very simple. It is composed in some-times imperfect couplets *(pareados)*, that is, pairs of lines riming in consonance. The number of syllables per line fluctuates, but the line, unbroken by caesura, seems to have a time-length of approximately nine syllables. The poet is exceedingly form-conscious—so much so, in fact, that he brags about his skill in the handling of verse: his poem is *acabada* (has "finish") and *bien rimada* (properly rimed) by someone who knows how such things should be done, by an *escolar*, that is, who has travelled abroad to learn all about *cortesía*—courtly behaviour, especially con-cerning ladies and love, and the art of writing poetry.

  Thematically there is a rather close relationship be-tween the *Razón de amor* and the troubadour lyric: the courtly love theme, with its praise of the lady, its love conversations and the parting of the lovers, the springtime with its trees and flowers and freshwater spring, the stylized maiden, the recognition after loving from a dis-tance, the love messenger, and the exchange of love tokens. It also touches upon the *debate (clérigo* vs. *caballero)* and, of course, leads to one.

  Rhetorically the poem lacks the sophistication and brilliance of the better Provençal works of the period though for its own language and time it shows the poet's firm command of relatively advanced poetic concepts and techniques. Certainly this poet is able to express more deli-cate and subtle feelings than was the one who extolled the exploits of the Cid, though he lacked that poet's depth of emotion and his earnestness. Like the author of the Cid poem he had a love for the pictorial, though he cared less for line and distinct drawing (and therefore for motion) and more for color, perhaps since lyric poetry generally tends to concern states and the relatively static. There is a marked subjectivity—egocentricity one might even be tempted to call it—manifest in the work, and, like the troubadours, the poet is highly sense-conscious. He makes a concerted, almost simultaneous, appeal to *all* the senses: the *sight* of the colorful springtime landscape, the *taste* and *color* of the wine and the water, the *feeling* of contrast between the heat of the day and the coolness of the spring, the *perfume* of the flowers, the *sound* of the love song and the tinkling of the dove's bell. This early thirteenth-century poet has learned some of the techniques of painting and is able to transfer them to poetry, and he knows something of the psychology of suggestion. He has made the first step toward the use of perspective—that is, he paints first his background of springtime landscape and then against it introduces his foreground figure, his lady, who, although she stands out distinctly against the background, nevertheless blends with it in freshness and in color, and becomes the final expression of it. The poet is careful to choose colors and other sense stimuli from the background picture for his painting of the portrait of his lady: the vermilion *(bermejo)* of the wine is the color of her lips (the adjective *bermejo* is used twice in describing her appearance); the lilies match her forehead; her face as fresh as an apple reminds of the apple tree holding the two vessels; the silk and gold of her brocade suggest both color and texture that could blend with those of any of the flowers. The lady, moreover, gathers flowers and sings as she enters, and thus brings with her, supposedly, their perfume. It will be noted that the poet himself had plucked a flower just as the *doncella* entered, and that he was about to sing of love. These examples illustrate a subtle use of parallelism and thematic repetition still widely found in lyric poetry in our own century (cf. Unamuno's use of white in his *El*

Cristo de Velázquez). There are similar and even more
subtle repetitions: the perfume of the flowers around the
spring would resurrect a dead man—the departure of the
lady left the poet almost dead; the color of the dove corres-
ponds to that of the *doncella*'s forehead and the lilies, and
the dove's entrance with the tinkling of the bell parallels
that of the *doncella* with her song; the olive tree provides
shade first for the poet and later for the couple.

The *Razón de amor* has certain features that will invite comparison in later works. One is the method the poet
employs to describe his landscape: he begins by indicating
immediately the month, "En el mes d' abril," an abstract
reference, and the time of day, "después yantar," a concrete reference. We thus are set on a time plane, of which
we are reminded later, first directly with the word *siesta*
(the midday hour), and then indirectly repeatedly through
reference to heat and shade, and finally again directly
with repetition of the word *siesta*. The impression of particular month or at least season is then subtly reinforced
by appeal to the senses of touch, taste, and smell: protection of the vessel from the heat, suggestion of thirst in the
expression of the poet's desire to drink the cold water, and
his preference for the water over the wine (literally, also,
the two are so placed), excessive heat that causes the poet
to disrobe, noticeable coolness around the spring in contrast
with the surrounding heat, perfume of the flowers whose
blooming season is spring (salvia, roses, lilies, violets),
cooling effect of the sip of water. Against this sense-
presented time plane the poet sets his picture and the motion of his narrative. The only tangible objects specifically
contributing to the landscape picture are two trees in an
orchard, a spring, turf, and four kinds of flowers, plus a
vague and massive *Otras tantas yeruas . . . , que sol' nom-*

bra no las sabría. We have, then, merely a few miscellaneous parts of a landscape, with no mention of their arrangement or relative position. The reader unconsciously creates
the picture according to his own fancy while the poet
distracts his conscious attention to the two vessels in the
treetop and to himself. The poet's attention to himself, and
his conspicuous role in the poem, constitute a noteworthy
feature of the work.

Intrusion of the author throughout the poem cannot
escape notice. In the introductory ten-line passage, a bio-
graphical sketch in the third person, the poet speaks well
of himself. In the next section, a forty-five-line background
description preceding the entrance of the *doncella,* he is the
first-person subject (understood) of thirteen verbs (over-
doing the subjective element!). The following two-line
nexus, *mas ui uenir una doncela, pues naçí non ui tan bella,*
contains three first-person subjects understood. After the
nexus comes a description ostensibly devoted totally to the
doncella, but the poet still is unable to resist the tempta-
tion of asserting himself, albeit he intrudes under a sort
of camouflage, when, in mentioning the lady's gloves, he
is impelled to note: *sabet, non ie las dio uilano.* Before many
lines have passed he sings his own praises on the tongue
of his lady:

> "Porque eres escolar,
> "quis quiere te deuría más amar.
> "Nunqua odí de homne deçir
> "que tanta bona manera ouo en sí."

He continues to be the subject of her discourse, at the end
of which he devotes a six-line section wholly to his own

praise, and then directs the conversation back to the subject of himself, and the ensuing dialogue and narrative, of which he is the principal subject, ends with her great extasy over *him*. At the parting his final words are an admonition to her concerning himself: *mas de mi amor pensat, fe que deuedes*. The poem finally ends with his account of his own emotional reaction to the situation. Here we have, now, the earliest known Spanish version of the theme of courtly love, certainly a most original interpretation of the faithful and devoted lover (!). Poet-lover has appeared in first, second, and third person singular, and first person plural *(Junniemos amos en par / e posamos so ell oliuar)*. He has been presented in the positive and, for contrast, with a touch of the negative, having reserved for himself the only examples of litotes: *sabet, non ie las dio uilano*, for example. In the matter of character and personality perspective techniques and of author-character participation in a literary work, the *Razón de amor* is the earliest major example in Spanish literature. No further comment is necessary, surely, on the element of subjectivity in this poem.

The subject of motion does call for comment. In the introductory passage serving as prologue, the poet immediately asks for the reader's or listener's approach to himself, that is, the poet, and from that point on all motion pivots around him, beginning with the wide sweep of motion (his travels) with which he encircles himself as he steps on the stage. The sharp contrast between that extensive motion and the inertia suggested in the following quiet repose in the shade of the olive tree emphasizes the passive attitude of the poet as the description is placed before the eye; the eye thereupon becomes the only moving object in the picture, though it seems to be not the eye itself that roves, but rather the abstraction *sight* in centrifugal motion centered in the poet and travelling from tree to tree and from vessel to vessel. The eight-line expository digression (lines 19-26) is first a miniature but only half-completed love-idyll with its indicative motions, one completed and the other as yet uncertain, and then the hypothetical motion, a shadow as it were, mimicking actual motions in the narrative proper. The near-static condition of the poet-observer, inert in the presence of centrifugal motion (sight with poet at center, and emanating the intangibles coolness and perfume with moving spring and illusorily static flowers as centers), is broken when the poet bestirs himself only for his own comfort or prestige and only sufficiently to engender centripetal motion. He holds the motion to a minimum and attracts direction to himself. Even the affection of the *otra dona* is said to be drawn to him. When the motion reverses direction and becomes once again centrifugal (exit of the *doncella)* in relation to the poet, he instantly becomes inert again, and resumes the static condition. Motion and direction thus emphasize subtly the egocentricity of the poet, and thus intensify the subjective element in the poem. In contrast, inertia, serving as introduction and conclusion, frames the description-narrative.

Particular attention should be given to one feature that links the *Razón de amor* closely to the *mester de clerecía* (note that the lady stated, and not idly: *pero dizem' un su mesaiero / qu' es clérygo e non caualero . . .).* That feature is the general composition of the poem, which is essentially a mosaic or pastiche made up of heterogeneous themes and poetic genres—in this case including among the latter a song and a *debate*. The composition is clearly sectional and the sections, of varying length, rather loosely related to each other, are held together by means of rapid-

transition connectives or none at all: the introduction (lines
(1-10) stands alone and unconnected, and so does the section (lines 11-32) on the wine and water vessels; the poet's
activity (lines 33-37), which frames the description of the
water spring and its surroundings, is introduced swiftly
with a single line *(Plegém' a una fuente perenal)* and dismissed neatly with another single line nearly paralleling
it in structure *(Prys' del agua un bocado)*, and at the same
time beginning a short enumeration of actions (lines 51-
56) that ends with the nexus, *mas ui uenir una doncela, /
pues naçí non ui tan bella*, terminating the account of the
poet's activity of the moment and introducing the description of the lady and her clothing (lines 58-75); this section
of description is skillfully brought to a close with mention of
gloves and the hand, so that there is a natural connection
(hand—flower gathering) between the description and the
brief account (lines 76-77) of the lady's actions, which are
summed up in two lines that introduce the song the lady
sings (78-97)—and so on through the natural-seeming but
unexpected introduction of the little dove *(Por uerdat quisieram' adormir, / mas una palomela ui)* that returns our
attention to the vessels of the early part of the poem; and,
finally, an entrancing bit of cinematographic artistry (lines
150-160) marks the close of the poet's waking experience
and introduces the subject of what undoubtedly represents
a dream: the fantasy of the debate between the water and
the wine. The soporific state into which the poet had fallen
following upon his near-death experience (lines 47-48) and
which he takes pains to report, and the consequent bit of
drama that his mind fancies, are both part of the allegorical
"vision" literature widely cultivated during the late Mediaeval period in the *mester de clerecía*. The superior artistry
of our poet in handling the transition between the waking

and the dream state, that is, omission of the expected statement to the effect that he was dreaming, sets this poem,
however, almost in a class by itself.

The water-wine theme particularly illustrates the *clerecía* technique of thematic interweaving: first, an early
presentation of elements that may be paralleled or utilized
after an interval of time (poet supine in conditions that
could invite drowsiness, vessels strategically placed, the
hint of magic power in the wine and enchantment in the
water, a setting of natural attraction for birds); second,
a subsequent presentation, plus variation, of elements selected from the first presentation (angle of vision from
supine position, near-unconsciousness, vessels still in place,
appearance of the dove); and, finally, further appearances
and variation of the same elements (the poet's sleeping
mind continues and intensifies the distortion begun by the
action of the dove, and develops the conflict already present
in the waking mind when the poet first contemplated the
wine and the water and gave preference to the water—a
preference paralleled by the water's having the last word
in the argument).

GONZALO DE BERCEO

Each century, from the twelfth through the Golden Age offers one truly outstanding poem or name of a poet whose work can be considered a contribution of the first magnitude to the development of Spanish poetic expression. In the twelfth century the anonymous author of the *Poema del Cid* fashioned out of almost nothing a vigorous poetic form and language that continue to command our respect and admiration even after eight centuries. In the thirteenth century the poet is Gonzalo de Berceo, the first Castilian poet whose name we know, the poet who first conceived the idea of making the vernacular—the Castilian dialect in this case—the vehicle of learned religious poetry. To achieve his end he set about accommodating a new meter, enriching vocabulary and rhetorical effects, and even adapting certain troubadouresque thematic materials to Christian use. The fourteenth century boasts its Juan Ruiz, Arcipreste de Hita, who contributed a wealth of themes, new modes of poetic expression, new outlooks and attitudes. Juan de Mena, in the fifteenth century, dissatisfied with the slow pace of poetic progress in Castilian, deliberately set about broadening the scope of poetic expression, creating new vocabulary and introducing the abundant use of the more complex rhetorical devices, finding new themes, and giving new interpretations to old ones. Garcilaso's innovations in the sixteenth century gave a tremendous impetus to the development of Spanish poetry, especially the lyric, and led directly to the brilliant climax of the Golden Age, in the seventeenth century, in the work of Góngora.

Berceo was born at the end of the twelfth century and lived until about the middle of the thirteenth. He was reared in a monastery, and became a priest. His literary efforts were devoted to the composition of religious poetry, in which he followed Latin, and possibly French, models: saints' lives (*Vida de Santo Domingo de Silos, Vida de San Millán, Vida de Santa Oria, El Martirio de San Lorenzo*), poems in honor of the Virgin (*Milagros de Nuestra Señora, Loores de Nuestra Señora, Duelo de la Virgen el día de la Pasión de su Hijo*), other religious pieces (*El sacrificio de la misa, Los signos del juicio*), including hymns. For him it was not sufficient merely to express himself in verse. His purpose was both artistic and didactic, and consequently he wrote in such a way that ordinary, unlettered people might understand, enjoy, and profit from his learning and share with him his religious devotion to Saint Mary—that is, he wrote in the vernacular, as he explains at the beginning of his *Vida de Santo Domingo de Silos*:

> En el nomne del Padre, que fizo toda cosa,
> et de don Ihesuchristo, fijo de la Gloriosa,
> et del Spíritu Sancto, que egual d' ellos posa,
> de un confesor sancto quiero fer una prosa. (*st.* 1)
>   Quiero fer una prosa en román paladino,
> en qual suele el pueblo fablar a su veçino,

ca non so tan letrado por fer otro latino,
bien valdrá, commo creo, un vaso de bon vino. (*st.* 2)

and in the introductory stanza of *El martirio de San Lorenzo:*

Quiero fer la pasión de sennor Sant Laurent
en romanz que la pueda saber toda la gent.

Berceo's notion of the purpose of literature obviously was that of *enseñar deleitando* (to teach by delighting, or pleasing), and so instead of merely setting down in verse the things he had read in Latin or had observed or originated, he dubbed himself "the Virgin's troubadour," he borrowed materials from his fellow troubadours, and he ornamented his poems with some of the trimmings of the current style. Although much of his work is narrative and expository, it also contains lyric elements, and occasionally a lyric passage. Perhaps the most famous of such selections is the lyric allegory serving as introduction to the *Milagros de Nuestra Señora,* in which the poet, speaking in first person, assumes the guise of a pilgrim who has wandered into a garden of surpassing beauty:

Amigos e vasallos de Dios omnipotént,
si vos me escuchásedes por vuestro consimént,
querríavos contar un buen avenimént:
terrédeslo en cabo por bueno veramént. (*st.* 1)
Yo maestro Gonzalvo de Berçeo nomnado,
iendo en romería caeçí en un prado
verde e bien sençido, de flores bien poblado,
logar cobdiçiaduero pora omne cansado. (*st.* 2)

Daban olor sobeio las flores bien olientes,
refrescaban en omne las caras e las mientes;
manaban cada canto fuentes claras corrientes,
en verano bien frías, en yvierno calientes. (*st.* 3)
   Avié hy grant abondo de buenas arboledas,
milgranos e figueras, peros e mazanedas,
e muchas otras fructas de diversas monedas,
mas non avié ningunas podridas nin açedas. (*st.* 4)
   La verdura del prado, la olor de las flores,
las sombras de los árbores de temprados sabores
refrescáronme todo, e perdí los sudores:
podrié vevir el omne con aquellos olores. (*st.* 5)
   Nunqua trobé en sieglo logar tan deleitoso,
nin sombra tan temprada, nin olor tan sabroso;
descargué mi ropiella por iaçer más viçioso,
poséme a la sombra de un árbor fermoso. (*st.* 6)
   Yaçiendo a la sombra perdí todos cuidados,
odí sonos de aves dulçes e modulados.
Nunqua udieron omnes órganos más temprados,
nin que formar pudiessen sones más acordados. (*st.* 7)
   Unas tenién la quinta, e las otras doblaban,
otras tenién el punto, errar non las dexaban;
al posar, al mover todas se esperaban;
aves torpes nin roncas hi non se acostaban. (*st.* 8)
   Non serié organista nin serié violero,
nin giga nin salterio, nin mano de rotero,
nin estrumént nin lengua, nin tan claro voçero,
cuyo canto valiesse con esto un dinero. (*st.* 9)

Peroque vos dissiemos todas estas bondades,
non contamos las diezmas, esto bien lo creades,
que avié de noblezas tantas diversidades,
que non las contarién priores nin abbades. (*st.* 10)

El prado que vos digo avié otra bondat:
por calor nin por frío non perdié su beltat,
siempre estaba verde en su entegredat,
non perdié la verdura por nulla tempestat. (*st.* 11)

Man a mano que fuy en tierra acostado,
de todo el laçerio fui luego folgado,
oblidé toda cuita, el laçerio passado:
¡qui allí se morasse serié bien venturado! (*st.* 12)

Los omnes e las aves quantas acaeçién,
levaban de las flores quantas levar querién,
mas mengua en el prado ninguna non façién:
por una que levaban, tres e quatro naçién. (*st.* 13)

Semeia esti prado egual de paraíso,
en qui Dios tan grant graçia, tan grant bendiçión miso.
El que crió tal cosa, maestro fue anviso;
omne que hi morasse, nunqua perdrié el viso. (*st.* 14)

El fructo de los árbores era dulz e sabrido.
Si don Adám oviesse de tal fructo comido,
de tan mala manera non serié deçibido,
nin tomarién tal danno Eva nin so marido. (*st.* 15)

Sennores e amigos, lo que dicho avemos,
palabra es oscura, esponerla queremos:
tolgamos la corteza, al meollo entremos,
prendamos lo de dentro, lo de fuera dessemos. (*st.* 16)

Todos quantos vevimos que en piedes andamos,
siquiere en presón, o en lecho iagamos,
todos somos romeos que camino andamos:
Sant Peidro lo diz esto, por él vos lo probamos. (*st.* 17)

Quanto aquí vivimos, en ageno moramos;
la ficanza durable suso la esperamos;
la nuestra romería estonz la acabamos
quando a paraíso las almas enviamos. (*st.* 18)

En esta romería avemos un buen prado,
en qui trova repaire tot romeo cansado:
la Virgen Gloriosa madre del buen criado,
del qual otro ninguno egual non fue trovado. (*st.* 19)

Esti prado fue siempre verde en onestat,
ca nunca ovo mácula la su virginidat,
post partum et in partu fue Virgen de verdat,
illesa, incorrupta en su entegredat. (*st.* 20)

Las quatro fuentes claras que del prado manaban,
los quatro evangelios esso significaban,
ca los evangelistas quatro que los dictaban,
quando los escribién, con ella se fablaban. (*st.* 21)

Quanto escribién ellos, ella lo emendaba,
eso era bien firme, lo que ella laudaba.
Pareçe que el riego todo d' ella manaba,
quando a menos d' ella nada non se guiaba. (*st.* 22)

La sombra de los árbores buena dulz e sanía,
en qui ave repaire toda la romería,
si son las oraçiones que faz Sancta María,
que por los peccadores ruega noche e día. (*st.* 23)

Quantos que son en mundo, iustos e peccadores,
coronados e legos, reys e emperadores,
allí corremos todos vasallos e sennores,
todos a la su sombra imos coger las flores. (*st.* 24)

Los árbores que façen sombra dulz e donosa,
son los sanctos miraclos que faz la Gloriosa,
ca son mucho más dulçes que azúcar sabrosa,
la que dan al enfermo en la cuita rabiosa. (*st.* 25)

Las aves que organan entre essos fructales,
que an las dulçes voçes, diçen cantos leales,
estos son Agustint, Gregorio, otros tales,
quantos que escribieron los sos fechos reales. (*st.* 26)

Estos avién con ella amor e atenençia,
en laudar los sos fechos metién toda femençia,
todos fablaban della, cascuno su sentençia,
pero tenién por todo todos una creençia. (*st.* 27)

El rosennor que canta por fina maestría,
siquiere la calandria que faz grant melodía,
mucho cantó meior el varón Ysaya,
e los otros prophetas onrada compannía. (*st.* 28)

Cantaron los apóstolos muedo muy natural,
confessores e mártires façién bien otro tal,
las vírgines siguieron la grant madre caudal,
cantan delante d' ella canto bien festival. (*st.* 29)

Por todas las eglesias esto es cada día,
cantan laudes ant' ella toda la clereçía,
todos li façen cort a la Virgo María:
estos son rossennoles de grant plaçentería. (*st.* 30)

Tornemos ennas flores que componen el prado,
que lo façen fermoso, apuesto e temprado:
las flores son los nomnes que li da el dictado
a la Virgo María Madre del buen criado. (*st.* 31)
 La benedicta Virgen es estrella clamada,
estrella de los mares, guiona deseada,
es de los marineros en las cuitas guardada,
ca quando essa veden, es la nave guiada. (*st.* 32)
 Es clamada, y eslo de los çielos Reyna,
tiemplo de Ihu Xpo, estrella matutina,
sennora natural, piadosa veçina,
de cuerpos e de almas salut e mediçina. (*st.* 33)
 Ella es velloçino que fue de Gedeón,
en qui vino la pluvia, una grant vissión.
Ella es dicha fonda de David el varón,
con la qual confondió al gigante tan fellón. (*st.* 34)
 Ella es dicha fuent de qui todos bebemos,
ella nos dio el çevo de qui todos comemos,
ella es dicha puerto a qui todos corremos,
e puerta por la qual entrada atendemos. (*st.* 35)
 Ella es dicha puerta en sí bien ençerrada,
pora nos es abierta pora darnos la entrada.
Ella es la palomba de fiel bien esmerada,
en qui non cae ira, siempre está pagada. (*st.* 36)
 Ella con grant derecho es clamada Sión,
ca es nuestra talaya, nuestra defensión.
Ella es dicha trono del rey Salomón,
rey de grant iustiçia, sabio por mirazón. (*st.* 37)

Non es nomne ninguno que bien derecho venga,
que en alguna guisa a ella non avenga;
non a tal que raíz en ella non la tenga,
nin Sancho nin Domingo, nin Sancha nin Domenga.
                                                    (*st.* 38)

Es dicha vid, es uva, almendra, malgranada
que de granos de graçia está toda calçada,
oliva, çedro, bálssamo, palma bien avimada,
piértega en que s' ovo la serpiente alzada. (*st.* 39)

El fust de Moysés enna mano portaba
que confundió los sabios que Faraón preçiaba,
el que abrió los mares e depués los çerraba,
si non a la Gloriosa, al non significaba. (*st.* 40)

Si metiéremos mientes en ell otro bastón
que partió la contienda que fue por Aarón,
al non significaba, como diz la lectión,
si non a la Gloriosa, esto bien con razón. (*st.* 41)

Sennores e amigos, en vano contendemos,
entramos en grant pozo, fondo no l' trovaremos,
más serién los sus nomnes que nos d' ella leemos
que las flores del campo del más grant que sabemos.
                                                    (*st.* 42)

Desuso lo dissiemos que eran los fructales
en qui façién las aves los cantos generales,
los sus sanctos miraclos grandes e prinçipales,
los quales organamos ennas fiestas cabdales. (*st.* 43)

Quiero dexar contanto las aves cantadores,
las sombras e las aguas, las devant dichas flores:

quiero destos fructales tan plenos de dulzores
fer unos poccos viessos, amigos e sennores. (*st.* 44)
   Quiero en estos árborés un ratiello sobir,
e de los miraclos algunos escribir:
la Gloriosa me guíe que lo pueda complir,
ca yo non me trevría en ello a venir. (*st.* 45)
   Terrélo por miráculo que lo faz la Gloriosa
si guiarme quisiere a mí en esta cosa:
Madre plena de graçia, reyna poderosa,
Tú me guía en ello, ca eres piadosa. (*st.* 46)

The poet comes directly to the point in his opening
stanza. He addresses the reader, states his purpose, and
anticipates the reader's reaction and, in a vague way,
introduces the mood of the poem. Note the doubling in his
salutation: *amigos e vassallos*. Doubling of this type was
to be employed frequently by poets for the next three centuries. We become aware of the poet himself, but have met
him only indirectly via the object pronoun *me*—note that
it is not the *subject* pronoun, which would give the author
greater prominence. The poet places himself, unselfishly,
in *third* place. He has placed his audience and God before
himself. When he does present himself directly in the first
line of the second stanza, he does so with all frankness and
simplicity, without the boasting or the vainglory of the
Razón de amor poet. He simply identifies himself as any
person naturally would do in becoming acquainted with
strangers. He thereupon turns attention away from himself to focus it on the subject uppermost in his mind and
spirit, returning later only long enough to place himself,
and with himself the reader, in a passive and restful position, the most appropriate for the pleasurable experience

of observing the beauty displayed all around, and for leaving the mind free for contemplation without interference from physical discomfort or fatigue. Note that this position gives the advantage of particular angle of vision. The poet *can* look and probably *is* looking upward, and his field of vision is on an unusual plane and covers an area unusual in both scope and bound. It will be noted, however, that description of the visual and olfactory and gustatory elements was completed while the poet was still on foot. After he places himself in horizontal position the appeal is primarily to senses of hearing and touch, and the concrete has given way largely to the abstract as the physical toil of travelling has ceded to relaxation and contemplation. We become more aware of intangible atmosphere than of tangible surroundings. From the intangibility of atmosphere we will progress to spirituality of the central message. As for the poet's presence, we are reminded of it only once more (stanza 12) and then only to share the sensation of utter relief and relaxation, this time both physical and spiritual *(oblidé toda cuita, el laçerio passado)*. The motif of memory (via its opposite *forgetfulness*, which is less "tangible" and more restful than memory) indirectly introduced at this point is, significantly, an *abstract* quality, in keeping with the intangibility of the atmosphere and the forthcoming emphasis on the spiritual, and lifts us one step above the atmosphere composed of perfume, music, and temperate air. From sense perception, then, we go to abstraction, to which an approach had been provided in stanzas 8 and 10 containing simple mathematical references. At the precise point of the introduction of this full-fledged abstraction *(oblidé, stanza 12)* and as if controlled by its meaning, the poet forgets himself until he is done with his message and must assume the role of author at the end of the selection. The poet, then, is present in his poem, which therefore makes evident the subjective element, but, unlike the poet of *Razón de amor*, he is concerned only incidentally with self—self is not the object of his devotion.

Coming back, now, to our second stanza, second line, we happen, with the poet, upon a meadow green, untouched, flower-filled, sandwiched between pilgrimage *(romería)* and tired man *(omne cansado)*. This first glance at the meadow, realistically enough, impresses on the mind only the salient characteristics most welcome to the weary pilgrim, but otherwise retains the imprecision of an impression gained only at first glance. The visual appeal of this stanza gives way to the olfactory in the beginning of the third, and here again it is the impression offered, general and imprecise, and not the distinguishing detail, that characterizes the description. Precision, then, only occasionally relieves the vagueness in the following stanzas, with the mention of the position of the springs (stanza 3, line 3), the kinds of fruit trees, the technical description of the birds' song, the ratio of replacement of plucked flowers. On the whole the poet is wont to persuade by profusion, accumulation, and statement of his own judgment and reaction rather than by direct presentation of fact. He tends further to weaken the effect of his description by the use of adjectives and adverbs so hazy in meaning as to be almost without meaning: *bueno, veramént, bien, cobdiçiaduero, sobeio*. An extreme example of such usage is found in stanza 6, in which the word in strongest position, that is, the rime word, is one of this weak type: *deleitoso, sabroso, viçioso, fermoso*. The result, of course, is anticlimax.

The effect of anticlimax results frequently also from

another characteristic of his stanza composition—the oft-repeated use of a last line containing a negative or a belittling statement even though it is intended to enhance the positive:

> logar cobdiçiaduero pora omne cansado (*st.* 2)
> mas non avié ningunas podridas nin açedas (*st.* 4)
> aves torpes nin roncas hi non se acostaban (*st.* 8)
> cuyo canto valiesse con esto un dinero (*st.* 9)
> que non las contarién priores nin abbades (*st.* 10)

More than a third of the strophes have a negative ending, bespeaking, perhaps, a certain negativism in the Mediaeval attitude on the one hand, expressed also in such negative comparisons as those in stanzas 5, 6, and 8, and, on the other hand, serving, perhaps, merely as a form of contrast. Contrast, however, had its more positive expression too, and is used even in complex fashion, as in stanza 3: *en verano bien frías, en yvierno calientes:* summer-winter, cold-hot, summer-cold, winter-hot.

The poet's laudable effort to compress sometimes results in crowding, as in stanzas 3 and 4, where the multiplicity of *fuentes claras* comes near creating confusion and makes it impossible for the reader to concentrate on any one, as he could do in the *Razón de amor.* We see, for example, practically the same trees in the two poems, but in the *Milagros de Nuestra Señora* there is a piling up of examples without their leading to a climax, and in the *Razón de amor* there is presented only what can be used at one time. The seeming congestion continued in stanzas 5 and 6 and the vagueness of some of the description is varied, as are most of the preceding stanzas, by reference to personal

reaction, so that the reader first receives the same stimulus
as the poet, learns the poet's judgment on it, and then
observes the poet's reaction to it, thus deriving his own
reaction and opinion from three distinct sources: one, directly from facts; two, indirectly through the poet's verbal
statements of opinion; and three, indirectly through the
poet's pantomime demonstration of opinion.

Strophes 8 and 9, in sharp contrast with the preceding
verses, present precise technical terms that might at first
seem to be a bit of pedantry on the part of the poet, but,
on the one hand, express the poet's feeling for harmony,
and, on the other, are necessary details in the allegory. They
contribute, moreover, to the sense of realism one derives
from the description as a whole, and, along with references
a few stanzas later to Biblical and hagiographic material,
reflect the poet's educational background, and set the work
on an intellectual plane.

Stanza 16, which serves as nexus between the concrete
and the abstract parallels of the allegory, begins the parallelism immediately with a new doublet salutation similar
to the first and forming a sort of chiasmus with it: *amigos
e vasallos—sennores e amigos*, in addition to involving a
contrast *(vasallos—sennores)*, and a repetition of both
vocabulary *(amigos—amigos)* and of rhythm. The two sections of the poem are thus immediately tied together; and,
furthermore, the possibility contained in the *Querríavos contar* of the first stanza has been converted to the accomplished *dicho avemos* of our nexus. Strophe 17 presents
clearly a major theme of the allegory, hinted in the *romería*
of the second strophe, and continues, thus, the parallelism
of the two parts of the poem: *todos somos romeos que camino andamos*. This theme, two centuries later to be exploited by Jorge Manrique in the *Coplas por la muerte de*

su padre, and at the height of the Golden Age by Góngora in *Las soledades,* is further developed in the next stanza, and the parallelism between the two parts of the poem continues in the explanation of the hidden meaning of the meadow. The poet continues to weave together systematically the two parts of the poem in this early and highly successful attempt at formal symbolism.

As the symbolism of the allegory develops we are gradually set on a new plane, a plane of spirituality, while we remain fully conscious of the original plane of the physical. In this manner, in the poetry of Berceo, the fictive work of the two-plane meaning is introduced to Spanish literature, and gradually will become characteristic of much of it and lead to such masterpieces as San Juan de la Cruz's *Cántico espiritual,* Cervantes' *Don Quixote,* Góngora's *Las soledades,* Benavente's *Los intereses creados.* This stress on the double plane of meaning, the realistic and the idealistic inseparable, is at this early date already firmly established as a trend in Hispanic literature. The dual plane is something more than mere symbolism—it is in reality two planes of simultaneous existence. This passage also is possibly the earliest extant example of a profane type of poetry, in this case the troubadouresque, converted to religious use, and foreshadowing a whole body of work termed *a lo divino,* common in later centuries, particularly the fifteenth and sixteenth.

Since both the *Razón de amor* and Berceo's introduction to the *Milagros de Nuestra Señora* are of the same period, and both are borrowings from the troubadour lyrics —the one via the Galician-Portuguese *cancioneiro* type, and the other through religious lore—and both employ the stylized springtime and praise of the lady as central themes, with imagery, motifs, vocabulary, and realistic detail often identical, with heavy emphasis on sense appeal, with like interweaving of objectivity and subjectivity and like motion of author and angle of vision as author enters and settles himself against the background, with almost identical background-foreground presentation technique, with similar sectional structure having a minimum of adhesive material between parts and occasionally protruding transition (cf. Berceo, stanza 16), comparison of the two is almost inevitable. In spite of striking similarities, differences are fundamental. The latter are most observable in the relative weight of the two pieces. The lightness of the *Razón de amor* is due not only to the metric form, but springs primarily from the very purpose of the poem—pure entertainment—and from the relative superficiality of the sentiment expressed. The anonymous poet's greater sophistication in style also helps create the impression of lightness—the poet knew when he had said enough, and avoided impeding himself with unnecessary obstacles. His attitude is positive, and he uses sparingly the negative and the unpleasant, of which there is such abundance in Berceo's work. The short-metered piece runs smoothly at an easy pace. Berceo's poem, with edification as its base, and the poet's consequent reliance more on expository than on narrative techniques, was perforce burdened with weighty content and more tedious method. The metrical form, called *cuaderna vía* (stanzas of four monorimed *alejandrinos*, that is, lines of seven-plus-seven syllables), was by nature more cumbersome than the ballad-like structure of the *Razón de amor*, especially since the syllables of the verses were carefully counted according to a system so rigid that it permitted only minor deviations from the rule of complete isolation of each syllable. The sincerity of religious devotion gives to Berceo's work a depth and a loftiness of feeling that are absent from

the lighter poem. Concern with life and its meaning, and
its relationship with time, adds a philosophic dimension to
the religious poem, lacking in the profane. Solidity of intellectual background suggested by religio-philosophic concern, by references to music and church literature, and by
allusion to historic characters in Berceo's poem is more
convincing than the vaunted worldly knowledge of the
escolar set on display by the troubadour. Even the physical
sensations produced in the reader by the weary pilgrim and
the idle plaint-singer carry different weights. Berceo's
poem is heavy with a massive and complex and varied
—albeit, perhaps somewhat naive—use of themes and
motifs. Massiveness of material, particularly in the descriptive section, tends to create congestion and even confusion,
for in a space probably no larger than that of the equivalent scene in the *Razón de amor*, there appear, without
specified arrangement, a meadow, countless flowers, four
springs, a *grant abondo* of trees (four kinds plus *muchas
otras fructas de diversas monedas*), while the air is heavily
laden with temperateness, perfume, and music, and, in addition, *de noblezas tantas diversidades* that not even priors
and abbots could count them. These components, moreover,
are not distinguished from each other by specific color as
they were in the *Razón de amor*. Berceo's scene is far from
being inert, however, or even characterized by the sense
of serenity and relaxation emanating from the near-static
and silent surroundings in the *Razón de amor*. Animation
and vitality are everywhere—abundance of springing water
and changing of its temperature, liveliness of bird-song
with its up and down of high and low notes and its unison
starting and resting, suggested hand movements on musical
instruments and sound and motions of singer, mental activity of counting and the suggested image of priors and

abbots in such activity, automatic replacement of plucked flowers with three and four times their number springing up. The very crowding itself and the variety and complexity, and even the negative qualities noted as missing, *podridas* and *acedas,* add life to the scene, to give deeper meaning to the theme of the pilgrimage of life woven directly into the poem. This animation leavens the conglomerate and offsets the weight of its uncontoured bulk.

Massiveness, combined with lack of color distinction, of clear line, of focus, engenders a certain haziness, and in this haziness we are unable to determine specific time or season. Seasons merge with each other. The season here presented, air redolent with perfume and ringing with birdsong, meadow green and flower-bedecked, surely must be spring. *El fructo de los árbores . . . dulz e sabrido* would argue for late summer or early fall. Two seasons only are mentioned by name, summer and winter (stanza 3). Both have the attributes of spring. The pilgrim's discomfort from the heat would indicate summer. This imprecision in the presentation of time, markedly in contrast with the precision of the *Razón de amor,* probably reflects the poet's concept of the timelessness of eternity, and helps to keep the poem on a superterrestrial abstract plane. Based on an expository and descriptive rather than a narrative technique, such as that employed in the *Razón de amor,* the poem follows some order other than the chronological, except for the three events that take place: arrival, disrobing, lying down. The order chosen is a logical one, spatial rather than temporal; gradual elevation of line of vision from earth to grass-and-flower-top level, to tree height, and from there one may suppose the sky beyond and infinity of space. In addition to visible gradation of the concrete, there is a corresponding upward direction of the intangible: the per-

fume from the flowers has risen to the level of perception
by the pilgrim afoot. Finally, the source and the effect of
the music, which may be at any level, give an impression of
carrying the attention beyond the trees and into the realm
of the spirit. Characteristically, Berceo fails to tell us
whether he lay prone or supine, whereas the poet of the
Razón de amor quickly lets his sight dwell on a relatively
precisely located concrete object, a vessel in a tree, thereby
giving us to understand that he was supine. The transfer
to the spiritual realm—that is, the introduction of music—
in Berceo's poem coincides with the poet's relinquishing his
toils and cares (that is, simultaneous with the act of lying
down). Thereafter, except for mention of the miraculous
replacement of plucked flowers (which mention, incidentally, delicately ties the introduction to the principal theme
of the whole work, the miracles of Our Lady), all concern
is with the intangible and the abstract, until finally we are
led to the equating of the meadow with paradise, and are
reminded of God. There is, then, a gradual motion upward
through the ethereal regions of perfume, or springwater-
cooled but balmy air, refreshing shade and atmosphere, and
music, to paradise and God, to a state of contemplation—
a motion, a direction, and a means of which we shall be
reminded when we read Fray Luis de León's *A Francisco
Salinas*. The dynamism of this upward-travelling line contrasts sharply with the static of the pilgrim's horizontal
position. The static quality of the individual would seem
somehow to reflect the Mediaeval attitude toward the individual human being and his relative unimportance in the
universe, and it is interesting to note here that in sixteenth-
century Fray Luis de León's poem to Salinas the poet himself, the individual, that is, himself seems to move upward.
We can assume a chronology in this progression of Berceo's

from the physical to the spiritual, and we have the datum of the pilgrimage to set time in a specific direction, even though virtually all the materials are achronologically presented within the frame, which in part is temporal: reality of present time, in which the poet is addressing his audience (note the verb tenses in the first stanza and in the final three stanzas).

This introduction to the *Milagros de Nuestra Señora* is, like *Razón de amor con los denuestos del agua y del vino*, related to the western European Mediaeval *visione* literature that reached its apogee approximately half a century later (around 1300) in Italy in Dante's *Divine Comedy*, and in Spain is found in a number of works of the fourteenth and fifteenth centuries, among them Francisco Imperial's *Decir al nacimiento del Rey Don Juan*, the anonymous *Decir a las siete virtudes*, and Juan de Mena's *Laberinto de Fortuna*. It, with other poems by Berceo, is the first known learned lyric, and first in the *mester de clerecía*, to exemplify the Marian literature so popular in the late Mediaeval period in Spain. It foreshadows, too, in some way, the Garcilaso eclogue and other pastoral or idyllic literature. We have already noted its significance in the development of the allegory and of symbolist poetry. Nexus, then, between troubadour and mystic, the poem, along with others by Berceo, stands as an exquisite example of the somewhat primitive learned lyric written for the pleasure of the non-erudite.

Berceo borrowed heavily from troubadour art and custom in expressing his own religious pleasures, particularly his adoration of the Virgin, to whom he commends himself and whose praises he versifies in the 233 *cuaderna vía* stanzas of his *Loores de Nuestra Señora*. After devoting the introductory stanza to his Lady, placing himself in her care, and identifying her by way of epithet and informative statement (cf. *senhal)*, the poet presents himself almost timidly and with the humility befitting the true lover, troubadour style. He makes known to her his wish to be her lover at the *entendedor* stage *(querría entender)* and, in place of the conventional kiss used to seal the agreement, expresses his desire to touch the hem of her skirt. He declares his unworthiness, and vows his faith and loyalty:

> A ti me encomiendo, Virgo, madre de piedat,
> que conçebiste del Spíritu Sancto, e esto es verdat,
> pariste fijo preçioso en tu entegredat,
> serviendo tu esposo con toda lealtat. (*st.* 1)

> En tu loor, sennora, querría entender,
> de las tus largas faldas una fimbria tanner,
> ca non me siento digno ante ti paresçer,
> maguer la tu feduza non la puedo perder. *(st.* 2)

He adroitly combines praise with a statement of his purpose in composing his poem and with an invocation and request for inspiration:

> En tu feduza, madre, de ti quiero dezir
> cómmo vino el mundo Dios por ti redimir;
> tú me da bien empezar, tú me da bien a complir
> que pueda tu materia quál o cómmo seguir. (*st.* 3)

The invocation becomes almost a requisite in long Mediaeval poems. The acts of the lover parallel, of course, those of the Holy Orders, and the *entendedor* stage translates to the priesthood. The transfer is easily made, since the troubadour "love" was equivalent to a religious cult.

It is particularly important to note the poetic intent expressed both in the title of the poem and *(entender, dezir)* in the last two stanzas quoted above. A composition of 233 stanzas of *cuaderna vía* does not lend itself easily to the sustaining of lyricism, and it is truly surprising that in the *Loores de Nuestra Señora* Berceo, although he frequently strayed from the strictly lyric by borrowing from both expository and narrative genres, and by recounting religious lore, elevates the whole poem well above the prosaic and devotes many lines to pure lyric expression. Whole sonnet-like sections are either almost totally or at least predominately lyric:

En ti se cumplió, sennora, el dicho de Isaya
que de radiz de Iesse una verga saldría,
et flor qual non fue vista d' ende se levantaría,
Spíritu Sancto con VII dones en la flor posaría. *(st.* 8)

Madre, tú fuisti la verga, el tu fijo la flor,
que resuçita los muertos con su suave odor,
saludable por vista, vidable por sabor,
pleno de los siete dones, sólo d' ellos dador. *(st.* 9)

Tú fuiste la cambariella que dize el Psalmista,
ende salió el esposo con la fermosa vista,
gigante de grandes nuevas que fizo grant conquista,
rey fue et obispo et sabidor legista. *(st.* 10)

La tu figura, madre, traié el vellocino
en qui nuevo miraglo por Gedeón avino;
en essi vino la pluvia, en ti el Rey divino;
por vençer la batalla tú abriste el camino. *st.* 11)

La maior esperanza nos en Dios la tenemos,

pero en ti, sennora, grant feduza avemos,
ca todo nuestro esfuerzo nos en ti lo ponemos:
Sennora, tú nos uvia ante que periglemos. (*st.* 196)

   Por ende eres dicha tú estrella de mar,
por que en tal periglo nos aves a uviar,
por el tu guyonage avemos arrivar,
et de aquellas ondas tan fuertes escapar. (*st.* 197)

   En la venida, madre, que fiçiemos primera,
por onde la salut vino, tú nos fuisti carrera;
en la segunda, madre, tú nos sey obrera
que non seamos presos en la mortal murera. (*st.* 198)

   Madre, tú eres dicha fuente de piadat,
Tú fuisti reliquiario pleno de sanctidat,
la tu merçed spera toda la christiandat,
ca por ti commo cree, ganará salvedat. (*st.* 199)

   Qui en ti entendió, nunca fue engannado;
quanto en ti metió, bien lo cogió doblado;
bien lo sabe Teófilo el que fue renegado,
ca por tu guyonage fue, madre, revocado. (*st.* 200)

   Dulçe es el tu nombre, dulçe toda tu cosa;
salió quando tú naçiste de la spina rosa.
Tú abriste los misterios commo natural cosa,
a ti reçebió don Xpo para ser su esposa. (*st.* 204)

   Ante la tu beltat non an preçio las flores,
ca tal fue el maestro que echó las colores;
nobles son las fechuras, las virtudes meiores,
onde te laudan tanto los tus entendedores. (*st.* 205)

   Toda tu cosa, madre, es tan bien adonada,

que quien en tu solaz entra una vegada
siempre toda su cosa es mejor allinada,
del diablo en cabo el alma emparada. (*st.* 206)

    Madre, la tu memoria e la tu mención
sabor face en oreias, dulzor en corazón;
mucho plaçe al alma quando oye tu sermón;
puso Dios en ti, madre, complida bendición. (*st.* 207)

    De todas las bondades fuisti, madre, cumplida,
fuisti de Sancto Spíritu larga-mente embebida,
pariste e mamantesti, et non fuisti corrompida;
porque non crede esto es Iudea perdida. (*st.* 208)

Berceo's attempt to maintain the lyric cast of the poem
is beautifully illustrated in the Creation and the Commandments passages in his use of a refrain-like theme that by
way of repetition-with-variation serves as a means of bind-
ing together sections that otherwise would be only loosely
related to each other. Like virtually all long Mediaeval
poems the *Loores de Nuestra Señora* is a miscellany, although, in its Biblical and Apochryphal derivation (for the
most part) and its exclusion of the profane, the source
of the subject matter is more limited than most. Unlike
the case of most long poems of the early period, however,
the individual parts of this poem, in addition to being held
together by the homogeneity of their subject matter, are
closely knit together by technical means. The *vita Christi*,
the Creation, the story of Noah, the Ten Commandments,
the stories of David and Susanna, the delightful discursion
on the day Sunday:

    El día del domingo día es consagrado,
  de muchos privilegios es privilegiado;

éste sólo es del nombre del sennor dirivado,
sobre todos los otros debe seer honrrado, (*st.* 104)
    En domingo sin dubda fue el mundo criado,
el çielo con la tierra tal día fue formado,
éste fue ante d' ellos, otro es fecho e alumbrado,
vaia dormir el sábbado ca ya perdió el fado. (*st.* 105)
    Mucho fue el domingo de don Xpo amado,
ca quiso en domingo seer resuçitado.
Guardemos el domingo commo nos es mandado,
e siguamos el curso commo es destaiado. (*st.* 106)

digressions on the fate of such *adversarios* as Judas, Herod,
and Pilate, and on the number seven, the Disciples and the
Apostles, Judgment Day:

    Otro grant privilegio aven estos varones,
el día del juiçio juzgarán las razones,
ellos con el tu fijo partirán los gualardones,
destaiarse an por siempre iamás las petiçiones. (*st.* 169)
    Allí vernemos todos en complida edat,
allí verná tu fijo con la su magestat,
allí verná la cruz e la humanidat,
allí se partirá por siempre mentira de verdat. *(st.* 170)
    Todos buenos e malos allí serán llegados,
los buenos de los malos bien serán apartados,
los corazones de cada uno serán manifestados,
justos e pecadores serán embergonzados. (*st.* 171)
    Mostrarnos ha don Xpo todas sus feridas,
las quales por nos ovo en la cruz resçebidas;

todas las negligençias y serán façeridas,
serán las elemosinas de los buenos gradidas. (*st.* 172)
    En sobeio porfazo nos somos a veer,
quando veremos la sangre de las plagas correr,
veremos las vertudes de los çielos tremer;
debíamos bien agora aquel día temer. (*st.* 173)
    Debíamos agora bien aquel día dubdar,
aguysar nuestras cosas quando avemos vagar,
confesar los pecados, penitençias tomar,
del mal nos departiendo en bien perseverar. (*st.* 174)
    Combidará los iustos Dios por regnar consigo,
desechará la paia, levarse á el trigo,
enviará los malos con el mal enemigo,
de cuya mano curie Dios a todo mi amigo. (*st.* 175)

followed by a typical Mediaeval "confession," but more
lively than most:

    Yo ¿cómmo parezré peccador en esse día,
que siempre fiçi e dixi vanidat e folía?
De bien nin dixi nin fiçi un dinero valía,
mezquino peccador, ¿quí faré aquel día? (*st.* 176)
    Oy mal Evangelios, amé siempre locura,
en los viçios carnales entendí sin mesura,
de partirme del mal nunca non ovi cura:
mezquino, ¿cómmo yré ante la su catadura? (*st.* 177)
    Guardé commo desleal la promesa jurada,
la que quando el baptismo resçebí, ovi dada,
siempre metí en punna en la cosa vedada,
mezquino, non ponía mientes en tal çelada. (*st.* 178)

Quando vedía las cosas del mundo floreçer,
e la su vana gloria en él resplandeçer,
parientes e amigos redor de mí seer,
non me membró que en esto me avía de veer. (*st.* 179)

Quando era en la iglesia las horas me enojaban,
los pensamientos vanos de seso me sacaban,
todas vanidades allí me remembraban,
mezquino peccador, tan mal me engannaban. (*st.* 180)

Guardémosnos de enganno, amigos e sennores,
ca aquellos porfazos y aquellos pavores,
de lo que vos oydes mucho serán mayores,
los viçios d' esti mundo tornarse an en dolores. (*st.* 181)

along with passages on the wages of sin and our blessings
from God, before the return to Mary, all follow in a sort
of conversational order that in the reading seems as natural and easy as talking itself, and yet neither the order
nor the connective material is the result of chance. In the
consecutive selections on the Creation, the Flood, and the
Ten Commandments, for example, the final line of each
stanza is a variation on the theme of the Passion, combined with an embryonic "confession," Passion and confession together implying redemption. Here are the Commandments:

Dio ley a judíos, en ella diez mandados,
los quales serán oy commo creo contados;
otros decretos ovo a esos acostados:
el actor de todo esto lazra por mis peccados. (*st.* 87)

Mandó creer un Dios en el primer mandado,

pecado de blasfemia en el otro fue vedado;
el terçero el sábbado mandó que fuese curiado:
agora por mis peccados véolo cruçificado. (*st.* 88)

Al quarto, los parientes mandó mucho onrrar,
sobre todo el quinto viédanos el matar;
al sexto, quita el forniçio, el séptimo vieda el furtar:
el que manda todo esto por mí le veo lazrar. (*st.* 89)

Vedar falso testimonio el octavo contiende,
el nono en cubdiçia mala quitar entiende,
el lecho del veçino el deçeno defiende:
Dios por que todo vino, por mí en la cruz piende. (*st.* 90)

The Passion had been presented previously, and the somewhat conventional Mediaeval "confession," quoted above, follows at some distance later. The refrain, in fact, issues from the Passion account, the end of which especially emphasizes Christ's *will* to die for the redemption of mankind. This repetitive device, which artfully juxtaposes Old Testament and New, creation and death, righteousness and sin, suffering of one for the salvation of another, and which replaces with poignancy what might otherwise have been monotony of enumeration, has a rhythm all its own and the force of tolling sweet and deep-toned bells, a force that gradually increases with the repetition until it rings out emphatically by appearing as both opening and closing lines in the same stanza before it modulates to a brighter variation (resurrection). It acts as a background melody connecting Passion, Resurrection and Confession. The effect is greatly enhanced within this series of selections by the introduction, several strophes previously, of the refrain's theme—itself an aftermath of the Passion account—and its repetition at irregular intervals in preparation for presentation of the coming passages. The poet does not drop the device at the close of the Commandments passage, but allows it to fade away in much the same manner in which it approached, and at the same time gradually, as the passage on the Resurrection comes near, turns it from the negative introspective attention focused on sin to the positive contemplation of life, goodness, upward motion, and finally sums up the joyous thought in a single climactic stanza in which the final line is a miniature paean resounding the principal theme of the poem:

Este libró a David del osso e del león,
mató al filisteo, un soberbio varón,
por ésti fue Judea quita de Babilón:
desóse matar agora por dar a mí perdón. (*st.* 91)

Esti salvó Susana del crimen que sabedes,
los tres ninnos del fuego, en esto non dubdedes;
sobre los machaveos fezo grandes merçedes:
por nos murió agora en cruz commo veedes. (*st.* 92)

Quanto en todo el mundo podría seer asmado
lo que saber podemos et lo que es çelado,
todo por esto fue fecho, fuera sea peccado:
agora por mis debdos veo a él prendado. (*st.* 93)

En grant verguenza yago, mezquino peccador,
quando veo por mal siervo muerto tan buen sennor;
yo falsé su mandado, él muere por mi amor,
en grant verguenza yago mezquino peccador. (*st.* 94)

Sennor, bien sé que vives maguer muerto te veo;
maguer muerto, que vives firme-mente lo creo;

tú mueres que yo viva, en esto firme seo;
la tu resurectión yo mucho. la deseo. (*st.* 95)
    Todas estas mezquindades que te veo sofrir,
a Isayas creo que las oy deçir;
quando lloró Iheremías esto vedía venir:
Sennor, ¡ seas loado porque quisiste morir! (*st.* 96)
    Si tú nunca morieses vivir yo non podría,
si tú mal non sofrieses yo de bien non sabría,
si tú non deçendiesses yo nunqua non subría:
¡ Loado seas Xpo, et tú virgo María! (*st.* 97)

Only a short passage separates this anaphora-marked stanza from the following account of the resurrection. This deliberate use of contrast of mood and the skilful modulation from the feeling of shame and remorse to one of release and joyfulness are the work of one who has devoted much study to the art of poetry.

This example is only one of many widely varied lyric techniques employed by Berceo to give unity and coherence to his composition and to avoid monotony. Even the general structure of the work is so patterned as to give symmetry and harmony to the whole. Despite its title and its stated purpose, only the opening and the closing of the poem are devoted directly to praises of the Virgin. The bulk of the work has to do with other themes, as noted above, outstanding among them the life of Christ. Only incidental and sporadic explicit mention of the Virgin appears in the large central portion of the poem, except for certain necessary references to her as concerned with Christ's life, and for the apostrophe (usually *Madre)* repeatedly interspersed as a constant, but almost as an undertone and as if she were more observer than participant in the events. Implicitly, of course, she is present in spite of this prolonged lack of focus on her, since her greatest glory is her being the mother of the central figure. The account of Christ's life, in turn, is interrupted continuously in favor of the somewhat extraneous but carefully blended materials mentioned above, as if the whole of man's consciousness and his universe were intimately a part of Christ's being and suffering.

One of the poet's greatest achievements in the *Loores de Nuestra Señora* is the frequent creation and control of mood to accord with the events in the Mother-Son life that furnish the basis of the poem. The first mood is one of serene confidence and security, the key words employed to establish it being the rime-words of the first stanza: *piedat, verdat, entegredat, lealtat.* With the eighth stanza before the Annunciation, the mood begins to expand in quiet happiness with the introduction of a lyric passage having a flower as its opening theme. By means of the flower image several senses are brought directly into play and the pleasurable sensation is thereby increased:

En ti se cumplió, sennora, el dicho de Isaya
que de radiz de Iesse una verga saldría,
et flor qual non fue vista d' ende se levantaría
Spíritu Sancto con VII dones en la flor posaría. (*st.* 8)

Madre, tú fuisti la verga, el tu fijo la flor,
que resuçita los muertos con su suave odor,
saludable por vista, vidable por sabor,
pleno de los siete dones, sólo d' ellos dador. (*st.* 9)

Tú fuiste la cambariella que dize el Psalmista,
ende salió el esposo con la fermosa vista,
gigante de grandes nuevas que fiso grant conquista,
rey fue et obispo et sabidor legista. (*st.* 10)

Uplifting of the spirit is accomplished through the repeated use of words suggesting lightness of weight, upward direction, liberation, and expansion: *que de radiz de
Iesse una verga saldría, se levantaría, Spíritu Sancto, verga,
resuçita, siete dones, salió, gigante, conquista, rey, obispo.*
A series of predictions interwoven throughout the first
part of the poem following the three-stanza introduction
and leading to the Annunciation proper contributes to a
mood of pleasurable expectation, even though the tense
and sense are historical. The evolving joyful mood that
is leading to the Annunciation is not allowed, however, to
expend itself hastily when the event arrives, but is tempered first by the gentle manner of the messenger, next
by the atmosphere of prayer that comes from the glossing
of the first part of the *Ave María,* and finally by the
humble attitude of the Virgin:

> Gabriel fue imbiado, con la mensagería,
> en la çibdat de Názareth, a ti, sennora mía;
> en tu çiella te trobó sin carnal compannía,
> dulçemente te saludó, díxote: "Ave María." (*st.* 21)
> Benedicta fuisti clamada et de graçia plena,
> conçebiste por virtut e pariste sin pena,
> por ti se fue afloxando la mortal cadena,
> por ti cobró su logar la oveia çentena. (*st.* 22)
> El tu fruto benedicto Ihu Xpo fue clamado,
> et el regno de David a él fue otorgado;
> el su poder non a fin, nin sería cantado:
> por él fue fecha la luz, e el mundo criado. (*st.* 23)
> El mensage reçebiste con grant humildat;
> lo que dixo conoçiste que era verdat;

la manera preguntesti de la prennedat:
él respondió e te dixo la çertenidat. (*st.* 24)

Throughout the densely detailed though relatively brief account of the events between the birth (stanzas 25-26) and
Holy Week (stanza 54) the historical tone varies but rarely
and slightly from the unemotional, though some feelings
of joy, peace, and wonder shield the passage from monotony, which in any case would be unable to prevail because of the growing feeling of apprehension and anguish
that gathers as the reader catches the first hint of tragedy
in the conditions in the stable and the fear with which
a certain prophecy had been made:

Falliéronte lugares, oviste grant angostura,
en pesebre de bestias posiste la criatura;
Abacuch lo dixera en la su scriptura,
que contezría assí e ovo en pavura. (*st.* 27),

and then witnesses Herod's outrage (stanzas 36-39) and
the Devil's endeavours and consequent frustration (stanzas
45-46), and finally learns of the poet's own emotion as the
time for recounting the fatal week approaches:

Las sus grandes merçedes ¿ quí las podría contar?
Madre, serié follía en sólo lo asmar:
pavor me va tomando d' esti logar pasar,
ca las falas del omne serán a porfazar. (*st.* 53)

Needless to say, Berceo's presentation of the Crucifixion
and surrounding events and circumstances is done with a
sensitivity that touches the reader deeply but strictly avoids

the maudlin. The mood is one of distress and remorse, but the quiet dignity of both character-subject and narrator balances that mood with one of trustfulness, of assurance, of steadfastness. This double-facet mood is sustained after the account of the Passion by means of the refrain-like stanza-ending discussed above, and by the same means the poet converts this mood into one of exaltation (see stanza 97, quoted above). At this point the refrain technique is dropped, but the mood is further developed by means of both subject matter and vocabulary. After an account of, and commentary on, the burial and the descent, the resurection itself is told briefly (stanza 103) and comes to a climax in the passage on the day Sunday (quoted above), a passage filled with a spirit of holy gladness. In the vocabulary we find such expressions as *resurreçión, tesoro, virtut, gozo* intermingled with the necessarily gloomy words concerning the burial and the descent to Hell, and then a sudden increase of the same type of bright expression when the resurrection is about to take place:

> Cambiemos la materia, en otro son cantemos,
> oyremos tales nuevas con que nos gozaremos:
> resuçitó don Xpo, mas la hora non sabemos,
> domingo fue de mannana segunt lo que leemos. (*st.* 103)

The discursion on Sunday momentarily holds in check the mounting joy, but, on its closing, the happy mood is suddenly given great impetus with a quick succession of joyous expressions in a single stanza:

> Visitó sus amigos, ¡Dios, tan grant alegría!
> Dos soles, Deo graçias, nasçieron aquel día,

mal grado aya toda la mala confradía:
Resuçitó don Xpo: ¡ Dios, qué grant alegría! (*st.* 107)

and the mood finally culminates in one envelope stanza of
elation, in which the Virgin is brought to the fore:

> ¡ Alégrate, sennora!, que alegrarte debes,
> ca buenas nuevas corren e nuevo tiempo vedes,
> lo que speresti siempre, sennora, ya vedes.
> ¡ Alégrate, sennora!, que alegrarte debes. (*st.* 112)

Thereafter the poem continues evenly and with only an
occasional marked fluctuation in mood. One notable exception is a "confession" similar to the earlier one, though
in a different tone, and having a similar refrain-like strophe
ending. Other exceptions include lyric expression in the
section of the praise quoted above, and the prayerful attitude evident in the final strophes.

At the conclusion of the poem Berceo finally declares
himself frankly not only the Virgin's troubadour, but also
her lover, and even specifically her lover at the stage of
entendedor:

> Aun merçed te pido por el tu trobador:
> qui este romançe fizo, fue tu entendedor. (*st.* 232)

and he ends his long poem by asking favors of her for
himself and his fellow man, completing (stanzas 213-214)
the gloss begun earlier on the *Ave Maria,* and bringing the
poem to a close on a positive note of the highest expectation and bliss, fitting climax to a poetic offering to his
Lady:

> Seas contra tu fijo por elli rogador,
> recábdali limosna en casa del Criador. (*st.* 232)
>   Ruega por la paz, madre, e por el temporal,
> acábdanos salut, e cúrianos de mal,
> gúyanos en tal guysa por la vida mortal,
> commo en cabo ayamos el regno çelestial. (*st.* 233)

The supplicatory tone with which he ends his poem and the reference to troubadour art recall immediately the opening stanzas, with which these final stanzas form a frame into which the main body of the poem is set and with which it merges harmoniously.

The many special effects obtained in the *Loores de Nuestra Señora* Berceo achieves through abundant and widely varied use of rhetorical artifice. Obviously well versed in the art of poetic composition as set forth by the troubadours, who in turn derived many of their artifices from the Ancients and earlier Mediaeval writers, he is fully aware of the purpose of their poetic devices and is both highly skilled and judicious in their use. The *cuaderna vía* itself is a variation of the old *cobla continuada* written in Provençal standard twelve-syllable measure. By means of anadiplosis, called also *lexaprende* or *dexaprende* (the repetition of all or certain parts of the last line of one stanza in the first line of the following stanza), Berceo frequently gives special emphasis to an event or an idea. Careful use not only of simple metaphor, but of sustained metaphor, particularly in reference to the Virgin, is one of his most lyric methods of praise:

> Por ende eres dicha tú estrella de mar,
> por que en tal periglo nos aves a uviar,

por el tu guyonage avemos arrivar,
et de aquellas ondas tan fuertes escapar. (*st.* 197)

Combined with zeugma it lends a special elegance to the stanza:

Madre, tú fuisti la verga, el tu fijo la flor
que resuçita los muertos con su suave odor,
saludable por vista, vidable por sabor,
pleno de los siete dones, sólo d' ellos dador. (*st.* 9)

Closely related to metaphor is simile:

commo paia en agua adessuso andidieron. (*st.* 151)

In the following example Berceo uses an image later refined and expanded by Góngora in *Las soledades:*

La lumbre commo lenguas paresçió derramada. (*st.* 156)

Anaphora is another means of emphasis, particularly effective when combined with a bit of climactic parallelism:

Allí vernemos todos en complida edat,
allí verná tu fijo con la su magestat,
allí verná la cruz e la humanidat,
allí se partirá por siempre mentira de verdat. (*st.* 170)

¿ Quál bien sería tan grande commo la cara suya veer,
cómmo nasçe el fijo del padre entender,
o cómmo salle el Spíritu de entre ambos saber,
o cómmo son un Dios todos tres connosçer? (*st.* 189)

A more complex type of series zeugmatically combined and involving some comparison and a touch of hyperbaton illustrates still another facet of Berceo's style:

> Vida da que non fin, e salut perdurable,
> claridat maior de sol, firme paz e estable,
> ligereza más de viento, sotileza mirable:
> tal regno de tan buen rey es mucho deseable. (*st.* 192)

He not only makes frequent use of series and enumeration of diverse kinds, but seems to be particularly fond of actual numbering (Creation, Commandments, Christ's appearances after death), and even the contemplation of a single number. The mystic number *seven* holds his attention for eleven strophes (143-153), in which by way of enumeration and facet presentation we are allowed to examine the number's significances and total value.

Antithesis is particularly useful to Berceo when he wishes to make a clear contrast between humanity and divinity, especially when suffering lies between:

Quando veo por mal siervo muerto tan buen sennor. (*st.* 94)

> Sennor, bien sé que vives maguer muerto te veo,
> maguer muerto, que vives firme-mente lo creo;
> tú mueres que yo viva, en esto firme seo (*st.* 95)

> Si tú nunca morieses vivir yo no podría,
> si tú mal non sofrieses yo de bien non sabría,
> si tú non deçendiesses yo nunqua non subría (*st.* 97)

In this last example, note not only the anaphora but also,

as in other lines above, that the positive, by being placed last in the contrasting pair, is given precedence over the negative. Other examples, chosen at random, include:

que me non aborrescas quando tant me quisiste (*st.* 98)
quant grant tesoro siede en tan poco lugar (*st.* 101)
en tierra de tristiçia tan grant gozo andaba (*st.* 102)
del mal nos departiendo en bien perseverar (*st.* 174)

Contrast is, of course, basic to the whole idea underlying the poem: the contrast between death and life, a contrast elaborated particularly in the Crucifixion-Resurrection passages.

Although Berceo has a marked preference for the strict and simple parallelism of correlative verse, he does not overlook the advantages of the balance formula of chiasmus, and the sensation of equilibrium it produces. Some of the lines that are built on this principle are:

adoremos la cruz et en Xpo creamos (*st.* 99)
cataron el sepulcro, la mortaia vidieron (*st.* 108)
Dexémosnos de aquesto, de lo meior digamos (*st.* 117)
Acróvolis esfuerzo, todo miedo perdieron (*st.* 160)
confesar los pecados, penitençias tomar (*st.* 174)
refrenemos la carne, al Criador sirvamos (*st.* 187)
Aquí yazremos siempre, nunca de aquí saldremos (*st.* 185)

This last line also contains a forcible antithesis *(siempre-nunca)*.

Hyperbaton is virtually inevitable in any poem restricted by predetermined line measure and by rime. The *Loores de Nuestra Señora* is no exception, but Berceo's

hyperbaton surely is not always the result of circumstance.
Combined with anaphora, as in strophe 97, quoted above,
or with parallelism of any sort, hyperbaton deepens the
impression of the message:

> En todas las façiendas, madre, mientes parabas,
> de dichos nin de fechos nada non olbidabas,
> en las humanas cosas al fijo ministrabas,
> en las que son durables a él te acomendabas. (*st.* 41)

> Acróvolis esfuerzo, todo miedo perdieron,
> cada uno por su parte a las tierras salieron,
> nueva ley predicaron, el mundo conquisieron,
> quequiera qui lis vino de grado lo suffrieron. (*st.* 160)

Hyperbaton is so much a part of the style of the work as
a whole, however, that the reader comes to expect it and
becomes almost unaware of its presence.

The psychomorphism that becomes so prominent in
the Golden Age, particularly in such poets as Boscán, Garcilaso, San Juan de la Cruz, and Góngora, is only barely
to be found in Berceo's *Loores de Nuestra Señora:*

Las piedras maguer duras con su duelo quebraron (*st.* 76)

This lone example, not particularly original, serves not
so much to indicate any interest in nature as it does to
emphasize the fact that every detail of the poem concerns
the mental and physical activity of human beings, and of
beings considered equivalent or superior to them in general
nature and physical form—that is, angels and members
of their orders, the Holy Ghost, the Devil. The work is
literally crowded with such human activity. References to

any other phase of Nature are rare and brief, simply and
directly stated, and of a more or less conventional form:
claridat maior de sol (*st.* 192), *ligereza más de viento* (*st.*
192), *estrella de mar* (*st.* 197), *fuente* (*st.* 199), *rosa* (*st.*
204), *flores* (*st.* 205), *rayo de sol* (*st.* 209), *estrella* (*st.*
211). The few passages in which such material is found
are among those having the greatest lyric value.

Exclamation in such passages as the *¡Alégrate, sennora
. . .* (*st.* 112, quoted above) and

¡O gente çiega et sorda, dura de corazón! (*st.* 15)

and rhetorical and semi-rhetorical question:

Las sus grandes merçedes ¿quí las podría contar? (*st.* 53)

¿Quí vio testimonio nunca tan sin color?
Dormiendo ¿quién podría veer el furtador? (*st.* 115)

Para el Spíritu Sancto tal cosa convenía,
por los siete sanctos dones que consigo traya:
cosa tan con recabdo ¿quí la ordenaría,
si non tu fijo, madre, por qui todo venía? (*st.* 153)

Dirán unos a otros: "Mezquinos, ¿qué faremos?
Aquí yazremos siempre, nunca de aquí saldremos,
que clamemos merçed oydos non seremos:
¿Qué faremos, mezquinos? Siempre en muerte vivremos."
(*st.* 185)

Diga, si non se tiene desto por entregada,
¿cómmo passó don Abacuc la puerta ençerrada?
La flama a los ninnos ¿cómmo fue tan temprada?
O despruebe, o crea, o diga: "Non sé nada." (*st.* 212)

vary the tone and invite the reader's imagination to contribute to the poetic creation.

Some of the most remarkable devices employed in the
Loores de Nuestra Señora are the highly developed gloss
forms, the paraphrase, and related amplifications, by means
of which Berceo inserts a veritable catechism into the poem,
in a manner so artful that the reader is unaware of the
fact that what he has enjoyed reading has been in large
part a *tratado de la doctrina cristiana.* One of the principal
reasons for the unobtrusiveness of the didacticism is the
extreme variation in the technical means of presentation
of the various parts of the dogma. The *Credo*, of course,
is fundamental to the whole structure, and consequently
the whole poem, exclusive of very few passages, is an explication of it largely by way of the *vita Christi* that occupies the central portion of the work. Indeed, in its relation to the act of faith, the figure of Christ is technically
equivalent to some of the later allegorical figures such as
the personifications of fortune, death, virtues, and vices
used to represent in concrete form an abstract idea. The
Creation and the Judgment passages are conspicuous elements of the work, no doubt illustrating the first and last
tenets within the first *Credo* sentence, that is, the one
having to do with the identification and the life of Christ.
The tenets contained in the second *Credo* sentence are scattered and variously presented: the *Spíritu Sancto* appears
independently in the first stanza, and sporadically thereafter (stanzas 5, 129, 153, 155, 189, 208), but is directly
presented as a member of the Trinity, and specifically as
part of the Creed, in the following:

> ¿Quál bien sería tan grande commo la cara suya veer,
> cómmo nasçe el fijo del padre entender,

o cómmo salle el Spíritu de entre ambos saber,
o cómmo son un Dios todos tres connosçer? (*st.* 189)
　　Esta es la verdat e bien sé que non miento:
todos tres son eguales e sin empezamiento,
una es la natura, non a departimiento,
de la sancta credençia éste es el çimiento. (*st.* 190)
　　Non es nuestro deçir quáles son sus riquezas,
oro nin plata nada non son contra las sus abtezas,
siempre de sus thesoros da nuevas estrannezas,
non sería asmado quántas son sus noblezas. (*st.* 191)

Brief but explicit is the statement concerning the *sancta iglesia:*

　　Toda sancta iglesia aquí ovo comienzo,
　　daquende ovo forma e todo ordenamiento. (*st.* 168)

This statement follows immediately upon a passage (stanzas 162-167) devoted to the concerted efforts and common endeavor and responsibilities of the four saints who happen also to be the four Evangelists:

　　Johanes e Matheo fueron los delanteros,
　　después Lochas e Marco vinieron postrimeros,
　　todos en corazón ovieron commo leales obreros,
　　el sennor de la vinna diolis buenos dineros. (*st.* 163)

The remission of sins is, naturally, a major theme of the *Loores de Nuestra Señora,* as the refrain-like repetition reminds us. As for the resurrection of the body, the poet affirms:

Dexémosnos de aquesto, de lo meior digamos,
resusçitó don Xpo, de firmes lo creamos,
apareçió a Peydro commo escripto trovamos,
resusçitó don Xpo, en buena nos levamos. (*st.* 117)
    Quando él resusçitó todos resusçitamos,
saliemos de prisión, enguedat recobramos;
a la virgo María todos graçias rendamos,
porque los peccadores tan grant merçet ganamos. (*st.* 118)

Life eternal, the last item of the *Credo,* is implied throughout the poem and contained in its final line:

commo en cabo ayamos el regno celestial. (*st.* 233)

Every detail of the *Credo* thus not only is deliberately
made an integral part of the *Loores* but receives full and
clear treatment without causing the slightest disfiguration
of the poem as poem. The artist is master of the pre-
ceptor. The beautifully veiled *Credo* exemplifies a level of
art that will seldom be achieved again in the immediately
following centuries.

In sharp contrast to the *Credo* representation is that
of the *Decalogue* (Ten Commandments, stanzas 87-90,
quoted above). Here we have the simplest form of enumeration, relieved only—but most appealingly—by the refrain-
like stanza-ending, which links *Decalogue* to *Confiteor* (confession). For presentation of this latter the poet employs
a technique completely different from those of *Credo* and
Decalogue. In the first place he speaks in a spontaneous
and personal manner, substituting a subjective reaction
of remorse for the more intellectual catechistic model—a
variation on the theme, that is, rather than a gloss or paraphrase—and in the second place, he divides his confession

matter into three separate bodies of material, each for producing an effect distinct from that of the others. The function of the refrain-like stanza-ending has already been discussed, and its leading eventually to a whole stanza devoted to the confession theme: *(En grant verguenza yago . . .)* just before the Resurrection theme appears has also been noted. This stanza stands as a sort of climax to the confession-ornamented *Decalogue,* and seems to bring the confession theme to a conclusion, though in reality it is a miniature confession foreshadowing the full-length one that appears later. The confession theme is suddenly dropped from attention at this point, and as suddenly, but completely naturally, it is found again as an aftermath of Judgment Day. Emotion is now tempered by the intellectual. Specific recollections, a bit of consternation, and self-interest give a new tone and a more pronounced feeling of the personal to the confession, (quoted above, stanzas 176-180, but introduced in the two preceding stanzas).

Berceo the artist avoids overworking a technique. Interestingly enough, he does not make a list of the Deadly Sins or even single any of them out as representing a fixed number, and the sins he admits having committed do not group themselves into any standard classification. Although he is fond of enumeration, he avoids this method of presenting such other doctrinal materials as the *Seven Gifts of the Holy Ghost,* to which he makes direct reference four times (stanzas 8, 9, 150, 153); the *Pater Noster,* mentioned as such once *(Mostrólis pater noster . . . ,* stanza 49), but not further elaborated; the *Seven Sacraments,* some of which he mentions directly, some by implication, but in scattered reference rather than a unit or a completed list: Baptism:

demostrólis la forma con la qual bapteassen *(st. 131)*

The Holy Eucharist:

> Estando a la çena fizo su testamiento,
> en el pan, en el vino fizo grant sacramiento,
> púsonos de su muerte un fuerte remembramiento,
> de sí labó los piedes, dio nuevo mandamiento. (*st.* 57)

Holy Orders:

> Fueron los cardenales en la fe confirmados,
> qué farían o qué non, fueron bien castigados,
> fueron de Sancto Spu una vez aspirados,
> los malos argumentos todos fueron falsados. (*st.* 129)

Penance:

> Descojó sus vasallos de los de vil manera,
> non quiso de los altos ó la soberbia era,
> mostrólis pater noster, metiólos en carrera,
> del perdón del xpiano liçençia dio larguera. (*st.* 49)

> Debíamos agora bien aquel día dubdar,
> aguysar nuestras cosas quando avemos vagar,
> confesar los pecados, penitençias tomar,
> del mal nos departiendo en bien perseverar. (*st.* 174)

This synecdochal type of reference, of course, is all that is necessary to call to the mind of any Christian of his time the whole or any of the parts. Berceo was above insulting the intelligent reader, and, despite his humble statements, it was for the adult literarily sophisticated reader that he was writing, certainly not for the mere child or the dolt.

So it is that he can leave to inference the list of the Works of Mercy if he merely reminds us that Christ

> mandó çebar al pobre et render bien por mal (*st.* 50)

or mentions the *perdón del Xpiano* (stanza 49). He does number, one by one, the days of the Creation and their events (stanzas 80-82), immediately preceding the *Decalogue*, and later the ten appearances of Christ between the Resurrection and the Ascension (stanzas 124-127), and takes delight in the number seven itself and the many facts and events connected with it *(El cuento septenario,* stanzas 143-153), but is content to state merely the total of twelve for the Apostles though he details the names of the four Evangelists (*st.* 162-165). Actual as well as suggested number and numbering, then, are the basis not only for presenting various phases of doctrine but also as a means of simplifying the presentation. Enumeration without numbering is utilized frequently throughout the poem, and most emphatically near the close where the poet charges the Virgin with the performance of a series of Works of Mercy:

> Acorri a los vivos, ruega por los passados,
> conforta los enfermos, converti los errados,
> conseia los mezquinos, visita los cuytados,
> conserva los pacíficos, reforma los yrados. (*st.* 227)
>
> Madre, contién las órdenes, salva las cereçías,
> alarga la credençia, defiende las mongías,
> siempre menester te avemos las noches e los días,
> ca nuestras voluntades de todo son bien vaçías. (*st.* 228)
>
> Esfuerza a los flacos, defiendi los valientes,

alivia los andantes, levanta los iaçientes,
sostién a los estantes, despierta los dormientes,
ordena en cada uno las mannas convenientes. (*st.* 229)

Here, with the aid of hypozeuxis, the poet not only reminds us again, indirectly, of our charge in regard to such works but brings the Virgin into sharp relief, and at the same time, apparently, paraphrastically incorporates into his work a selection used in a Church service: "Esta petición es muy semejante a la que contiene la antífona, *Sancta Maria, sucurre miseris, juva pusillanimes,* etc., y parece traducción parafrástica de ella," notes Tomás Antonio Sánchez, early editor of Berceo's works. Strict parallelism and asyndeton in the first strophe and other portions of this passage replaces numbering, with the result that attention is fixed on the individual idea contained in each clause rather than on its relative position in the series, and endlessness in the possible number of works of mercy is suggested. This implied infinity is well placed here, approaching the end of a poem whose aim, expressed in its final lines, is to lead the reader to celestial eternity:

guyanos en tal guysa por la vida mortal,
commo en cabo ayamos el regno çelestial. (*st.* 233)

It would be idle to single out all the rhetorical devices that make up the stylistic personality of the *Loores de Nuestra Señora.* Suffice it to say that they are all necessary for the relief from what otherwise is essentially a long series of the simplest kind of narrative and declarative statements plus a few imperative supplications. These devices give the poem much of the quality that elevates it above the prosaic, that makes it the work of the *trobador* as distinguished from that of the *juglar.*

Whereas the *Loores de Nuestra Señora* is a composite work, a synthesis of Christian doctrine, and a blended sampling of literary genres, Berceo's 210-stanza poem bearing the title *El duelo que fizo la Virgen María el día de la pasión de su fijo Jesu Christo*, and commonly known as *El duelo de la Virgen*, is an expansion of a single subject, the Passion and the Virgin's reaction to it. Since this work involves intense emotion, and is an amplification of detail, there is virtually complete thematic unity and wide variety of lyric techniques. The result is that *El duelo de la Virgen* not only surpasses the *Loores de Nuestra Señora* in lyricism, but is probably the best example we have of the learned lyric before the *cancionero* period.

It goes without saying that Berceo utilized in this poem essentially the same rhetorical devices that contributed to the success of his other works, but emphasis of certain ones in this poem helps to differentiate this work from the others. One such detail is the miniature amplification paralleling the general concept and structure of the whole work, and well exemplified in the lines on *día:*

"Bien ploren los mis oios, non çesen de manar,
"el corazón me rabia, non me puede folgar,
"açiago es oy, bien nos debe membrar,
"los siervos de mi Fijo débenlo bien guardar. (*st.* 140)

"A los del nuestro vando miémbrelis esti día,
"día tan embargoso, tan sin derechuría,
"día en qui yo pierdo mi sol, Virgo María,
"día que el sol muere, non es complido día. (*st.* 141)

"Día en qui io pierdo toda mi claridat,
"lunne de los mis oios e de toda piadat,

"ploran los elementos todos de voluntat:

"io mesquina si ploro, non fago liviandat. (*st.* 142)

The amplification of *amargura*, largely by way of hypotyposis, is much more elaborate and subtle. The Virgin's sorrow is bitter to her, and the bitterness is intensified through contrast with the sweetness she finds inherent in her Son. We are introduced first to sweetness in its literal sense:

"prissiemos Corpus Domini, unos dulçes bocados (*st.* 15)

and shortly thereafter we find it appearing figuratively and synesthetically:

"del mi fiio dulçíssimo ambas eran sus tías (*st.* 20)

just before we find the expression *amargo duelo* (*st.* 21), which states the major theme of the poem. Stress falls again on the sweet:

"tendió a todas partes la su dulz catadura (*st.* 36)

not long before the account of the mockers' literal gall:

"diéronli mal bebraio commo malos e chanes.

   "Diéronli mal bebraio amargo sin mesura,

"fiel vuelta con vinagre, una crúa mixtura:

"él non lo quiso tragar, ca era cosa dura,

"todo fincó en ellos e en la su natura. (*st.* 39-40)

Vicarious suffering and therefore the increasing of bitterness is played up when Mother almost literally duplicates the actions and the attitude of Son, first resisting and then enduring:

"Fraire, verdat te digo, débesme tú creer:
"querríe seer muerta más que viva seer;
"mas al Rey del çielo no l' cadió en plaçer,
"oviemos del absinçio larga-mente a beber. (*st.* 45)

The poet wisely avoids turning the effective to the maudlin by immediately enumerating pleasant qualities, the final one being *dulzor,* significantly, riming with *sabor:*

"Con rabia del mi Fiio, mi padre, mi sennor,
"mi lumne, mi confuerto, mi salut, mi pastor,
"mi vida, mi conseio, mi gloria, mi dulzor
"nin avía de vida nin cobdiçia nin sabor. (*st.* 46)

More than two dozen stanzas elapse before unpleasant taste is found again, and then the reference is broad:

"Tú sufres el laçerio, io los malos sabores (*st.* 73)

and is rather soon followed by an apostrophe to the *Fiio dulz e sombroso* (*st.* 76). In the next three mentions, one of which is illative, the bitterness is shifted back to the Son, who reflects the Mother's suffering as she had reflected his:

" 'más me amarga esso que los colpes mortales (*st.* 81)

and confesses his willingness figuratively to drain the cup for the sake of mankind:

" 'Madre, será aína el vaso agotado (*st.* 93)
" 'Si io el vaso bebo commo me es mandado (*st.* 94)

thereby bringing a measure of comfort to the Mother:

"vos bebedes por todos vinagre e amargura (*st.* 100).

Recollection of the bitterness returns, nevertheless, but in recollection the acuteness of specific taste is missing and the unpleasantness is shared:

"qua mal muesso tragamos, e fuer vaso bebiemos (*st.* 148)

This tempering precedes by four stanzas one of the few instances of relief from the aloed:

"diziendo: '¡Ay fijo la mi dulzor complida!' (*st.* 152)

which, in turn, gives way as soon to bitterness full-force and quadrupled:

"veía io mesquina amarga assadura. (*st.* 155)
  "Vedía assadura amarga io mesquina,
"amargos coçineros e amarga coçina:
"en título en lengua ebrea e latina
"en griego la terçera, pan de mala farina. (*st.* 156)

Here the literal and the figurative are so nearly fused that it is diificult to distinguish between the two. The flavor permeates consciousness:

"El viernes en la noche fasta la madrugada
"sofrí grant amargura, noche negra e pesada (*st.* 161)

"Todas façíamos planto e duelo sin mesura;
"mas la que lo pariera soffría maior cochura,
"levaba maior cuyta, tenía maior ardura,
"ca tenía por pitanza amarga asadura. (*st.* 164)

"Rodía cruda maiella, amarga pitanza,
"sabíali más amarga que grant colpe de lanza, (*st.* 165)

Cantaban los trufanes unas controvaduras
que eran a su Madre amargas e muy duras (*st.* 177).

Like an unexpected burst of sunshine from behind clouds,
joy suddenly takes precedence over bitterness:

Resusçitó don Xpto: ¡Dios, tan grant alegría!
Dos soles, Deo graçias, nasçieron essi día:
resusçitó don Xpto, e la Virgo María
toda la amargura tornó en alegría. (*st.* 196)

and bitterness thereupon disappears from the poem.

Taste is perhaps the most difficult of the senses for
a poet to use extensively in his work, especially in a work
as long as is the *Duelo de la Virgen*. Berceo uses it both
lyrically and dramatically, first in scattered mention, artfully and literally giving us a foretaste of, and as if to
prepare us for, the actual taste of the gall, and later the
parallel emotional bitterness to be experienced from the
taunts of the guards of the sepulchre. Three techniques
particularly make his use of taste outstanding. One is the
synesthetic play on sweet-bitter, with a preponderance of

the bitter, to parallel the account of torture victim's character and mockers' gall. The second is the parallelism itself, by means of which the closeness of the relationship, the mutual concern, and the inseparability of feeling of Mother and Son are so clearly demonstrated. The third is the careful control of dynamics and therefore of emotional tension. The above quotations indicate the distribution of taste reference throughout the poem and the variation from specific to broad. The two clusters of references (stanzas 39-40 and 155-156) are widely spaced, though placed well within the poem, and constitute the parallel climaxes (of the literal and of the figurative) toward which the gradual accumulation of sporadic isolated references, interspersed in varying tempo and pulsating force, builds or from which it recedes, finally to disappear altogether in the appropriate circumstances.

Concealment of technique in the presentation of bitterness is virtually complete. Attention is drawn away from it to center on certain useful ornaments with which the composition is adorned. One of these that catches the ear immediately is the frequent repetition of *lexaprende* in many variations:

"ruégote que m' condones esto que io te digo. (*st.* 79)
  "Ruégote que m' condones esto que io te pido (*st.* 80)

" 'non quiso que ioguiessen en tal enfermería. (*st.* 86)
  " 'Non quiso que ioguiessen en tan pudio valleio (*st.* 87)

" 'io e tú, Madre mía, no l' podemos verter. (*st.* 91)
  " 'Yo e tú, Madre mía, lo debemos gostar (*st.* 92)

More than two dozen examples cause nearly a fourth of the stanzas to be involved in this special type of linking,

not to mention the many repetitions of the same patterns
within the stanza. Berceo even combines *lexaprende* with
chiasmus:

"façiéndoli boçines iudíos e paganos. (*st.* 49)
  "Iudíos e paganos vaçiéndole boçines (*st.* 50)

"ca nunca parió Madre Fiio de tal natura. (*st.* 60)
  "Fiio de tal natura de Madre non nasçió (*st.* 61)

"nin reçibió colpada que li uslase tanto. (*st.* 110)
  "nunqua priso colpada que tanto li uslase (*st.* 111)

plus anaphora:

"fiçieron las oveias despessar al pastor. (*st.* 71)
  "Fiçieron las oveias al pastor enforcar (*st.* 72)

"veía io mesquina amarga assadura. (*st.* 155)
  "Vedía asadura amarga io mesquina. (*st.* 156)

"no li membró del dicho del su sancto Esposo. (*st.* 109)
  "No li membró del dicho de su Esposo sancto (*st.* 110)

In chiasmus, it will be noted, the second half of the
combination stands virtually as a mirror image of the first,
and so produces a reflective effect. In the *Duelo de la Virgen* a special type of anaphora also contributes to the impression of mutual reflection of feeling in Mother and Son,
an impression already noted in the use of the theme of bitterness. In a series of eight stanzas (73-80, and cf. 123-129)
the Virgin lamentingly and imploringly addresses the Son.
She begins with an exclamation:

"¡ Ai Fiio querido, sennor de los sennores! (*st.* 73)

and thereafter each stanza except the last begins with the vocative *Fiio*. In the last stanza (80) the *Fiio* is held until the beginning of the third line. Intensification of the word through additional anaphora in the third stanza, the last two lines of which begin with *Fiio*, so that four of five consecutive lines bear the initial *Fiio*, seems to reflect the intensity of the Virgin's emotion. Emotional intensity and compositional unity thus are in part simultaneously produced by means of this anaphora that seems to spring so spontaneously from distress. Four consecutive stanzas (74-77) plus the last (80) of this series contain the word *Madre* at mid-verse stress position. The Son's answer to the Mother's grief and supplication begins with this word (stanza 81), which is the initial word of the following two stanzas and sporadically of others thereafter. Deliberate enmeshing in set pattern thus once more symbolizes the insoluble Mother-Son bond and so stresses the poignancy of reciprocity and therefore the intensification of the suffering.

By means of carefully selected reciprocity devices such as those just discussed, in addition to the dialogue form in which the poem is cast, and which together form what may be termed a "mirror" technique, Berceo creates for his purpose a most unusual and original kind of perspective, in which the two figures, through simultaneous reflection of each other's feelings, set up a possible infinity of duplications, each one increasing the total and therefore penetrating to great depth. Naturally, a great portion of the poem is devoted to the Virgin's suffering alone for each incident of the Passion, but nearly complete identification of Mother with Son occurs several times:

"Conviene que fablemos en la nuestra privanza
"del pleito del mi duelo, de la mi mal andanza,

"cómmo sufrí martirio sin gladio e sin lanza,
"si Dios nos aiudara fer una remembranza. (*st.* 44)
"oviemos del absinçio larga-mente a beber. (*st.* 45)
"agora so ferida de muy mala colpada (*st.* 122)

and Mother's reaction to the first incident leading to Crucifixion is a foreshadowing parallel to the whole sequence
of events—to be noted are such details as loss of blood,
simulation of death, revival:

"Con esta sobrevienta que nos era venida,
"perdí toda la sangre, iogui amodorrida;
"querría seer muerta más que sofrir tal vida;
"si muerta me oviessen, oviéranme guarida. (*st.* 17)
　"Quando cobré el sesso, catém' a derredor,
"nin vidi los disçípulos, nin vidi al pastor:
"lo de primas fue queta, mas ésta muy maior,
"non havía conseio de haver nul sabor. (*st.* 18)

and her reaction to the fact of death is precisely a death-
like state:

"Quando rendió la alma el Sennor glorioso,
"la gloriosa Madre del mérito preçioso
"cadió en tierra muerta commo de mal rabioso,
"no li membró del dicho del su sancto Esposo. (*st.* 109)
　"No li membró del dicho de su Esposo sancto,
"tanto priso grant cueyta e tan manno crebanto,
"ca nunqua li viniera un tan fiero espanto,
"nin reçibió colpada que li uslase tanto. (*st.* 110)

Correspondingly, the Son's suffering is increased by the witnessing of the Mother's reaction:

> "El mi Fiio preçioso, sennor de grant imperio,
> "más se dolié de mí que non de su laçerio,
> "façié complida-mientre todo su ministerio,
> "commo nos lo demuestra el Santo Evangelio. (*st.* 30)
>   "Recudió el Sennor, dixo palabras tales:
> " 'Madre, mucho me duelo de los tus grandes males,
> " 'muévenme tos lágrimas, los tus dichos capdales,
> "más me amarga esso que los colpes mortales. (*st.* 81)
>   " 'Madre, cata mesura, atiempra más to planto;
> " 'Madre, por Dios te sea, non te crebrantes tanto,
> " 'a todos nos crebantas con essi tu quebranto;
> " 'Madre, que tú lo hagas por Dios el Padre sancto. (*st.* 98)

Mutual concern is made manifest without recourse to words:

> "Io cataba a elli porque tanto lazdraba,
> "e él cataba a mí que tanto me quesaba;
> "entre todas las cueitas a mí non oblidaba,
> "quando io daba voçes, elli bien me cataba. (*st.* 29)
>
> "Estaba estordida, non podía fablar,
> "con la rabia del Fiio non podía folgar,
> "ca era un mal muesso pesado de tragar,
> "más que la sierva cruda que es un mal maniar. (*st.* 35)
>   "Estando en la cruz la santa creatura
> "tendió a todas partes la su dulz catadura:
> "vio a mí mezquina triste con grant cochura,
> "clamando: "¡Fiio, Fiio!" a una grant pressura. (st. 36)

Sharing is inevitable:

> " 'Otra guisa non puede esti mal guareçer
> " 'nin por otro escato, nin por otro saber,
> " 'fuera por esti vaso que debemos beber:
> " 'io e tú, Madre mía, no l' podemos verter. (*st.* 91)
>   " 'Yo e tú, Madre mía, lo debemos gostar,
> " 'io sufriendo las penas e tú el grant pesar:
> " 'deben todas las gentes por ende te loar,
> " 'lazdrar tú e tu Fiio por las almas salvar. (*st.* 92)

Intensification of suffering is increased by still another use of perspective, that of time. The fiction of vision or dream so often employed by Mediaeval writers to lend a poetic air and an illusion of distance to a work is replaced in the *Duelo de la Virgen* by memory. The realistic depiction contained in the recollection underscores the poignancy of the original feelings—so acute were they that they remain fresh even after lapse of time, joy of triumph, and bliss of beatitude. Acuteness of the sorrow is further stressed through the reluctance with which the Virgin agrees to call to memory her bitter experiences, to *refrescar las mis penas:*

> "Fraire," disso la duenna: "esme cosa pessada
> "refrescar las mis penas, ca so glorificada;
> "pero la mi fetila non la he oblidada,
> "ca en el corazón la tengo bien fincada." (*st.* 13)

Grief, moreover, is perhaps the cause of noticeably more extensive (though still minimal) use of psychomorphism in the *Duelo de la Virgen* than in the *Loores de Nuestra Señora:*

"Non era maravella si la que lo parió
"con duelo de tal Fiio si se amorteció:
"en los signos del çielo otro tal conteçió,
"todos fiçieron duelo quando elli morió. (*st.* 113)
"el sol perdió la lumne, oscureçió el día (*st.* 114)

"El velo que partié el tiemplo del altar
"partiós' en dos partes, ca non podié plorar;
"las piedras porque duras quebraban de pesar, (*st.* 115)
"De los sepulcros vieios de antiguas sazones
"en qui iaçién reclusos muchos sanctos varones,
"abriéronse por sí sin otros azadones,
"revisclaron de omnes grandes generaçiones. (*st.* 116)

"Mientre que por el mundo corrién estos roydos,
"los elementos todos andaban amortidos;
"recudí io mesquina a esos apellidos,
"ca cuidábanse todos que serién destruidos. (*st.* 118)

"Día en qui io pierdo toda mi claridat,
"lunne de los mis oios e de toda piadat,
"ploran los elementos todos de voluntat:
"io mesquina si ploro, non fago liviandat. (*st.* 142)

Several poetic genres are clearly discernible in the
work, as would be expected in a *mester de clerecía* composition. Narrative frequently sustains the movement of the
poem and serves to hold some of the semi-independent sections together. Dialogue, which bears some relationship to
the Mediaeval poetic debate, is the form of which most of
the poem is comprised. The prayer appears several times.
Lyric devices are largely responsible for homogenizing the

whole. One song, *¡Eya velar!*, bodily inserted in the poem, after proper introduction to avoid obtrusiveness, provides an early example of the fusion of the popular and the learned, a feature of Spanish poetry conspicuous in the work of such poets as the Marqués de Santillana, Lope de Vega, Góngora, and García Lorca.

The *¡Eya velar!* is one of the rare examples left to us of thirteenth-century popular song, and for its style and meaning as well as its form it has been a favourite in anthologies. In this *canción de vela*, Berceo has employed a semi-dialogue form in which the speaker apparently addresses alternately his companions (stanzas 178-179, 181, 183, 187-190) and entombed Christ (stanzas 180, 182, 184-186), but does not wait for an answer other than the refrain *¡Eya velar!* With its immediate introduction the song is:

> Tornaron al sepulcro vestidos de lorigas,
> diçiendo de sus bocas muchas suçias nemigas,
> controbando cantares que non valían tres figas,
> tocando instrumentos, çedras, rotas e gigas. (*st.* 176)
> Cantaban los trufanes unas controvaduras
> que eran a su Madre amargas e muy duras:
> "Aljama, nos velemos, andemos en corduras,
> "si non, farán de nos escarnio e gahurras." (*st.* 177)

> *Cántica. ¡Eya velar, eya velar, eya velar!*
> [*To companions:*]   Velat, aliama de los iudiós,
> *¡Eya velar!*
> que non vos furten el Fijo de Dios,
> *¡Eya velar!*   (*st.* 178)

ca furtárvoslo querrán

¡Eya velar!

Andrés e Peidro et Iohán.

¡Eya velar!   (*st.* 179)

[*To Christ:*]   Non sabedes tanto descanto

¡Eya velar!

que salgades de so el canto.

¡Eya velar!   (*st.* 180)

[*To companions:*]   Todos son ladronçiellos

¡Eya velar!

que assechan por los pestiellos.

¡Eya velar!   (*st.* 181)

[*To Christ:*]   Vuestra lengua tan palabrera

¡Eya velar!

a vos dado mala carrera.

¡Eya velar!   (*st.* 182)

[*To companions:*]   Todos son omnes plegadizos,

¡Eya velar!

rioaduchos, mescladizos.

¡Eya velar!   (*st.* 183)

[*To Christ:*]   Vuestra lengua sin recabdo

¡Eya velar!

por mal cabo vos a echado.

¡Eya velar!   (*st.* 184)

Non sabedes tanto de enganno

¡Eya velar!

que salgades ende este anno.

¡Eya velar!   (*st.* 185)

Non sabedes tanta razón
¡Eya velar!
que salgades de la prisión.
¡Eya velar!   (*st.* 186)

[*To companions:*]   Tomaseio e Matheo
¡Eya velar!
de furtarlo han grant deseo.
¡Eya velar!   (*st.* 187)

El disçípulo lo vendió,
¡Eya velar!
el Maestro non lo entendió.
¡Eya velar!   (*st.* 188)

Don Fhilipo, Simón e Iudas
¡Eya velar!
por furtar buscan ayudas.
¡Eya velar!   (*st.* 189)

Si lo quieren acometer,
¡Eya velar!
oy es día de paresçer.
¡Eya velar!   (*st.* 190)

The final stanzas of the *Duelo de la Virgen* constitute a poem complete in itself, a fusion of paean and prayer well expressing the characteristically joyfully devout and confident attitude of Spain's earliest known great lyric poet:

Reyna de gloria, Madre de piedat,
sennora de los ángeles, puerta de salvedat,

conseio de las almas, flor de grant onestat,
tú me da connoçençia de sancta caridat. (*st.* 205)
    Tú eres benedicta carrera de la mar,
en que los peregrinos non puedan periglar;
tú los guía, sennora, que non puedan errar:
mientre por ti se guíen pueden salvos andar. (*st.* 206)
    Madre plena de graçia, tú seas bien laudada,
tú seas gradeçida, tú seas exaltada,
tú seas bien venida, tú seas bien trobada,
que sofriste tal pena e ffuste tan lazdrada. (*st.* 207)
    Madre, a ti comendo mi vida, mis andadas,
mi alma e mi cuerpo, las órdenes tomadas,
mis piedes e mis manos, peroque consegradas,
mis oios que non vean cosas desordenadas. (*st.* 208)
    Sennora de los çielos, plena de bendiçión,
abri las tus oreias, udi mi petiçión:
io ofrir non te puedo ninguna oblaçión,
mas la tu sancta graçia tenga la mi razón. (*st.* 209)
    Madre, que a Teófilo que era desperado
tú li ganesti la graçia del tu sancto criado,
tú aguisa, sennora, pora mí tal mercado,
porque nunqua me vea en premia del pecado. (*st.* 210)

The tone of this selection and the manner of the handling of its materials are similar to those of the hymns included among Berceo's works. In the hymns also the poet shifts smoothly from invocation to praise. The hymns, which scholars claim are adaptations of Latin liturgical hymns, are addressed one each to the Holy Ghost, to Saint Mary, and to Christ. The hymn to Christ has a first stanza

strikingly filled with brilliance, followed by a stanza of
contrasting night:

> Tú, Christe, que luz eres, que alumnas el día,
> que tuelles las tinieblas, fáçeslas ir su vía,
> bien creo que luz eres, lumne de alma mía,
> e que predigas lumne e toda bien fetría. (*st.* 1)
> Sennor e Padre Sancto, a ti merçet pedimos,
> por ti en esta noche seamos defendidos
> que folguemos seguros de nuestros enemigos,
> ayamos noche buena los de ti redemidos. (*st.* 2)

The hymn beginning *Veni, Creator Spiritus*, perhaps because of the ethereal nature of the Holy Ghost, remains on a
higher level of abstraction than does any selection of com-
parable length in Berceo's works:

> Veni, Creator Spiritus, pleno de dulçe lumne,
> visita nuestras mientes de la tu sancta lumne,
> purga los nuestros pechos de la mala calumne,
> ímplelos de tu graçia commo es tu costumne. (*st.* 1)
> Tú eres con derecho dicho confortador,
> dono dulz preçioso de Dios nuestro Sennor,
> fuent viva, fuego vivo, caridat e amor,
> unçión con que sana la alma pecador. (*st.* 2)
> De la tu sancta graçia, de la tu caridat
> manan los siete dones de grant actoridat.
> Tú eres dicho dedo del Rey de magestat,
> tú façes a los bárbaros fablar latinidat. (*st.* 3)
> Ençiende la tu lumne en el nuestro sentido,
> que ayan nuestras almas en ti amor complido;

la pereza del cuerpo que anda amortido
sea resuçitada por el tu don complido. (*st.* 4)

Del mortal enemigo tu graçia nos defienda,
dános cómmo vivamos en paz e sin contienda;
tú sei guión nuestro, cúbranos la tu tienda,
que escusar podamos toda mala façienda. (*st.* 5)

Dános sen que sepamos el Padre entender,
a vueltas con el Padre al Fijo connoçer,
de ti cómmo tengamos creençia e saber,
cómmo eres con ambos un Dios e un poder. (*st.* 6)

Loor sea al padre e al su engendrado,
a ti Creator Spiritus, de ambos aspirado;
el Fijo que por nos fo en cruz martiriado
envíenos la graçia del Spíritu sagrado. Amen. (*st.* 7)

EL LIBRO DE ALEXANDRE

El libro de Alexandre, commonly dated mid-thirteenth
century, formerly attributed to Berceo and more recently
to Juan Lorenzo Segura (de Astorga) or to an anonymous
poet, was written purportedly to give a historical account
and to extol the exploits of King Alexander the Great
(Macedonia and Greece, 356 B.C.). It contains more than
ten thousand lines in the *mester de clerecía* mode. The
poet is proud of his craftsmanship:

> Mester trago fermoso, non es de ioglaría,
> mester es sen peccado, ca es de clerezía,
> fablar curso rimado per la quaderna uía
> a síllauas cuntadas, ca es grant maestría. (*st.* 2)

It is an encyclopedic miscellany, typical of the period,
and at the same time the most comprehensive general compendium remaining to us from the early centuries of Castilian literature. One of the most entertaining of Mediaeval books, it reads like a digressive novel interspersed with
interpolations from other genres, including the lyric. Some
of the entertainment derived by present-day readers was

not intended by the author, but today's readers are amused by the anachronic: Alexander, for example, is dubbed knight and accompanied by his Twelve Peers. Anachronisms and legend-for-history notwithstanding, the poem is an animated present-day-lifelike presentation of history seldom, if ever, found in historical writing. The poet had a vivid vision of the past, an acute sense of the perennial. Even when he speaks at length on his contemplation of death and the grave, his account is a cinematographic one of both physical and psychological activity. Certainly he was inspired by idealism and the heroic in both deed and thought. The first pages of the poem give us an early portrait of the ideal prince, and in it we find an interest in both the idealistic and the practical, a combination that is later to interest several of Spain's master writers.

From the *Libro de Alexandre* it is possible to select a number of passages that give evidence of the relatively advanced stage of development of the thirteenth-century non-religious lyric. The wide variety of subjects, each evoking a distinct mood, and the individualized techniques of composition employed to relate subject and mood, indicate that Castilian had rapidly become a major literary language. The following selections will give some idea of the breadth of interest in the lyric at the early date of mid-thirteenth century.

The desire to include as much encyclopedic information as possible in the work gives rise to a particular minor and most enchanting genre, that of the miniature breviate paralleling the general structure of the poem. One of these miniatures, *La obra de las armas que Achilles mandó far*, is a description of Achilles' arms, which presents a panoramic view of the earth and the to-and-fro of its occupants' activities upon it, all with the serenity of detach-

ment provided by spatial and emotional distance perspective and an appreciation of the poetic qualities of existence.
Man, beast, bird, and natural phenomena, planets included,
are one in this existence; they are held in one view, are
governed by one law:

> En pocas de palabras vos quiero destajar
> la obra de las armas que Archiles mandó far,
> que sy por orden todo lo quesiesen notar
> serié vn breujario que prendrié grant logar.
> > (Paris ms. *st.* 637)
> Ome que por espaçio lo quesiese asmar
> > (Paris ms., *st.* 638)
> hy uerrían los peçes quántos son enno mar,
> las unas naues yr e las otras tornar,
> las unas pereçer e las otras arribar. (*st.* 609)
> Hy estauan las tierras por poblar e pobladas,
> las aues e las bestias por domar e domadas,
> la torre que fezioron las yentes periuradas. (*st.* 610)
> Hy estauan contrarios los tiempos por yguales,
> cada uno cuémo corren, o quáles temporales,
> cuémo naçen los truenos e los rayos mortales,
> cuémo son en el anno IIII. tiempos cabdales. (*st.* 611)
> Estaua don Enero con nieues e con geladas,
> el uerano con flores e dulçes maçanas,
> agosto con soles e miesses espigadas,
> ochubre uendimiando e faziendo pomadas. (*st.* 612)
> Eran hy los XII. signos del sol bien compassados,
> los unos de los otros ygualmente taiados,

e los VII. planetas cuémo tienen sus grados,
quáles son más rauiosas o quáles más pagadas.
(st. 613)

Non es ombre tan neçio que uiesse el escudo,
que non fuesse buen clérigo sobre bien entendudo:
el maestro que l' fizo fue tan mientes metudo
que metió en escudo granado e menudo. (<i>st.</i> 614)

From the universal the poet is able to turn to the
particular and to the appreciation of a single aspect of
nature, and to the mood prompted by natural phenomena
and created by man's activity. The burst of the red dawn
coincidental with man's resounding annunciation of imminent bloodshed gains response from earth and heaven:

Ya quería en tod' esto apuntar el aluor,
querié tornar el çielo en uermeia color,
mandó mouer las huestes el bon emperador,
ca non podié de sy partir el mal sabor. (<i>st.</i> 802)
Las trompas e los cuernos ally fueron tannidos,
fueron los atambores de cada parte feridos:
tanto eran grandes e fieros los roydos,
semeiauan las tierras e los çielos mouidos. (<i>st.</i> 803)

If man seems capable of moving the earth and the sky
above, he succumbs, nevertheless, to the dictates of contrasting elements in them:

El mes era de julio un tiempo escalentado,
quando el león ha el sol en su grado:

auíe ya del mes XV. días andado,
segundo esto pareçe bien era mediado. (*st.* 835)
   El tiempo era fuerte, e el sol muy feruiente,
querié de calentura morrer toda la gente,
Cecilia sobre todas auié aer caliente,
ca el ardor del sol la quexa fiera miente. (*st.* 836)
   Va por medio la uilla una agua cabdal,
que segundo la tierra bona una conal
façe en bona sierra, desçende por bon ual,
pareçe so la agua crespo el arenal. (*st.* 837)
   Preso el rey sabor de bannarse en ella,
ca corrié tan fremosa que era marauiella;
ouiera hy contida por poco grant mazella,
mouiera todo 'l mundo del río la querella. (*st.* 838)

The poet is as relentless with his heat-shafts as the mid-July sun and atmosphere are with theirs. The zodiacal figure of Leo is particularly apt here, representing as it does not only the ferociousness of the lion itself but also Leo's command of the fiery, the hot, and the dry in zodiacal interpretation, and astrologically the day house of the sun. This type of astronomical reference with its many implications appears again and again in Spanish poetry in the following centuries and most beautifully, perhaps, and with suggestiveness remarkably similar to that of this poet's verse, by Góngora at the beginning of *Las soledades*. The two stanzas of heat and dryness find a sudden contrast in two stanzas of invitingly cool running mountain water. As usual in this poem, nature and man go together, constantly interacting with each other, and so the king in his toils is here exhausted by one element and refreshed by another.

Neither the *Razón de amor* poet nor Berceo was superior to the author of the *Libro de Alexandre* in portraying the tree-shaded and spring-tempered natural retreat. In fact, this author is more convincing than the others in that he singles out a specific tree known for its dark-green foliage and standing alone in an open and elevated space, and around this centralized figure and sloping away from it he places a limited number of essential accessory details in a natural order and proportion. Instead of cramming by simple enumeration or conglomeration, he offers only what reason can accept, and he expands lyrically on each item: the time-laden aseasonal evergreen laurel on the hillcrest, the natural spring whose waters temper the surroundings and run down the slope, the sweet-and fresh-scented air as a natural consequence of tree and spring located on a knoll, the birds delighting in their surroundings and their busyness, and finally the meadows flowering in response to the gentle movement of the water. This poet is not content to stylize or to accept the conventionalized concept of springtime; he chooses a simple landscape picture that he has observed from nature first-hand; and he paints realistically as well as artistically, and in so doing makes the reader almost literally breathe the refreshing air of the shaded hillock, and soothe all his sense organs in his perception of the surroundings. Significantly, he does not disturb the greenness and the shade and the water with direct mention of sunlight or specific bright color, though these are implicit in the *prados* with their *flores colorados*. He creates a sense of momentary peace and harmony amidst the perennial war and discord of successive events, and he does so partly by the utter simplicity of the picture and partly by holding the picture completely within the bounds of verisimilitude and so placing no strain on

credulity—for, after all, laurels *are* evergreen, springs in
certain localities *do* run the year round, trees and springs
do attract birds, birds *do* sing in the morning, spring water
does flow down-hill and create flowering meadows that attract various animals. One of the notable features of this
scene is that of its relationship with the surrounding area.
It is not a completion within itself appearing almost out of
nothingness, as in the case of the *Razón de amor* and the introduction to the *Milagros de Nuestra Señora*, but occupies a
perfectly natural and accessible place in the general landscape. The picture has an air of timelessness and a hint
of solitude in it—the aged, solitary, fruitless tree forever
green, the setting itself standing alone above the surrounding terrain. This bit of ruggedness, and the unusual plane
of the terrain differentiate this piece immediately from the
other known Castilian poetic landscapes of the early centuries:

> En medio del hueste auié un colladiello,
> d' ella e d' ella parte era alto un poquiello,
> era enna cabeça sano e uerdeziello,
> era un logareio por uerdat apostiello. (*st.* 888)
>
> Estaua en medio un lorer ançiano,
> los ramos bien espessos, el tronco muy sano;
> cobríe la tierra un uergel muy loçano,
> siempre estaua uerde ynuierno e uerano. (*st.* 889)
>
> Manaua de siniestro una fuente perenal,
> nuncas mingua ca era natural:
> auié so el rozío fecho un regaral,
> por hy fazié su curso cuemo una canal. (*st.* 890)
>
> Exié de la fontana una blanda frior,

de la sombra del áruol un temprado sabor,
daua el aruolorio sobre buena olor,
semeiaua que era huerto del Criador. (*st.* 891)
    Que por buena solombra, que por la fontana
ally uenién las aues tener la meridiana,
ally fazién los cantos dulzes a la mannana,
mas non cabrié hy aue sy non fues palaçiana. (*st.* 892)
    El agua de la fuente deçende a unos prados,
teniélos siempre uerdes, de flores colorados,
auié hy grant auondo de diuersos uenados,
de quantos en el mundo podíen ser osmados. *(st.* 893)

Not always, however, was our author so faithful to the
natural; at times he added to the natural a touch of the
supernatural—and as a result composes a rather commonplace description (stanzas 1121 ff. and stanza 1331).

In the rather extensive lapidary (stanzas 1306-1330)
the author apparently strives more to be informative concerning the magic virtues of each stone than poetic in displaying the visual qualities. This lapidary, typical of Mediaeval catalogue verse, is part of the *pleyto de Babilonnia*
(stanzas 1299 ff.) in which the poet demonstrates his skill
in inventorying.

In the *pleyto de Babilonnia* the poet turns his attention easily from natural assets to man-made wonders, from
his usual lively portrayals to the static of solid masonry,
and gives us our earliest known cityscape in Castilian
poetry:

La çerca es estranna, en penna çimentada,
pero yaz en penna, es bien carcauada;

la cárcaua es bien fonda, d' agua bien rasada,
naues traen por ella ca es fonda el agua. (*st.* 1361)

Vn trecho de balesta es alto el muro,
de bona argamassa e de pedernal duro,
en ancho otro tanto si mal no lo mesuro:
el que estouiés de dentro deuiés seer seguro. (*st.* 1362)

Las torres ha espessas, segundo aprisiemos,
atantas son que cuenta dar non les podriemos:
los días de un anno dizen que serién diezmos;
del que las non uiesse creydos non seriemos. (*st.* 1363)

Las amenas son de canto menudas e granadas,
las otras son de mármol redondas e quadradas;
éstas con aquéllas son assy afferradas
que sean las unas de las otras suiugadas. (*st.* 1364)

Ay sen llos postigos XXX. portas cabdales;
guárdanlas sendos reys, que pocos á de tales,
todos por natura son reys naturales;
dizen que todos tienen regnos generales. (*st.* 1365)

El real es en medio fecho a marauellas,
y es el sol pintado, la luna e las estrellas,
y están las columnas, los espeios en ellas,
en que s' miran todas casadas e ponçellas. (*st.* 1366)

Son dentro enna uilla los naturales bannos
a que uienen las aguas so tierra por cannos;
están apareiados de cappas e de sayos;
non uien hy ombre a que menguassen pannos. (*st.* 1367)

Tienen a IIII. cantos IIII. torres cabdales,
plus claras son que uidrio, ca son finos cristales;

se fazen por la uilla furtos o cosas tales,
ally lo ueen luego entre las sinnales. (*st.* 1368)

A more melancholy expression of the sentiment of
patriotism than any we have met previously or shall meet
for some time is the six-stanza passage begining *El omne
en su tierra* . . . Here once again we find the theme-with-
variations structure. Totally unlike the poet of the *Poema
de Fernán González,* the author of this selection, unwit-
tingly no doubt, creates a mood of utter pessimism. In spite
of the cheerfulness in his opening line and most of the
first stanza, the poet's negative, even sour, approach to
his subject of patriotism is hardly relieved by a lone half-
stanza of warmth and pleasant image:

Los fijos e las fijas dulces son de ueer,
an de su companna los parientes plazer (*st.* 1474)

Although this poem is not in the least satiric, it foreshadows the work of such great pessimist-satirists as Pero
López de Ayala, the Archpriest of Talavera, and Quevedo.
The selection is a fine example of almost pure subjectivity,
for in spite of the author's complete exclusion of self from
his poem, and in spite of the fact that attention is altogether directed to earthly reality having no perceptible connection with the author as a person, we are struck far
more forcibly by the author's state of mind and his attitude
toward life and death than we are by the statements he
makes. In this selection the poignant verses are written between the lines—by the reader-cocreator. The poet's mood
is transferred to the reader by a sort of dramatic technique: constant activity in pantomime, silent movie
"shorts," so to speak.

This selection is important in the history of the development of Spanish poetry because it is one of the earliest —possibly, indeed, the earliest—elaboration on the theme of the physical aspect of death, which became almost an obsession of some fourteenth-and fifteenth-century poets:

El omne en su tierra uiue más a sabor,
fázenle a la morte los parientes honor;
los ossos, e l'alma an folgança maor
quando muchos parientes están aderredor. (*st.* 1470)

Los omnes de la uilla al que es estranno
en cabo del fossario lo echan orelano,
danle cuemo a puerco enna fossa de mano,
nunca diz más nadi: "Aquí iaz fulano." (*st.* 1471)

Mas el omne que es de cruda uoluntad
cuyda que los otros son sen piadat:
cuemo assy él es leno de maluestat,
ten que ennos otros non a caridat. (*st.* 1472)

Non serién las mugieres tan desuergonçadas
que por dulda del sieglo non fuessen defamadas,
que non lieuen a la eglesia candelas e obradas
e non fagan clamores tanner a las uegadas. (*st.* 1473)

Los fijos e las fijas dulces son de ueer,
an de su companna los parientes plazer:
encara no los puede tanto auorreçer
que descobierta-miente le quieran falleçer. (*st.* 1474)

Amigos, quien quesier creer e ascuchar,
non plantará maiuelo en aieno lugar:
buscará cuemo pueda a su tierra tornar:
crudo es e loco quien su casa quier desamparar.
                    (*st.* 1475)

The *Libro de Alexandre,* being an excellent example
of the multiple-genre *mester de clerecía,* would not be complete without a sample of the Mediaeval courtly poets'
"lady" description, in which the poet was supposed to give
an item-by-item laudatory analytic portrait of the idealized
beloved. By the fourteenth century this type of praise had
become so standardized and commonplace that Juan Ruiz
made it the object of satire in his *Libro de buen amor.* Our
poet converts the beloved to the somewhat aggressive Calectrix *la reyna.* Calectrix differed from the usual "lady" in
that she was not only a queen but an Amazon, which two
facts the poet apparently wished to make his description
reflect:

Venía apuesta-miente Calectrix la reyna,
vestía preçiosos panos de bona seda fina,
açor en su mano que fue de la marina,
serié al menos de doz mudas ayna. (*st.* 1710)

Avíe bon corpo, era bien astilada,
correa de IIII. palmos la çinnia doblada,
nunca fue en el mundo cara meior taiada,
non podría por nul pleyto ser más meiorada. (*st.* 1711)

La fruente auié blanca, alegre e donzella,
plus clara que la luna quando es duodena:
non auría fremosura cerca ella la Filomena
de la que diz Oraçio una grant cantilena. (*st.* 1712)

Tales ha las sobreceias cuemo listas de seda,
yguales, bien abiertas, de la nariz hereda,
trae solombrera tan mansa e tan queda,
non serié coprada por nenguna moneda. (*st.* 1713)

La beldat de los oios era fiera nobleza,
las pestannas mesturadas de continual adeça,
quando bien los abría era fiera fadeza,
a cristiano por fecho tolrrié toda pereza. (*st.* 1714)

Era tan a rrazón la nariz leuantada
que non podría Apelles deprender la posada:
los beços auenidos, la boca mesurada,
los dientes por iguales brancos cuemo quaiada. (*st.* 1715)

Blanca era la duena de muy fresca color,
auría grant entrega en ella un emperador:
la rosa del espino non es tan genta flor,
el roçío a la mannana non parece meior. (*st.* 1716)

De la su fremosura non quiero más cuntar,
temo de uoluntat fazer algún pesar:
los sus ensennamientos non los sabrié faular
Offreus el que fizo los áruoles cantar. (*st.* 1717)

Our versatile poet moves rapidly from theme to theme
and from mood to mood. When Maytime catches his fancy,
he pauses a moment to enjoy it:

El mes era de mayo un tiempo glorioso
quando fazen las aues un solaz deleytoso,
son uestidos los prados de uestido fremoso,
da sospiros la duenna, la que non ha esposo. (*st.* 1788)

Tiempo dolçe e sabroso por bastir casamientos,
ca lo tempran las flores e los sabrosos uientos,
cantan las donzelletas, son muchas ha conuientos,
fazen unas a otras buenos pronunçiamientos. (*st.* 1789)

Caen en el verano las bonas roçiadas,
entran en flor las miesses ca son ya espigadas,
entón casan algunos que pues messan las uaruas,
fazen las duennas triscas en camisas delgadas. (*st.* 1790)
    Andan moças e uieias cobiertas en amores,
van coger por la siesta a los prados las flores,
dizen unas a otras: "¡Bonos son los amores!"
y aquellos plus tiernos tiénense por meiores. (*st.* 1791)
    Los días son grandes, los campos reuerdidos,
son los passariellos del mal pelo exidos,
los táuanos que muerden non son aún uenidos,
luchan los monagones en bragas sen uestidos. (*st.* 1792)

It is difficult to imagine that the author who so aptly
spoke for the disillusioned traveller of *El omne en su tierra*
should have composed a poem in the lively and "glorious"
mood of *El mes era de mayo.* Both these selections are
unique and significant for the creation and sustaining of
mood. Although the moods of the two pieces are extreme
opposites, the principle technique involved in producing
them is the same: representation of constant activity in
pantomime. Not content, though, with *showing* us the lively
season, the poet would have us also *hear* it (birds and
maidens singing), *feel* it (flowers and breezes tempering,
showers falling, ladies frolicking, women flower-gathering,
gadflies not yet biting, boys romping), *taste* it (via synesthesia: delicious bird-singing, sweet and tasty weather for
planning marriages), and no doubt even *smell* it in the
flowers and breezes together tempering it, grain forming,
flower-gathering.

The May theme, a Mediaeval favourite, undoubtedly

has its origin in the distant past, in purely popular song
and dance that come almost spontaneously, impelled by the
season itself. We shall meet it again in a favourite ballad:

> Por el mes era de mayo
> cuando hace la calor,
> cuando canta la calandria
> y responde el ruiseñor . . .

In literature it is related to the general springtime theme.
If we compare our present selection with the *Razón de
amor* or with the introduction to Berceo's *Milagros de
Nuestra Señora* we will notice at a glance fundamental
differences. Without benefit of extensive landscape description, the poet of *El mes era de mayo* plunges immediately
into the depicting of the activity of typical human beings
in uninhibited and spontaneous reaction to the season, and
along with people other aspects of nature join in the activity. The human element, the psychology of stimulus and
reaction, active human participation in spring rather than
passive enjoyment of it, at once differentiate this poem
from the other two under discussion. Berceo's description
stands midway between this Maytime piece and the *Razón
de amor* in its account of the animation of the scene.

With the attention of engineer, of architect, and of
decorator, the poet focuses on the splendor and the palatial
elegance of the royal residence and transmits to us a sense
of the magnificence of royalty. Tour-fashion, the well-
informed author guides us through the many marvels of
human workmanship, of man-made beauty. The passage
is a real tribute to man in his artistic endeavour, and an
appreciation of the product of that endeavour in several
media:

La obra del palaçio non es de oluidar,
pero non la podriemos derechamientre contar:
porque mucho queramos de la uerdat lexar,
aún aurán por esso algunos a duldar. (*st.* 1956)

El lugar era plano, rica-ment assentado,
auondado de caça se quier e de uenado,
las montanas bien çerca do paçié el ganado,
verano e innuierno era bien temprado. (*st.* 1957)

Furon los palaçios de bon mestre assentados,
furon maestramientre a quadra compassados,
en penna uiua furon los çimientos echados,
per agua nen per fuego non serién desatados. (*st.* 1958)

Eran bien enluziadas e firmes las paredes,
non le fazíen mengua sáuanas nen tapedes,
el techo era pintado a laços e a redes,
todo d' oro fino, como en Dios creedes. (*st.* 1959)

Las portas eran todas de marfil natural,
blancas e reluzientes como fino cristal;
los entaios sotiles, bien alto el real,
casa era de rey, más bien era real. (*st.* 1960)

Quatroçientas colunpnas auié en essas casas,
todas d' oro fino capiteles e basas:
non serién más luzientes se fussen biuas brasas
ca eran bien brunidas, bien claras e bien rasas. (*st.* 1961)

Muchas eran las cámaras, todas con sus sobrados,
de çiprés eran todos los maderos obrados,
eran tan sotil-mientre entre ssí enlaçados,
que non entenderié omne do furan aiuntados. (*st.* 1962)

Pendién de las colunpnas derredor de la sala
vna muy rica uinna, de meior non uos incala:
leuaua foias d' oro grandes como la palma:
querría de grado auerlas tales, se Dios me uala. (*st*. 1963)

Las vuas eran fechas muy de grant femençia,
piedras son preçiosas todas de grant potençia,
toda la peor era de grant magnifiçençia:
el que plantó la uinna fu de grant sapiençia. (*st*. 1964)

Como todas las vinnas son de diuersas naturas,
assí las piedras son de diuersas figuras:
las unas eran uerdes e las otras maduras,
nunca les faz mal gielos nen calenturas. (*st*. 1965)

Ally fallaría omne las bonas cardeniellas,
e las otras maores que son más tempraniellas,
las blancas alfonsinas que tornan amariellas,
las alfonsinas negras que son más cardeniellas. (*st*. 1966)

Las bonas calagrannas que se quieren alçar,
las otras moleias que fazen las uieias trotar,
la torronts amorosa bona pora 'l lagar,
quanto uos omne non podrié dezir nen cuntar. (*st*. 1967)

Dexemos nos la vinna que era muy loçana,
que leuaua la uendimia tardía e temprana:
digamos del áruol que enna vinna estaua,
que asié hy riqueza fiera e adiana. (*st*. 1968)

En medio del encausto un logar apartado
seye rico áruol en medio leuantado,
nen era muy grueso nen muy delgado,
d' oro fino era, sotilmientre obrado. (*st*. 1969)

Quantas aues en çielo an uozes acordadas,
que dizen cantos dolçes menudas e granadas,
todas en aquel áruol pareçién figuradas,
cada una de su natura en color diuisadas. (*st.* 1970)
    Todo los estrumentos que usan los ioglares,
otros de maor preçio que usan escolares,
de todos auía hy tres o IIII. pares,
todos bien temprados por formar sus cantares. (*st.* 1971)
    A la rayz del áruol bien a XV. estados
venién unos canones que abién soterrados,
eran de coure duro por en esso laurados,
todos eran en el áruol metidos, ençerrados. (*st.* 1972)
    Soprauan cuemo bufetes en aquellos canones,
luego dezién las aues cada uno sus sones,
los gayos, las calandras, tordos e los gauiones,
el rossinol que diç las fremosas cançiones. (*st.* 1973)
    Luenga serié la cunta de las aues cuntar,
la noche ua ueniendo e quiero destaiar:
ya non sé quál quisiesse de las otras echar,
quando la çigarra non quiso delexar. (*st.* 1974)
    Voluí a los estrumentos a buelta connas aues,
encordauan açierto las cuerdas connas claues,
alçando e apremiando fazién cantos suaues,
tales que pera Orfeo de formar serién graues. (*st.* 1975)
    Ally era la música cantada per razón,
las dobles que refieren coytas del coraçón
las dolçes de las baylas, el plorant semitón;
bien podién toller preçio a quantos no mundo son.
                       (*st.* 1976)

Non es en el mundo omne tan sabedor
que dezir podiesse quál era el dolçor;
mientre omne uiuisse en aquella sabor
non auríe sede, nen fame, nen dolor. (*st.* 1977)
 Podédesuos per otra cosa mucho marauillar,
se quisiesse las medias solas farié cantar,
se quisiesse la terçia, si quisiesse un par,
sotil fu el maestre que lo souo laurar. (*st.* 1978)
 Ouo Alexandre por fiera estraneza,
dixo que non uira tan estranna riqueza,
todos tenién que era muy adapte nobleza,
non auíen oydo tan noble apteza. (*st.* 1979)

The poet's idea of Heaven was a simple one:

El Criador que fizo todas las creaturas,
con diuersos donarios e con diuersas figuras,
ordenó los lugares de diuersas naturas
do reçebían las almas lazerios e folguras. (*st.* 2171)
 Fizo pora los bonos que lo aman a seruir,
que so auer non duldan con los pobres partir,
el regno del parayso, do non pueden dormir,
do non podrién un punto de lazerio sofrir. (*st.* 2172)
 Ally serán en gloria qual non sabrían pedir,
qual non podrié nul omne faular nen comedir:
pornán toda su forçia en a Dios bendezir,
al que fue, al que es, al que á de uenir. (*st.* 2173)
 Nunca sentirá teniebra nen frío nen calentura,
verán la faz de Dios, muy dolçe catadura,

no s' fartarán d' ella a tan grant abondadura:
quien ally heredar, será de grant uentura. (*st.* 2174)

Static Heaven did not challenge the poet's imagination,
but the Hell he draws is both lively and complex:

Pora los otros malos que fazen mala uida,
que an la carrera derecha auorrida,
fue fecho l' infierno, çibdat mala complida:
assaz ha mal forado sen nenguna exida. (*st.* 2175)
  Fondo yaz infierno, nunca entra y lumbre,
de sentir luz nenguna non es su costumbre,
muros de piedra sufre presos de ueguedumbre
que no los romperíen nenguna fortedumbre. (*st.* 2176)
  Siluan per las riberas muchas malas serpientes,
están días e noches aguzando los dientes,
assechan a las almas, non tienen a al mientes,
per éstas peligraron los primeros parientes. (*st.* 2177)
  Quando ueen uenir las almas peccadriçes
tráuanles de los beços, préndenlas a las narizes,
fázenles entornar sen grado las çeruizes:
las que ally non furen teners' an por felizes. (*st.* 2178)
  Nunca fartarse pueden, están muertas de fame,
están todas cargadas de mala uedegambre,
non apertarién tanto cadenas de arambre,
Dios liure todo christiano de tan mala pelambre. (*st.* 2179)
  En todas sus cámaras non azen nunca flores,
se non spinas duras e cardos ponnidores,
touas que fazen fumes e amargos pudores,
peniscales agudos que son mucho peores. (*st.* 2180)

The seven personified deadly sins dwell around Hell's gateway busily plying their various nefarious trades—in a long and detailed passage (stanzas 2181-2247).

The panoramic view from a height is a theme that is treated periodically in Spanish poetry from the *Poema del Cid* through the Golden Age. Our poet's view is quite similar to that of fifteenth-century Juan de Mena's in the *Laberinto de Fortuna*. Even the means to the point of vantage will give a similar sensation. Here the poet tells how the ingenious king arranged for himself an airlift powered by hungry griffins straining for food dangling barely out of reach, and so was able to ride at will above the earth and to see its marvels below him:

Tanto pudo el rey a las nuues poiar,
que uee montes e ualles de iuso so sí estar:
veya entrar los ríos todos en alta mar,
mas cómo yaze o non nunca lo pudo asmar. (*st.* 2340)

Veyé en quales puertos son angostos los mares,
veyé muchos perigros en muchos de lugares,
veyé muchas galeras darnos pinescales,
otras salir a puerto, aguisar de iantares. (*st.* 2341)

Mesuró toda Africa cómo yaz assentada,
per quál logar seríe más rafez la entrada;
luego vio per u podría auer meior passada,
ca auié grant exida e larga la entrada. (*st.* 2342)

Luengo seríe de todo quanto vio contar,
non podríe el medio del día auondar,
mas en una hora sopo mientes parar,
lo que todos auedes no lo sabrié asmar. (*st.* 2243)

"Alexander's tent" is one of the best known passages of the poem. It concerns for the most part a static representation of animation, and so harmonizes well with the almost constant depiction of activity throughout the work. The tent itself is imposing in its proportions and its ornamentation. It betokens the splendor of the king, and with the splendor the completion of a time cycle— the twelve-month year—perhaps intended as a foreshadowing of the imminent completion of a life-cycle, the king's:

Ante que a las parias entremos reçebir,
quiérouos de la tienda, de su obra dezir:
segund que lo entiendo cuydo lo departir,
quien meior lo podier auerle que gradir. (*st.* 2375)
Larga era la tienda, redonda e bien taiada,
a dos mill caualleros darié larga posada:
Apelles el maestro la ouo debuxada,
non faría otro omne obra tan esmerada. (*st.* 2376)
El panno de la tienda era rico sobeio,
era de seda fina, de un xamet uermeio,
como era teçido ygualmente pareio,
quando el sol rayaua luzía como espeio. (*st.* 2377)
El çendal era bono sotilmientre obrado,
de pedaços menudos en torno compassado:
como era bien presso e bien endereçado,
no l' deuisaría omne do era aiuntado. (*st.* 2378)
Cargólo el maestro de somo a fondón
de piedras de preçio, todas bien a rrazón,
non falleçié nenguna de las que ricas son,
toda la más sotil era de grant missión. (*st.* 2379)

Tenié enna cabeça tres maçanas de bon oro,
qualsequier de todas ualía grant thesoro,
nunca tan ricas uio iudío nen moro,
si en el mundo fussen saberlas ya Poro. (*st.* 2380)

Non querría el tiempo ennas cordas perder,
ca auríe grant rato en ellas a poner:
eran de seda fina, podrían mucho ualer,
las laçadas d' oro do yuan a prender. (*st.* 2381)

Las estacas cabdales que las cuerdas tyrauan,
toda la otra obra essas lo adobauan:
las unas a las otras ren non semeiauan,
como omnes espessos tan espessas estauan. (*st.* 2382)

Mas de la otra orden que tiran las uentanas,
de todas las meiores semeiauan ermanas:
de oro eran todas, de obra muy loçanas,
teníen en su mano sennas ricas maçanas. (*st.* 2383)

Querría a la obra de la tienda entrar,
en estas manezuelas non querría tardar,
auriemos hy un rato assaz que deportar,
yrsenos ye domientre guisando de iantar. (*st.* 2384)

Bien pareçié la tienda cuando era alçada,
suso era redonda, enderredor quadrada,
de somo fasta fondo era bien estoriada,
quál cosa conteçió a omne, quál temporada. (*st.* 2385)

Era enna corona el çielo deboxado,
todo de creaturas angélicas poblado,
mas el logar do fura Luçifer derribado,
todo está yermo, pobre e desonrrado. (*st.* 2386)

Criaua Dios al omne pora enchir es' lugar,
el malo con enbidia óuogelo a furtar,
por el furto los ángelos ouioron grant pesar,
fu iulgado el omne pora morir e lasdrar. (*st.* 2387)

Cerca estas estorias, e çerca un rancón
alçauan los gigantes torre a grant missión:
mas metió Dios en ellos tan grant confusión,
perque auién a hyr todos a perdiçión. (*st.* 2388)

Las ondas del deluuio tanto querién souir,
per somo de Tyburio fascas querién salir;
Noé beuié el uino, no lo podié sofrir,
asié desordenado, queríalo encobrir. (*st.* 2389)

En un de los fastiales luego enna entrada
la natura del anno sedié toda pintada:
los meses con sos días, con su luna contada,
cada uno quál fazienda auié acomendada. (*st.* 2390)

Estaua don Janero a todas partes catando,
çercado de çenisa, sus çepos acarreando,
tenié gruessas gallinas, estáualas assando,
estaua de la percha longaniças tirando. (*st.* 2391)

Estaua don Feurero sos manos calentando,
oras fazíe sol, oras sarraçeando:
verano e inuierno yualos destremando,
porque era más chyquo seyésse querellando. (*st.* 2392)

Marçio auié grant priessa de sus uinnas laurar,
priessa con podadores, e priessa de cauar;
los días e las noches fazíelos yguar,
faze aues e bestias en çelo entrar. (*st.* 2393)

Abril sacaua huestes pora yr guerrear,
ca auié alcaçeres grandes ya pora segar;
fazié meter las uinnas pora uino leuar,
creçer miesses e yeruas, los días alongar. (*st.* 2394)

Sedié el mes de Mayo coronado de flores,
afeytando los campos de diuersas colores,
organeando las mayas, e cantando d' amores,
espigando las miesses que sembran lauradores. (*st.* 2395)

Maduraua don Junio las miesses e los prados,
tenié redor de ssí muchos ordios segados,
de çeresas maduras los çeresos cargados,
eran a mayor siesto los días allegados. (*st.* 2396)

Seya el mes de Julio cogendo segadores,
corriénle per la cara apriessa los sudores,
segudauan las bestias los moscardos mordedores,
fazié tornar los uinos de amargos sabores. (*st.* 2397)

Trillaua don Agosto las miesses per las serras, [las eras]
auentaua las paruas, alçaua las çeueras,
yua de los agrazes faziendo uuas ueras:
estón fazía Outunno sus órdenes primeras. (*st.* 2398)

Setembrio trae uaras, sacude las nogueras
apretaua las cubas, podaua las uimbreras,
vendimiaua las uinnas con fuertes podaderas,
non dexaua los pássaros llegar a las figueras. (*st.* 2399)

Estaua don Othubrio sus missiegos faziendo,
yua como de nueuo sus cosas requiriendo,
yua pora sembrar el inuierno ueniendo,
ensayando los uinos que azen ya feruiendo. (*st.* 2400)

Nouembrio secudía a los puercos las landes,
caera d' un roure, leuáuanlo en andes;
compiezan al crisuelo uelar los aueçantes,
ca son las noches luengas, los días non tan grandes.
                                        (*st.* 2401)
Mataua los puercos Deçembrio por mannana,
almorzauan los fégados por amatar la gana,
tenié nyubla escura siempre per la mannana,
ca es en es' tiempo ela muy cotiana. (*st.* 2402)

In addition to the months, other themes are worked into
the paintings on the tent silks, among them the mapamundi,
which provides a much better panoramic view of the world
than the one Alexander was able to command from his
griffin vehicle:

En el panno terçero de la tienda ondrada
era la mapamundi scrita e notada:
bien tenié quien 'a fizo la tierra decorada,
como se la ouiesse con sus pies andada. (*st.* 2412)
Tenié 'l mar en medio a la tierra çercada,
contra la mar la tierra non semeiaua nada,
y éssa muy más yerma que poblada,
d' ella azié pasturas, d' ella asié laurada. (*st.* 2413)
Las tres partes del mundo yazen bien deuisadas,
Asia a las otras auiélas engannadas,
Europa e Africa yazen bien ranconadas,
deuíen seer frías, semeiauan andadas. (*st.* 2414)
Ally fu el maestro sotil e acordado,

non oluidó çiudat, nen castiello poblado,
nen oluidó enperio, nen nengún bon condado,
nen río nen otero, nen yermo nen poblado. (*st.* 2415)

   Tajo, Doyro, e Ebro tres aguas son cabdales,
cólgala Montcayo enfiesto dos poales,
en Espanna ha estos çinco sinales,
con mucho bon castiello, con uillas naturales. (*st.* 2416)

   ¿Qué meiores querades que Burgos e Panpalona,
Seuilla, Toledo, León e Lixbona?
Per Gasconna corre el río de Garona,
en ésta yaz Bordel, uezina de Bayona. (*st.* 2417)

   La çiudat de París yaz en medio de Françia,
de toda la clerizía auié y abondançia,
Tors yaz sobre Leyre, uilla de grant ganançia,
más delantre corre Ródano, río de abondançia. (*st.* 2418)

   Azién en Lombardía, Pauía e Milana,
pero otras dexamos, Tolosa e Uiana,
Bolonna sobre todas pareçe plaçiana,
de lees e de derechos éssa es la fontana. (*st.* 2419)

   En cabo de Toscana, Lombardía passada,
en ribera de Tybre asié Roma poulada:
abié el que la ouo primero çimentada
de ssu ermano mismo la cabeça cortada. (*st.* 2420)

   Se quisiéssemos todas las tierras ementar
otro tanmanno liuro podríe y entrar,
mas quiero en la cosa a destaio andar,
ca soe yo cansado, querríame ya folgar. (*st.* 2421)

   Los castiellos de Asia con todas sus heredades

ya uos faulemos d' ellas, se uos bien acordades:
los tribos, los gigantes, los tiempos, las edades,
todo asié en ella con sus propredades. (*st.* 2422)
 Alexandre en esto lo podié reçebir
quanto auié conquisto, quanto por conquerir:
non se lle podié tierra alçar nen encobrir,
 qu' él no la sopiesse buscar e combatir. (*st.* 2423)

Almost as if Alexander's life were already done, as indeed,
unbeknown to him, it virtually was, Alexander's exploits
are summed up *en el IIII. fastial* (stanzas 2424-2430) like
a flashback moments before his death.

 Strikingly Romantic in his mood-building technique
employed in the passage filled with foreboding of treachery
and portending of death, the poet makes use of irony (in
the imperial procession moving to the musical accompaniment of the *Te Deum laudamus*), of psychomorphism, of
darkness, of contrast both explicit and implied:

 Quando fu la fazienda toda bien deliurada,
fu çerca de nona muy bien passada:
el emperador del mundo, proçessión ondrada,
 con *Te Deum laudamus* tornó a su posada. (*st.* 2437)
 Fu la noche uenida fort e peligrosa,
amaneçió la mannana çiega e tenebrosa,
venié robal mundo de la flor preçiosa,
 que era más preçiada que lilio nen rosa. (*st.* 2438)
 Las estrellas del çielo por el día durar
andauan a pereça, dáuanse a grant uagar:
tardaua el luzero, no s' leuantar,
 apenas le podioron las otras fer andar. (**st.** 2439)

> Essa noche uioron, solésmoslo leer,
> las estrellas del çielo entre sí conbater:
> que como fuertes signos ouo en el naçer,
> viron a la muerte fortes apareçer. (*st.* 2440)

Note the parallelism, mentioned by the poet himself, that frames the life of the hero.

The poem ends (discounting the poet's address of leave-taking from his audience) with a lugubrious lyrico-philosophico-moral thought cast in a sonnet-like form:

> Sennores, quien quisier su alma bien saluar,
> deue en este seglo muy poco a fiar:
> qui en el poder del mundo no la quiera dexar,
> deue a Dios seruir, e déuelo rogar. (*st.* 2505)
> La gloria deste mundo quien bien la quisier amar,
> más que la flor del campo no la deue preçiar,
> ca quando omne cuyda más seguro estar,
> échalo de cabeça en el peor lugar. (**st.** 2506)
> Alexandre que era rey de tan gran poder,
> que mares nen tierra no lo podién caber,
> en una fuessa ouo en cabo a caber,
> que non podié de término doze pies tener. (**st.** 2507)

POEMA DEL CONDE FERNAN GONZALEZ

In the anonymous *Poema del Conde Fernán González*, written between 1250 and 1271 and concerning the mid-tenth-century Count of Castile, we come upon some primitive and rather crude examples of patriotic poetry in which the patriotic spirit is quite the contrary of that expressed in the epic, which deals with the extolling of battle and other aggressive behavior. The poet looks with nostalgia to the golden days of a utopian past:

Era estonçe Espanna todos de vna creençia,
al Fyjo de la Virgen María fasían todos obediençia,
pesava mucho al diablo con tanta obediençia,
non avya entre ellos enbydia nin contienda. (*st.* 38)
    Estavan las yglesias todas vyen ordenadas,
de olio e de açeyte e de çera estavan bien avastadas,
los diesmos e las preminençias leal-mente eran dadas,
e todas las gentes en la fe vyen arraygadas. (*st.* 39)
    Vesquían los labradores todos de su laçeryo,
las grrandes potestades non eran rrobadores,
guardavan vyen sus pueblos commo leales sennores,

todos vesquían de sus derechos los grandes e los menores.

(st. 40)

> Estava la façienda toda en ygual estado,
> avya con este vyen grran pesar el diablo:
> rrevolvyó atal cosa el mal aventurado,
> el goço que avya, en llanto fue tornado. (st. 41)

Although he is dismayed by the evil that has befallen, he is also moved by his love for the country as it stands in the present, abounding in good things. His is a quiet and intimate patriotism that expresses the love for one's home and familiar surroundings. The selection on the present state of his homeland reads not entirely unlike a Chamber of Commerce advertisement, but it does reveal the sentiments of pride and sincere appreciation for many blessings. The theme-with-variations technique is elaborated largely by way of simple enumeration. The poet lists strictly realistic and practical materials and assets, giving sometimes a panoramic view, sometimes a close-up, but nothing between. Animate and inanimate are indiscriminately mixed, and in the first half of the poem the materials do not build up to a climax or follow any kind of order. The poet counts on persuading by weight of sheer mass. The second half of the poem, however, does show more dramatic progression, and rather loosely does lead to a climax. After the list of useful products comes a statement about the fine knights of the land, who are given a whole stanza. Next, the apostles get two stanzas, and the saints and martyrs share one. These are followed by a bit of naive flattery of fellow countrymen, and then by highest praise of Castile, the best part of which, we are finally informed, is Old Castile. The selection is of the same general type as the much longer *pleyto de Babilonnia* in the *Libro de Alexandre* (stanzas 1299 ff.), to which it is inferior in regard to poetic technique, but superior in sincerity of feeling:

Por eso vos digo aqueso, que byen lo entendades:
mejores son que otras tierras en las que vos morades,
de todo es bien conplida en la que vos estades
desirvos he agora quántas a de vondades. (*st.* 146)

Tyerra es muy tenprada, syn grrandes callenturas,
non façen en yvyerno destenprradas fryuras;
non es tierra en el mundo que aya tales pasturas,
árvoles para fruta, syquiera de miles naturas. (*st.* 147)

Sobre todas las tierras, meior es la montanna,
de vacas e de oveias non ay tierra tamanna,
tantos hay de puercos que es fyera façanna,
syrvense muchas tierras de las cosas de Espanna.
(*st.* 148)

Es de lino e lana tierra mucho avastada,
de çera sobre todas vuena tierra provada,
non será de açeyte en todo el mundo tal fallada,
tierra de Ingla e tierra de Françia desto es mucho
[avondada. (*st.* 149)

Buena tierra de çera e buena de venados,
de río, de mar, muchos buenos pescados,
quien los quere rreçientes, quen los quiere salados,
son de estas cosas tales pueblos muy abastados. (*st.* 150)

De panes e de vynos, tierra muy comunal,
non fallaría en el mundo otrra meior nin tal,

muchas de buenas fuentes e mucho buen rrío cabdal,
e otrras muchas más fuertes de que façen la sal. (*st.* 151)
    A y muchas venas de fyerro e cal [e plata]
en syerras e valles, e mucha de buena mata,
todas llenas de grrana para façer escarlata,
a y venas de oro que son de meior varata. (*st.* 152)
    Por lo que ella más val, avn non vos lo diremos,
de los buenos cavalleros avn mençión non fyçiemos,
meior tierra es de las que quantas nunca vyemos,
nunca tales cavalleros en el mundo nunca viemos. (*st.* 153)
    Dexarvos quero d' esto, que asás vos he contado,
non quero más deçir, que podría ser errado,
pero non oluidemos al apóstol Santyago honrrado,
fijo del Cebedeo, Santyago llamado. (*st.* 154)
    Fuertemente quiso Dios a la Espanna honrrar
quando al santo apóstol quiso ay enbyar,
de Inglaterra e Françia, quísola meiorar,
e sabet que non yaçió apóstol en todo aquel logar. (*st.* 155)
    Onrróle otra guisa el preçioso sennor:
fueron y muchos santos muertos por su sennor,
que de moryr a cochyllo non ovyeron temor,
muchas vírgenes y santas e mucho buen confesor. (*st.* 156)
    Commo ella es meior de las sus veçindades,
asy sodes meiores quantos en Espanna morades,
omnes sodes sesudos e mesura heredades,
d' esto por todo el mundo gran preçio heredastes. (*st.* 157)
    Pero de toda Espanna, Castylla es lo meior,
porque fue de los otrros el comienço mayor,

guardando e temiendo syenpre a su sennor,
quiso acreçentarla ansy el nuestro Sennor. (*st.* 158)

Avn Castylla la Vyeia, al mi entendimiento,
meior es que lo hal, porque fue el çimiento,
ca conquirieron mucho, maguer poco convento,
byen lo podedes ver en el acabamiento. (*st.* 159)

Like other *mester de clerecía* works the *Poema del
Conde Fernán González* contains selections from various
genres, the most notable of those belonging more or less to
the lyric being the prayer, the vision or dream, and the
philosophico-poetic sermonet. The prayer of supplication
(as in passages beginning with stanzas 106, 186, 231, 390,
541) follows the usual formula of the times, and shows
no advance over that of Jimena in the *Poema de Mío Cid.*
The vision (as in passages beginning with stanzas 401,
549) likewise has little new to offer except once, when
sent by evil powers instead of the usual heavenly rulers,
it lends both drama and fiery coloring to the poem, reliev-
ing it momentarily of its somberness:

Vyeron aquella noche vna muy fyera cosa,
veníe por el ayre vna syerpe rauiosa,
dando muy fuertes grytos la fantasma astrosa,
toda venié sangrienta commo vermeia, asy commo rrosa.
(*st.* 467)

Façía ella senblante que feryda venía,
semeiava en los gruytos que el çielo se partya,
alunbraua las vestes el fuego que vertya,
todos ovyeron grran miedo que quemarlos venía. (*st.* 468)

Non ovo ende ninguno que fuese tan sforçado,
que grran miedo non ovo e fuese espantado,
cayeron muchos omnes en tierra del espanto,
ovyeron muy grran miedo todo el pueblo crruçado.

(*st.* 469)

Despertaron al conde, que era ya dormido,
ante qu' él veniese, el culuebro era ydo;
falló todo el su pueblo commo desmaydo,
demandó del culuebro, cómmo fuera venido. (*st.* 470)

Dyxéronselo todo, de quál guisa veniera,
commo cosa ferryda, que muy grandes gritos diera,
por que se marauillaban cómmo la tierra non la
                                    [ençendiera,
vuelta venía en sangrue aquella vestya fyera. (*st.* 471)

Reflecting both the pensive mood that prevails in most
of the poem and the poet's frequent concern with moral
matters, the sermonet as it appears in the *Poema del Conde
Fernán González* is well in line with those that will be
written by moralists of the following two or three centuries. Perhaps the best example from our work is the one
beginning *Sy omne su tiempo en valde lo quiere pasar.*
Even though this piece lacks the vivacity of some of the
later examples of the genre, the piece is neatly developed
and presents a positive point of view that will not find
better expression until Jorge Manrique, some two centuries
later, writes his *Coplas por la muerte de su padre.* Balance
and interplay of the time-death-fame themes, of death-
the-equalizer subservient to man-the-master-of-his-own-
destiny (free will) are handled with the simplicity and lack
of affectation characteristic of the style throughout the

work. The principal theme, time, is presented in the opening line; man's earthly existence terminated by death, along
with a hint of possible triumph over death, are the related
sub-themes developed in the remainder of the first stanza
(346); death the would-be equalizer and man's will prevailing over it are the themes of the second stanza that
seem to spring spontaneously from those of the first; the
moral explication in the third stanza follows as a natural
conclusion of the previous statement and introduces the
requisite specific examples the enumeration of which concludes the argument, which is summarized in the final
stanza. The selection is part of a speech by the good Count,
of whom the poet affirms:

> ese fyrme varón,
> avya grran conplimiento del seso de Salamón,
> nunca fue Alexandre más grrande de coraçón. (*st.* 343)

It serves to illustrate these qualities in the Count's character as portrayed by the poet:

> Sy omne su tiempo en valde lo quiere pasar,
> non quiere deste mundo otrra cosa levar
> synon estar viçioso e dormir e folgar,
> deste atal muere su fecho quando viene a fynar. (*st.* 346)
>
> El viçioso e el laçerado amos an de moryr,
> el vno nin el otrro non lo puede foyr:
> quedan los buenos fechos, estos han de vesquir,
> d' ellos toman enxyenplo los que han de venir. (*st.* 347)
>
> Todos los que grran fecho quisieron acabar,
> por muy grrandes trabaios ovyeron a pasar,

non comen quando quieren, nin çenan nin an yantar,
los viçios de la carne anlos de oluidar. (*st.* 348)
   Non cuentan de Alexandre las noches nin los días,
cuentan sus buenos fechos e sus cavalleryas,
cuentan del rrey Davyt que mató a Golías,
de Iudas el Macabeo, fyjo de Matavyas. (*st.* 349)
   Carlos, Valdovinos, Rroldán e don Ogero,
Terryn e Gualdabuey e Vernaldo e Oliuero,
Torpyn e don Rrivaldos et el gascón Angelero,
Estol e Salomón e el otrro conpannero. (*st.* 350)
   Estos e otros muchos que vos he nonbrado,
sy tan buenos non fueran, oy seryén oluidados,
por lo que ellos fyzieron serán syenpre ementados,
serán los buenos fechos fasta la fyn contados. (*st.* 351)

A typical Mediaeval mixture of pagan and Christian
ideas, and one of the earliest allusions to the wheel and
the whims of Fortune, and with it the use of metonymy, are
to be found in another of the Count's sermonets:

   Ligera cosa es la muerte de pasar,
muerte de cada día, muy mala es de endurar,
sofryr tanto laçerio et ver tanto pesar,
ver los sus enemigos lo suyo heredar. (*st.* 438)
   Contesçe eso mismo a la gente renegada,
heredan nuestra tierra e tyénenla forçada,
mas enderesçerse ha la rueda que está trestornada,
serán ellos vençidos, la fe de Cristo onrrada. (*st.* 439)
   Non es dicha fortuna por ser siempre en vn estado,

de vno ser syenpre ryco e otrro ser menguado,
camia estas dos cosas la fortuna pryado,
al pobre façe ryco e al ryco menguado. (*st.* 440)
    Quiere façer las cosas ansy el Cryador,
de dar e de quitar él es el façedor,
por entender que él es sobre todos el meior,
el que suele ser vençido será el vençedor. (*st.* 441)

The *Poema del Conde Fernán González* gives superficially the impression of being a hybrid in form. Although
the poet's primary purpose and accomplishment were the
extolling of the character and exploits of the Count Fernán
González, which one might ordinarily expect would place
the poem among the epics of the *mester de juglaría,* the
digressions involving extraneous materials and modes and
the techniques of their insertion are sufficiently numerous
to justify a classification of the work as *mester de clerecía.*
The meter *(cuaderna vía)* also would show the author's
preference for the learned mode. The poet was far less
affected than was Berceo by the troubadour style and
poetic inspiration, though he was not altogether ignorant
of chivalric and courtly love codes. As far as the development of lyric poetry is concerned, the *Poema del Conde
Fernán González* represents a stage somewhere between
that of the *Poema de Mío Cid* and the work of Berceo. The
fairly high quality of his lyrics and the amount of lyric
sentiment—and interest in lyric poetry—he displays indicate that lyric poetry in Castilian was making advances
relatively independently of the troubadour influence.

HISTORIA TROYANA

In the anonymous *Historia Troyana*, which R. Menéndez Pidal dates around 1270, a number of poems are interspersed in the prose tale, which itself occasionally has poetic overtones, so that there is no sharpness of division between the two media. Each poem, moreover, is carefully prefaced by introductory matter in the prose passages preceding it, analogous to what happens regularly with lyric passages in the *mester de clerecía*. Similar combinations will later be found in the pastoral novel of the Golden Age. Content, verbal expression, and meter of the poems all offer indication of troubadour influence. The meter immediately attracts special attention because of its variety and the preference shown for short lines—only one selection is done in *cuaderna vía* and the others in eight-syllable verse except for one in seven-syllable and one in a combination of four- and eight-syllable verse. Menéndez Pidal has observed that the anonymous author of the *Historia Troyana* is " . . . el primero que se esfuerza en adaptar el verso y la estrofa al carácter de cada tema tratado." We might stress that, if the date of *ca.* 1270 for the composition is correct, the work attests to the early existence in Spanish of a variety of meters, themes, styles, and genres in poetry, and also indicates an early date for the probable widespread use of verse types current in the early *cancionero* period (late fourteenth and early fifteenth centuries) and would offer, in *Poesía XI*, the earliest example of one of the most virile of the minor forms of the *romance*, that is, the *romance* in couplets. The eleven poems vary in length from 24 to 180 lines each. Some are predominately narrative, others lyric. They serve as poetic interludes, original with the author, and expand on themes suggested by the story, which is adapted from a foreign model.

Aptly suiting meter and other poetic artifices to mood, the author creates a veritable incantation in Cassandra's prophecy of the fall of Troy:

Profeçía de Casandra

"¡ Gente perdida,
"mal fadada,
"confondida,
"desesperada,
"gente syn entendemiento,   (*l.* 5)
　"gente dura,
"gente fuerte
"syn ventura,
"dada a muerte,
"gente de confondimiento !   (*l.* 10)
　"¡ Ay gentío
"mal apreso,
"de gran brío
"mas syn seso,
"gentío de mala andança !   (*l.* 15)

"¡ ay catiuos
"syn conseio,
"sodes biuos
"mas sobejo
"es graue vuestra esperança!   (*l.* 20)
 "¡ Mal fadados,
"¿ qué fazedes?
"¡ Despertados!
"¿ non veedes
"quántos mueren cada día?   (*l.* 25)
 "ya el suelo
"non los coje;
"sequier duelo
"vos enoje
"por dexar esta porfía;   (*l.* 30)
 "vuestros muertos
"son atantos
"que ya huertos
"e plados quantos
"ha en Troya non los caben.   (*l.* 35)
 "¡ Ay mesquinos!
"vos auedes
"adeuinos,
"bien sabedes
"entre vos muchos que saben   (*l.* 40)
 "el mal fado
"que uos presto,
"mal pecado,

"es por esto
"que uos a mí non creedes.   (*l.* 45)
   "Mal apresos,
"mal andantes,
"bien commo estos
"vos enantes
"de mucho tiempo, moriredes;   (*l.* 50)
   "vuestra joya
"e vuestro bien,
"todo Troya
"que uos tien
"asy arderá a fuego.   (*l.* 55)
   "Griegos ternán
"muy grand bando,
"a vos vernán
"sagudando,
"Ylión entrarán luego.   (*l.* 60)
   "¡ Ay qué quexa,
"qué quebranto
"que aquexa
"a mí tanto
"que non podría más syn falla!   (*l.* 65)
   "¡ ay qué coyta,
"mal apresa,
"qué acoyta
"que me pesa
"de aquesta negra batalla!   (*l.* 70)
   "¡ Ay qué pena

"e qué tanta
"que me pena,
"que quebranta,
"fazme loca de despecho!   (*l.* 75)
   "¡Ay catiuos
"de g . . . íos
"pues . . . ivos
"d' estos bríos
"e dexad aqueste fecho!   (*l.* 80)
   "Gente mala,
"mala gente,
"non vos sala
"ya de mente
"sequiera la vuestra vida;   (*l.* 85)
   "grande pena
"vos es presa
"por Elena
"sy aquesta
"guerra non fuere partida.   (*l.* 90)
   "Gente loca,
"gente dura,
"e ¡qué poca
"es la cura
"que de uos mesmos auedes!   (*l.* 95)
   "mas bien sé yo,
"malfadados,
"bien lo veo
"por pecados

"que todos por ende morredes.   (*l.* 100)
  "¡ Ay astrosos,
"non oydes!
"pereçosos
"¿non vos ydes
"por non caer en aquesto?   (*l.* 105)
  "¡ Ay qué grand mal
"pasaredes!
"¡ ay qué mortal!
"non veedes
"cómmo vos está presto?   (*l.* 110)
  "¡ Ay coraçón
"quebrantado!
"¿por quál rrazón
"mal fadado
"no te partes por mill logares,   (*l.* 115)
  "si podieses,
"que este dapño
"non lo vieses,
"pues tamaño
"e de tantos pesares?   (*l.* 120)
  "¡ Troya rrica
"e nonbrada,
"ay qué chica
"mal fadada
"que será la vuestra onrra!   (*l.* 125)
  "Vos ardida,
"despoblada,

"cofondida
"e arada
"seredes por grand desonrra.   (*l.* 130)
   "¡ Ay troyanos
"caualleros,
"muy loçanos
"e guerreros,
"cómmo seredes lorados!   (*l.* 135)
   "¡ Mas ninguno
"que uos lore!
"ca sólo vno
"que aquí more
"non fincará por pecados."   (*l.* 140)
   Esto dezía
la infanta
e más quería
adelante
dezir, mas non la dexaron;   (*l.* 145)
   fue tomada
por sandía,
ençerrada
noche e día;
commo a loca la guardaron.   (*l.* 150)

Here the reader is caught in the deep monotone of the word-flow, the hypnotic repetition of rhythmic unit and specific word, and the gradual swell of evil and fate. The closely spaced consonantal rimes, the frequent anaphora, the hammering near-trochaic rhythm, the abundance of simple series, have a spell-binding effect. The cumulative force of repeated *¡ay!*, of *mal* and *fado* with their synonyms and derivatives and combinations *(malfadado,-os,-a)*, and like expressions, intensifies the feeling of impending doom. Strict parallelism of brief phrases, broken only once by chiasmus, *Gente mala, mala gente* (lines 81-82), that simply increases the bewitchment, adds stress to the implacable aggressive martial gait of the trochee moving fatefully on, spelling war in the background. In one passage (lines 61-75) the repetition takes on the additional forms of alliteration *(¡Ay qué quexa,/qué quebranto/que aquexa . . .)* and *derivatio (quexa-aquexa, quebranto-quebranta, coyta-acoyta, pena-pena)*, together giving the effect of annominatio, to add force to the simulation of the ritual of magic. Negative expressions and symbols of destruction abound, making their contribution to the mood. The purpose of all these devices constituting virtually a conjuration of the powers of the supernatural is quite probably to enhance the reputation of Cassandra as a prophetess, to create in the reader a sort of superstitious acceptance of the occult powers Cassandra supposedly possesses. In the matter of causing every detail of form to contribute to a single effect of mood, it would be difficult to find a Romantic poet who could surpass the author of the "Profecía de Casandra."

In "Agamenón aconseja matar a Héctor" *(Poesía III)* the poet aims to put in Agamemnon's mouth a volley that will convince by sheer force of repetition. Of the poem's twenty-four lines, eighteen, including the first nine, begin anaphorically with the word *éste*, and in two others *éste* is the second word. Most of the remaining words are the verb *es* and predicate nouns; a few constitute brief and simple declarations breaking the monotony of the hypozeuxis. There is a certain charm in the simplicity of the

construction and the continuous change of perspective on
the character and personality of Hector, whose great worth
transluces even his enemy's evaluation:

Agamenón aconseja matar a Héctor

"Este es su esfuerço e su bien,
"éste es su castiello fuerte,
"éste es el que los mantién,
"éste los guarda de muerte;
   "éste es su anparamiento,   (*l.* 5)
  "éste es toda su fuerça,
"éste es su acostamiento,
"éste es toda su esperança,
  "éste es toda su creençia,
"sin pendón e sin señal;   (*l.* 10)
"éste es la su mantenençia,
"éste es su seña cabdal;
   "éste es su señor e su rrey
"es, en cuyo poder son,
"éste es su dios, éste es su ley,   (*l.* 15)
"éste los guya e otro non;
   "ést es su rrecobramiento,
"su escudo e su manto;
"éste es el su ardimiento,
"mas éste es nuestro quebranto.   (*l.* 20)
    "Por éste somos vençidos,
"ellos por él enxalçados,
"éste nos ha cofondidos,
"éste nos ha quebrantados."

Enumeration and series are the poet's staple. Cinematographic focus on section after section, first in a series of close-ups and later in a view of and from a nearby tower, reproduces the action and the butchery of battle and the observer's reaction to it, in the "Descripción de la sexta batalla" *(Poesía IV)*, done in *cuaderna vía*.

The love of Troilus and Cressida (Briseida) inspires the author to compose a group of poems *(Poesías V-VIII)* built to some extent on troubadour themes and with troubadour techniques but depending, too, on the poet's own vicarious experience in the grief of the lovers whose cruel and unforeseen separation, resulting from a war bargain, throws them into despair. Step by step the poet follows first Troilo's and then Briseida's reaction to the news of their imminent separation, and their struggle between love and duty, duty in the form of patriotism and personal honor. Troilo's lament *(Poesía V)* is versified in the work's only heptasyllables, later in Spanish literature a favourite meter for the *endecha*. Troubadour-fashion, Troilo exalts his lady, attributing to her all good that has befallen him, and is thrown into despair at the thought of separation from her:

Lamento de Troilo

"El mi bien, el mi seso,
"la mi vida viçiosa,
"todo lo tiene preso   (*l.* 15)
"la mi señora fermosa;
   "mi plazer, mi cuydado
"en ella lo he puesto;
"sy yo soy esforçado
"o ardit o apuesto   (*l.* 20)

"por ella lo soy todo.
"Quanto al en el mundo veo
"todo me semeja lodo
"e nunca al deseo
　　"de bien synon veerla;　(*l.* 25)
"mas non puedo auer
"plazer nin bien syn ella;
"ca sy oy quanto auer
　　"en el mundo touiese
"nin quanta otra nobleza,　(*l.* 30)
"non creo que perdiese
"cuydado nin tristeza,
　　"sy fuese de mí partida
"o fuese alongada
"la que tien mi vida　(*l.* 35)
"toda de sy colgada.
　　"E yo esto mesquino,
"sienpre ge lo yo dezía
"e era adeuino
"de lo que auer auía,　*(l.* 40)
　　"ca ya agora soy yo
"en lo que adeuinaua,
"mi muerte ya la veo
"ver non la cuydaua.
　　"¿Quién sería que creyese　(*l.* 45)
"que Troya la viçiosa
"asy partir quisiese
"a quien es vna cosa?

"E çerca es mi muerte,   (*l.* 70)
"pues que auer non podiere
"Breyseda mi conorte.
   "Lorando con ojos
"serán muertos o çiegos
"anbos estos mis ojos   (*l.* 75)
"pues vier para griegos
   "mi señora, mi defesa,
"¡e vaya muy bien dicha
"ca de tal rrey promesa
"nunca será desdicha!   (*l.* 80)
   "e de mí non se quexe,
"por mí no se desconorte,
"ca maguer me ella dexe
"non me dexará la muerte.

After rejecting the tempting thought of deserting his
country to go with her, he contemplates suicide, but con-
siders that dishonorable also, and finally decides to excel
on the battlefield. The poet portrays in few and sure
strokes the vicissitudes of Troilo's emotions:

   "Por ende val más agora
"que yo mesmo me mate
"por vuestro amor, señora,
"e nada al non cate,
   "mas temo que despecho   (*l.* 105)
"me ouiésedes syn falla,
"sy faziendo buen fecho

"en aquesta batalla,
  "muerte prender podiese,
"e por mí me matase;   (*l.* 110)
"temo quien lo oyese
"que por muy vil me contase."
  Troylo en aquesto
yaquanto asosegaua;
muy alegre e muy presto   (*l.* 115)
e muy sabroso estaua
  atanto que saliese
el plazo e se acabasen
las treguas, que se metiese
en logar do lo matasen   (*l.* 120)
  los griegos, e feziese
él en ellos tal fecho
que, en cuanto beuiese
Breyseda, fuese ende rretrecho.

Breseida, having no battlefield and no choice, calls upon death and expends her grief in more violent fashion, well described by the poet in *Poesía VI:*

Lamento de Briseida

  "Mays pues asy es, la muerte
"se duela desta catiua   (*l.* 70)
"e la guarde que en tan fuerte
"coyta que fasta cras non biua,
  "ca pues yo tal pesar veo,
"tal daño e tal quebranto,

"morir codiçio, deseo,   (*l.* 75)
"non quiero otra cosa tanto."
    Esto dezía e loraua,
prendedero nin toca
en su tiesta non dexaua,
daua bozes commo loca,   (*l.* 80)
    e rronpié los sus cabellos,
ante sy los allegando,
fazía grand lanto sobr' ellos
a Troylo ementando.

Drama takes over as the lovers spend their last hours together. Dramatic narration as well as dialogue, both directly and indirectly reported, overshadow the lyric. Even the short passages that reflect the troubadour *alba* (dawn-song recounting the parting of lovers at dawn) have their pathos deepened more by the dramatic situation than by lyric feeling *(Poesía VII):*

    Amores de Troilo y Briseida

    Aquella noche, maguera
en que ellos asy estodieron,
que les fue la postremera
que anbos en vno touieron   (*l.* 100)
    jamás en toda su vida,
besauan e abraçauan
muy fuerte por espedida,
maguera que nunca quedauan
    de lorar, anbos pensando (*l.* 105)

en el plazo que venié,
catando el alua quándo
vernié e los partirié.

    Aquella noche a su grado
por sienpre les durarié;   *(l.* 110)
mill rrazones han fablado
por ver cómmo podrién,
    por quál guisa o por quál arte
por ellos ser desfecho
por engenio o por arte   (*l.* 115)
aquel tan esquiuo fecho.

    E pues que uos mucho diga,   (*l.* 145)
en aquel viçio lorando
stido con la su amiga
el infante muy cuytado
    besando la noche toda,
mas vieno claro el día   (*l.* 150)
que partió aquella boda,
partió aquella alegría.

Employing one of his favourite devices, anaphora, the poet
joins in parallel the grief of the two *(Poesía VIII):*

    Briseida va al campo de los griegos

    Oras piensa el infante
de rretener la donzella   (*l.* 30)
que non vaya adelante,
oras de se yr con ella;

oras lora, oras dize
mal a sy porque nasçió,
oras ventura maldize   (*l.* 35)
porque le esto acaesçió;
 oras maldize el fado,
ora quanto los dios le fezieron,
oras a sy mal fadado,
oras quantos lo ordieron;   (*l.* 40)
 oras maldezía a su padre
que lo asy ha cofondido,
ora dize: "Por Dios, madre,
"vos auedes me perdido".

 muy cuytada la donzella,
toda salía de su seso,
apenas podién tenerla   (*l.* 75)
los tres infantes en peso,
 con coyta de derribarse
del palafrén en que yua:
gran coyta auié de matarse
sy podiese la catiua.   (*l.* 80)
 Amenudo sospiraua
e la rrienda amenudo
la tenié, de sy loraua;
todo el seso ha perdido.
 Amenudo entristeçié   (*l.* 85)
e tornáuase amariella,
amenudo se dezié
malfadada e mesiella;

amenudo yua catando
a Troylo, el infante,   (*l.* 90)
amenudo se llamando
cuytada e malandante;
    amenudo se torçié
las manos con la gran coyta,
amenudo maldezié   (*l.* 95)
amor que la asy acoyta;
    amenudo paresçié
que tenía el lorar presto,
mucho amenudo dezié
contra Troylo aquesto: (*l.* 100)
    "Por mi mal voz fizo dios,
"ay Troylo, tan apuesto;
.... [*line missing*]
.... [*line missing*]
    "por mi mal tan enseñado   (*l.* 105)
"e tan ardit vos ha fecho,
"tan de plez, tan rrazonado,
"por mi mal todo ha fecho;
    "por mi mal tan corajoso,
"tan lidiador en batalla,   (*l.* 110)
"por mi mal atan fermoso,
"por mi mal todo syn falla.
    "Por mi mal es quanto bien,
"don Troylo, vos auedes,
"en sy espentado lo tien   (*l.* 115)
"este coraçón que veedes

"por ende morrá mal andante".
Pues sabe que asy venieron
Breyseda e el infante
fasta que se departieron.   (*l.* 120)

The conventional troubadour lover portrait appears in some detail in *Poesía X*, which enumerates all the essential characteristics of the lovelorn gentleman, in this case Dio- medes seeking the grace of Briseida:

Diomedes gana el amor de Briseida

Mas commo quier que oviesen
algunos grand alegría
e jugasen e rriesen,
Diomedes de noche e de día
    sienpre cuytado andaua;   (*l.* 5)
nin jugaua nin reya
....   [*line missing*]
con grand amor lo seguíe:
nunca lo dexaua dormir,
nunca lo dexaua folgar,   (*l.* 10)
amor le fazía morir,
no le dexaua sosegar.
    Amenudo sospiraua,
amenudo era yrado,
amenudo pensaua,   (*l.* 15)
amenudo era pagado,
    amenudo se ensañaua,
amenudo rreya,

amenudo se alegraua,
amenudo entresteçía.   (*l.* 20)
 Tan grand era el amor
que amenudo mudaua
Diomedes de la color
.... [*line missing*]
 De sí vna calentura   (*l.* 25)
le tomaua al coraçón,
tan grande e tan sin mesura
que le era muerte e al non;
 e dolíanle las quexadas,
ca muchas vezes avenié   (*l.* 30)
que estas tales caualgadas
aman contra los que tiene
 en su poder ençerrados,
e aquestas penas tales
sufren los enamorados   (*l.* 35)
.... [*line missing*]
 Nin folgará, si quisiere,
nin podrá auer sabor
el que amor preso toviere,
tal es la cuyta de amor.   (*l.* 40)
 E pues en este cuydado
de amor tan grande que vedes
está preso e ençerrado
el cuytado Diomedes
 por Breçayda la fermosa,   (*l.* 45)
que más que a sí amaua;

mas bien sabe vna cosa:
que nunca jamás cuydaua
   alcançar el su amor,
e por ende noche e día   (*l.* 50)
biue en esta pena,
nunca avié alegría.

   E quando avié bien pensado,
non fallaua otra guarida,
si su amor le fuese negado,   (*l.* 55)
sinon perder la vida.

   E yua con grand amor
a fablar e a estar con ella,
ca todo el su sabor
e su bien era veerla,   (*l.* 60)

   e sospiraua amenudo;
mas sesuda la donzella
entendía bien que perdido
andaua con amor d' ella,

   e por ende le era más dura   (*l.* 65)
e más braua e más desdeñosa;
ca, amigos, tal manera
a toda mujer fermosa,

   que desque supiere
que muy grand bien la queredes,   (*l.* 70)
que al non cobdiçiades,
por ella ensandesçedes,

   allí vos desdeñará,
allí vos será más fuerte,

allí vos despreçiará,   (*l.* 75)
menazarvos a de muerte;
    allí con el su engaño,
allí con las sus maldades,
vos buscará un tal daño
por que el cuerpo perdades   (*l.* 80)

After five more stanzas of similar generalizations, the author sets about portraying Briseida as the typical disdainful lady *(la belle dame sans merci)*, another troubadour subject that is to receive widespread treatment in the Spanish *cancioneros,* though this poet, no doubt influenced by Book Three of Andreas Capellanus's *Art of Courtly Love* or a related work, waxes downright misogynistic in his portrayal.

The *Historia Troyana* typifies in its verse passages several traits to be found in Juan Ruiz's *Libro de buen amor* and later in the *cancioneros:* metric variety, thematic and rhetorical partial dependence on troubadour poetry. It stands, along with our few other extant remnants, as evidence of a flourishing art in Castilian at an early period.

JUAN RUIZ, ARCIPRESTE DE HITA

Whenever the literary expression of an idealized state of life becomes so saturated with exaggeration and so spent with artificiality that it results in commonplace, it invites ridicule, usually in the form of parody. The lyric expression of troubadouresque courtly love is no exception. Sometimes a parody overshadows and outlives the work it satirizes, as when in *Lazarillo de Tormes* the picaresque adventure replaces the heroic of the tales of chivalry, or in *Don Quixote* the absurdity of knight-errantry is laid relentlessly bare. So it is with the troubadouresque. Better remembered than any one extant example of troubadour-influenced poetry in early Spanish is a miniature masterpiece parody of a typical troubadour love-lyric situation, *Aquí dise de cómo fue fablar con donna Endrina el Arçipreste*, of which the Arcipreste, of course, is Juan Ruiz, Archpriest of Hita (1283?-1350?), and the selection is from his *Libro de buen amor*, best known of the works of the *mester de clerecía*. The selection begins thus:

¡Ay, Dios! ¡y quán fermosa viene donna Endrina por la
[plaza!
¡Qué talle, qué donayre, qué alto cuello de garza!

¡Qué cabellos, qué boquilla, qué color, qué buenandanza!
Con saetas de amor fiere quando los sus ojos alza. (*st.* 627)
   Pero tal lugar non era para fablar en amores:
a mí luego me vinieron muchos miedos e temblores,
los mis pies e las mis manos non eran de sí sennores,
perdí seso, perdí fuerza, mudáronse mis colores. (*st.* 628)
   Unas palabras tenía pensadas para le desir,
el miedo de las compannas me fasién al departir,
apenas me conosçía nin sabía por do ir,
con mi voluntat mis dichos non se podían seguir. (*st.* 629)
   Fablar con muger en plaza es cosa muy descobierta:
a veses mal perro anda tras mala puerta abierta.
Bueno es jugar fermoso, echar alguna cobierta:
a do es lugar seguro es bien fablar cosa çierta. (*st.* 630)
   "Sennora, la mi sobrina, que en Toledo seía,
"se vos encomienda mucho, mil saludes vos envía,
"si oviés' lugar e tiempo, por quanto de vos oía,
"deséavos mucho ver, et conoçervos querría. (*st.* 631)
   "Querían allá mis parientes casarme en esta sazón
"con una donçella rica, fija de don Pepión.
"A todos di por respuesta que la non quería, non,
"de aquélla sería mi cuerpo que tiene mi corazón." (*st.* 632)
   Abajé más la palabra, díxel' que en juego fablaba,
porque toda aquella gente de la plasa nos miraba;
desque vi que eran idos, que omen aí non fincaba,
comenzél' desir mi quejura del amor que me afincaba:
                        (*st.* 633)
               .... [*line missing*]

.... [*line missing*]

"Otro non sepa la fabla, d' esto jura fagamos:

"do se çelan los amigos, son más fieles entramos. (*st.* 634)

"En el mundo non es cosa que yo ame a par de vos;

"tiempo es ya pasado de los annos más de dos

"que por vuestro amor me pena, ámovos más que a Dios.

"Non oso poner persona que lo fable entre nos. (*st.* 635)

"Con la grant pena que paso, vengo a vos desir mi quexa:

"vuestro amor he d' esto que me afinca e me aquexa,

"non me tira, non me parte, non me suelta, non me dexa,

"tanto me da la muerte, quanto más se me alexa. (*st.* 636)

"Reçelo he que non me oídes esto que vos he fablado:

"fablar muncho con el sordo es mal seso e mal recabdo.

"Cret que vos amo tanto que non ey mayor cuydado;

"esto sobre todas cosas me traye más afincado. (*st.* 637)

"Sennora, yo non me trevo a desir vos más rasones

"fasta que me respondades a estos pocos sermones:

"desitme vuestro talánt, veremos los corasones."

Ella dixo: "Vuestros dichos non los preçio dos pinnones.

[(*st.* 638)

"Bien así engannan munchos a otras munchas Endrinas;

"el ome tan engannoso así enganna a sus vesinas.

"Non cuidedes que so loca por oyr vuestras parlinas:

"buscat a quien engannedes con vuestras falsas espinas."

[(*st.* 639)

The fun begins with the title, and the enterprise promises
to be a thorny one, since the poet must deal with Lady Sloe.
Endrina (sloe) is apparently a pseudonym *(senhal)*—all

in proper troubadour style—that is, the device with which the lover was wont to cover the identity of his beloved, for the sake of protecting her reputation. From the pseudonym here chosen we are at liberty to imagine that the fair lady who has won the poet's heart is dusky as the sloe and that to reach her the way is hard as its wood, and thorny or at least prickly. The appearance of the sprightly and seductive beloved while the poet is still in the *fegnedor* (aspirant, or first) stage in his service of love, as he explains, brings about a standard reaction of fear and trembling, near-fainting, loss of physical strength, sudden pallor, stammering. Secrecy in affairs of love is the rule, and here advisable, for, anticipating (though he has not achieved) the position of *entendedor* (third stage, recognized suitor), he reasons that to let the cat out of the bag is to loose trouble. Pent-up love, so the lady hears as the poet enters the *precador* (second stage, suppliant) position, has been causing the poet's death, harassing him, never leaving him, having become his greatest care. The cold type *(la belle dame sans merci)* sends him on his way, shattering any dreams he may have harbored of becoming *entendedor* (third stage, recognized suitor) and finally *drut* (fourth stage, accepted lover). Since further and extensive reasoning still fails to convince the lovely lady, the lover gives up (as no true lover was supposed to do) his attempt to win her by means of his own worthiness, and leaves her service to enlist the aid of an experienced go-between, upon whom he bestows, contrary to custom, the *senhal* Doña Urraca (Lady Magpie), also called *Trotaconventos* (Convent-trotter), and who eventually deceives the lady into submission. The poem parallels, in addition to the formal love plaint, a common *serranilla* pattern, in which the rustic maiden is unimpressed by the gentleman's beguiling chat-

ter. Doña Endrina, it should be added, is a widow, and
widowhood for the beloved is a state not generally provided
for in either troubadour love song or *serranilla*.

With a smile the reader will now call to mind the
Razón de amor and the first conversation of its lovers,
followed by their parting. This reminiscence invites a comparison of the two selections. The early poem's seclusion
and privacy of the springtime garden has given way now
to the busy town square, where in place of discreet trees
we find people not wont to mind exclusively their own
affairs. Pert and disdainful—and most probably swarthy-
skinned—Doña Endrina entering the square with darting
glance, with graceful step and elegant bearing, gives the
impression of being somewhat lacking in the modesty and
the unselfconsciousness of the fair-complexioned, nameless,
and lovelorn *doncella* who comes singing her way into the
flowering garden, though in both poems the eye of the lover
falls on much the same details of the lady's anatomy, and
at such a sight both lovers come near fainting. The space
taken up by the *doncella* in reporting on the assets of her
lover is ceded by Doña Endrina to the lover himself, who
concocts a tale of material goods and family scheming and
worldly aspirations. The messenger employed successfully
by the earlier poet is dispensed with—for the moment, at
least—by the Archpriest: why let the cat out of the bag?
reasons he (moreover, as we shall soon see, there are other
persuasive reasons for one's bearing one's own messages—
and gifts). The ease with which the *escolar* of the early
poem makes his way in the lady's affection, even before
the first meeting, leaves the *Razón de amor* almost without
climax, whereas the Archpriest's fervent solicitation is
climaxed with acid and thorny rebuff (in parody of the
courtly lady's expected initial withholding of acceptance

of the lover's offer of servitude). The *escolar* settles down to a nap as a sequel to his ego-satisfying love dialogue, but the Archpriest must change his patter and embark upon an exhaustive and exhausting peroration as a consequence of his ego-deflating amorous monologue.

In a previous poem in the *Libro de buen amor* the poet (in addition to displaying his skill in playing with antanaclasis) had taken up the matter of the troubadour's messenger—the bearer of messages, of tidings, and of gifts that are to introduce the troubadour to his beloved and win for him her favorable attention and, it is hoped, even her love:

> *De lo que contesçió al Arçipreste*
> *con Fernand Garçía, su mensajero*
>
> Mis ojos no verán lus
> pues perdido he a Cruz (*st.* 105)
>
> Cruz cruzada panadera
> tomé por entendedera:
> tomé senda por carrera,
> como andalús. (*st.* 106)
>
> Coidando que la avría,
> díxelo a Fernand Garçía
> que troxiese la pletesía
> et fuese pleytés e dus. (*st.* 107)
>
> Díxome que l' plasía de grado
> e físose de la cruz privado,
> a mí dio rumiar salvado,
> él comió el pan más dus. (*st.* 108)
>
> Prometiól' por mi consejo

trigo que tenía anejo,
e presentól' un conejo
el traidor falso marfús. (*st.* 109)
   Dios confonda mensajero
tan presto e tan ligero;
no medre Dios tal conejero
que la caza ansí adús. (*st.* 110)
   Quando la crus veía, yo siempre me omillaba,
santiguábame a ella do quier que la fallaba,
el companno de çerca en la cruz adoraba,
del mal de la crusada yo non me reguardaba. (*st.* 111)
   Del escolar goloso compannero de cucanna
fise esta otra trova, non vos sea estranna,
ca de ante nin después non fallé en Espanna
quien ansí me fesiese de escarnio magadanna. (*st.* 112)

It is no wonder that the Archpriest excused himself
with Doña Endrina for having failed to employ the convention of messenger in his suit. What he carefully avoided
mentioning to her, however, was the possibility that he
might follow the advice of Don Amor, who had appeared
to him in a dream (parody of the "vision" literature of
the time), and take into his employ a substitute messenger
chosen, with the prudence born of humiliating experience,
from *her* sex, not again from *his*, and selected for proven
professional competence and trustworthiness in the messenger business. For this role Juan Ruiz created his beloved Trotaconventos, worthy prototype of Celestina. Although her possible forebears were several and ancient,
including the Old Woman of the twelfth-century anonymous dramatic poem entitled *Pamphilus,* from which much

of the Endrina episode is borrowed, Trotaconventos must in part certainly be derived from troubadour lore, travestied messenger performing duties analogous to those of original troubadour messenger, but with selfish motive and evil intent. As the story continues, Trotaconventos tricks the pretty widow into the arms of the lover, who, upon engaging the old bawd, had bestowed upon himself (!) the *senhal* of Don Melón de la Huerta. He later confesses that the Endrina episode was not his own experience but rather that of the earlier *Pamphilus*. With one possible exception, subsequent attempts of Trotaconventos to procure willing ladies for the Archpriest are failures, and so the would-be *drut* remains unwillingly in the ideal state of the true lover: desiring but not desired. His hopes for altering that state are dashed by the death of his gobetween. In his desolation he composes a mock dirge and funeral oration in her honor, and for the preservation of her memory and fame, an epitaph. The dirge begins bombastically with a stanza bedecked with exclamation, prosopopoeia, alliteration, palilogy, paronymy, anaphora, and hyperbaton:

De cómo morió Trotaconventos, et de cómo el Arçipreste
fase su planto denostando et maldesiendo la muerte

¡Ay, Muerte! ¡muerta seas, muerta, e mal andante!
Mataste a mi vieja, matases a mí ante,
enemiga del mundo, que non has semejante,
de tu memoria amarga non es que non se espante. (*st.* 1494)
Muerte, al que tú fieres, liévastelo de belmés,
al bueno e al malo, al rico et al refés,

a todos los egualas e los lievas por un pres,
por papas et por reyes non das una vil nues. (*st.* 1495)
 Non catas sennorío, deudo nin amistad,
con todo el mundo tienes continua enemistad;
non hay en tí mesura, amor nin piedad,
si non dolor, tristesa, pena e grand crueldad. (*st.* 1496)
 Non puede foír omen de ti nin se asconder,
nunca fue quien contigo podiese bien contender;
la tu venida triste non se puede entender:
desque vienes, non quieres a ome atender. (*st.* 1497)
 Dexas el cuerpo yermo a gusanos enfuesa,
al alma que lo puebra, liévastela de priesa,
non es omen çierto de tu carrera aviesa,
de fablar en ti, Muerte, espanto me atraviesa. (*st.* 1498)
 Eres en tal manera del mundo aborrida,
que por bien que lo amen al omen en la vida,
en punto que tú vienes con tu mala venida
todos fuyen dél luego como de res podrida. (*st.* 1499)
 Los que l' aman et quieren, et quien ha habido su
 [companna,
aborrésçenlo muerto como a cosa estranna,
parientes et amigos todos le tienen sanna,
todos fuyen del fuego como si fuese aranna. (*st.* 1500)
 De padres et de madres los fijos tan queridos,
amigos e amigas, deseados et servidos,
de mugeres leales los sus buenos maridos,
desde tú vienes, Muerte, luego son aborridos. (*st.* 1501)
 Fases al mucho rico yaser en grand poblesa,

non tiene una miaja de toda su riquesa;
el que vivo es bueno e con mucha noblesa,
vil, fediondo es muerto, aborrida villesa. (*st.* 1502)
    Non ha en el mundo libro nin escrito nin carta,
ome sabio nin neçio que de ti bien departa,
en el mundo non ha cosa que con bien de ti se parta
salvo el cuervo negro que de ti, Muerte, se farta. (*st.* 1503)
    Cada día le dises que tú le fartarás:
el omen non es çierto quándo et quál matarás;
el que bien faser podiese hoy le valdría más
que non atender a ti nin a tu amigo cras. (*st.* 1504)

El petafio de la sepultura de Urraca

    Urraca so que yago so esta sepultura,
en quanto fui al mundo, hove viçio e soltura,
con buena rasón muchos casé, non quise locura,
caí en una hora so tierra del altura. (*st.* 1550)
    Prendióme sin sospecha la muerte en sus redes;
parientes et amigos, ¿ aquí non me acorredes?
Obrad bien en la vida, a Dios non lo erredes,
que bien como yo morí, así todos morredes. (*st.* 1551)
    El que aquí llegare sí Dios le bendiga,
e sí l' dé Dios buen amor et plaser de amiga,
que por mí pecador un *Pater noster* diga,
si desir non lo quisiere, a muerta non maldiga. (*st.* 1552)

    The macabre ideas developed in these two poems,
especially in the invective against Death, are part of the
Mediaeval death theme, particularly as it was handled in

Spanish during the next century or two, that is, with
stress on the physical aspects of death, on the equalizing
power of death, and on death viewed as if at close range,
without the reflection and the emotional tempering af-
forded by time lapse. Although Juan Ruiz expresses melancholy, his melancholy is permeated with the bitterness of
frustration and the abhorrence at decay of the flesh; it
lacks the grave nostalgia and the philosophic overtones of
Jorge Manrique's *Coplas por la muerte de su padre* or even
of Ferrán Sánchez Calavera's *Dezir* on the death of the
Almirante Ruy Díaz de Mendoza. Death the terrifying
and repulsive agent of decay here differs also from Death
the active and magnetic levelling force as it appears some
decades later in the *Danza de la Muerte*. These poems give
us an opportunity to glimpse Juan Ruiz in a lugubrious
mood, at a time when his mockery sounds a bit hollowed
by dread.

Many aspects of troubadour love are satirized in the
Libro de buen amor. In place of the sophistry and refined
courtship of the lover, especially as advised by Andreas
Capellanus, Juan Ruiz employs pandering. The "love from
afar," like that represented in the *Razón de amor*, is
burlesqued in the episode of Doña Garoça, with whom the
Archpriest is persuaded by Trotaconventos to fall in love
through the enticement principally of promised table deli-
cacies. Whereas the lover was supposed to be faithful to
his lady, our poet-lover moves freely from lady to lady.
In the courtly tradition, love to be pure must never be con-
summated but the desire for consummation must constantly
and wilfully be increased in order to perfect the love and
ennoble the lover. In the *Libro de buen amor*, desire whetted
by continence is the usual lot of the lover, but through
the ladies' choice, not his—or through deceit of the mes-

senger. Ladies worth desiring are hard or impossible to
persuade. On the other hand, the rustic wench, who, according to Andreas Capellanus might with impunity be
first flattered and then embraced by force, does not wait
for the poet's advances, but aggressively takes the lead
(in the four *serranas*). The poet thus is able to parody
not only Andreas Capellanus's remarks but the *pastorela*
type of early poem in particular and courtly love in general, as well as to poke fun at himself as representative
of the male sex at the mercy of the wiles of women. Underlying the parody of courtly love, however, can be dis-
cerned a progression in love parallel to that envisaged by
the courtly love idealists. By dint of unfulfilled desire, and
undesired fulfilment *(serranas)*, the poet gradually im-
proves the quality of his love, particularly with the aid
of a virtuous nun, and after completion of his book devotes
many stanzas to pure praise of the Virgin.

Turning to realism, in fine, all the idealism of the
troubadours' code of love, Juan Ruiz candidly shows us
the under side of the picture, but he satirizes with a smile,
not a scowl. He laughs at himself and his own weaknesses
before he points a finger at his neighbor. In his emotional
maturity he accepts life as it is for him, human nature
as it is for him, and he has a good understanding of the
seamy side of human behaviour. On the surface, at least,
he is not worried about the shortcomings of his fellow
man—or about his own. He seems to feel that life on this
earth must—or if not must, will—be enjoyed, and he has
found one way of enjoying it to his own satisfaction, and
is ready to show that way to anyone who will heed him,
though he clearly warns that *the* way is by no means necessarily the one that most people take in following the dictates of the animal portion of their being, for underneath

the underside of the picture there is a way to spiritual
perfection, which is also a way of pleasure.

Other Mediaeval literary and semi-literary types draw
their share of ridicule as they are transfigured under the
pen of the poet. The burlesque epic, in which the dreaded
leader of the enemy forces is a lady, holds a prominent
place in the collection, in *De la pelea que hobo don Carnal
con la Quaresma*. Sir Flesh (Don Carnal), the conquering
hero, is obliged to muster all his forces—barnyard poultry,
hams, bacons, beef, lambs, deer and boar, and a great array
of others, many armed with pots and pans—and do strenu-
ous battle in order to be able to vanquish Lady Lent (Doña
Quaresma), who is backed by her loyal subjects, stalwart
salts from river and sea—the list is long and detailed. The
merry battle between appetite and abstinence serves to
point up indirectly the battle between the sexes, and so
to give a double meaning to this mock allegory while thus
relating it directly to the central theme of the collection:
love (Sir Flesh).

The debate, the allegory, and symbolism are together
hilariously parodied in the *Disputaçion que los griegos et
los romanos en uno ovieron*, ostensibly illustrating the
lesson that

> non ha mala palabra, si non es a mal tenida;
> verás que bien es dicha si bien fuesse entendida. (*st.* 54)

but giving at the same time, among many, a lesson in perspective and one on the insufficiency of both learning and
brute force employed independently of each other. The difference between learned ignorance and boorish ignorance
is cleverly drawn as the debate proceeds in total silence
and the pantomime symbolism, reduced to the lowest possible level of expression, is understood by nobody. Here

Juan Ruiz, humorously building the story on the figure of asteismus, replacing words with pun-gestures, is also informing the reader indirectly that there is more than one possible interpretation to his own *Libro de buen amor*, a refined one and a coarse one and any that lies between. Paradoxically, it is often the passage having a coarse meaning on the surface that has the refined meaning underneath, and vice versa; and likewise with the book as a whole, for the bantering obvious one overlays at least one of deadly seriousness (revelation of corruption, for example). In other words, the *Libro de buen amor* is typical of many of the outstanding works of Spanish literature in that it has more than one plane of meaning, certainly at least two, running parallel throughout the work. As a matter of fact, the *Libro de buen amor* is a composite containing numerous laminae of varying length and pattern, so tightly pressed together that they have become fused. In the fusion a certain ambiguity for the modern reader sometimes results. Such ambiguity is due not so much to the poet's desire to perplex the reader as to amuse him by means of a special manipulation of the only artistic medium at his disposal, the *mester de clerecía*. To the concatenation method of achieving continuity in the accumulation of heterogeneous materials, Juan Ruiz adds overlap, sometimes partial and sometimes complete, and not always of two layers only, but frequently of several.

The debate is also combined with one of Juan Ruiz's favourite genres, the fable, in a lengthy series of ancient fables constituting an argument between Trotaconventos serving as the Archpriest's mouthpiece, and Doña Garoça, the attractive and prudent nun.

Legal perorations and verbiage are derided in the lawyers' presentation of their case and the reading of the deliberately nerve-wrackingly monotonous verdict when the Archpriest *Aquí fabla del pleyto que 'l lobo e la raposa hobieron ante don Gimio alcalde de Buxía* (stanzas 311-361).

Not even church literature is spared. Prayers, sermons, parables, funeral orations, and epitaphs are all turned to sport. Even a Biblical text, basis of a mock sermon, is made to serve the cause of humor, as Professor Green has explained in *Spain and the Western Tradition.* In a solemn enough sermon on the subject *De quáles armas se debe armar todo christiano para vençer el diablo, el mundo e la carne* (stanzas 1553-1579), pronounced immediately following the dirge and funeral oration in honor of Trotaconventos and the reading of her epitaph, the poet speaks, without so much as batting an eyelash, of "El santo sacramento de orden saçerdotal" (*st.* 1565) and soon thereafter proceeds to "vos abreviar la predicaçión" by giving his famous sermonet on the subject *De las propiedades que las duennas chicas han,* in which he employs troubadouresque theme-with-variations technique to pay back-handed compliments to small women, concluding that they are to be preferred to their sisters because of the relatively smaller amount of evil they are able to contain—of the kind of evil, one may surmise, from which the wise man should flee. Note that the epiphonema contains half the requisite palinode (parodied) as an antidote to worldly love, but here with a merry meaning:

Quiero vos abreviar la predicaçión,
que siempre me pagué de pequenno sermón
e de duenna pequenna et de breve rasón,
ca poco et bien dicho afíncase el corazón. (*st.* 1580)
    Del que mucho fabla ríen, quien mucho ríe es loco.
Es en la duenna chica amor et non poco,

duennas hay muy grandes que por chicas non troco,
mas las chicas e las grandes, se repienden del troco.

[(*st.* 1581)

De las chicas que bien diga, el amor me fiso ruego,
que diga de sus noblesas: yo quiero las desir luego;
desirvos he de duennas chicas, que lo habredes por juego.
Son frías como la nieve e arden como el fuego. (*st.* 1582)

Son frías de fuera, con el amor ardientes,
en la calle solás, trevejo, plasenteras, rientes,
en casa cuerdas, donosas, sosegadas, bien fasientes,
mucho al y fallaredes a do bien paredes mientes. (*st.* 1583)

En pequenna gergenza yase grand resplandor,
en azúcar muy poco yase mucho dulzor,
en la duenna pequenna yase muy grand amor,
pocas palabras cumplen al buen entendedor. (*st.* 1584)

Es pequenno el grano de la buena pimienta,
pero más que la nues conorta et calienta,
así duenna pequenna, si todo amor consienta,
non ha plaser del mundo que en ella non sienta. (*st.* 1585)

Como en chica rosa está mucho color,
en oro muy poco grand preçio et grand valor,
como en poco blasmo yase grand buen olor,
ansí en duenna chica yase muy grand sabor. (*st.* 1586)

Como robí pequenno tiene mucha bondat,
color, virtud e preçio e noble claridad,
ansí duenna pequenna tiene mucha beldat,
fermosura, donayre, amor et lealtad. (*st.* 1587)

Chica es la calandria, et chico el ruysennor,

pero más dulçe canta que otra ave mayor;
la mujer que es chica por eso es mejor,
con donneo es más dulçe que azúcar nin flor. (*st.* 1588)

    Son aves pequennas papagayo e orior,
pero cualquier d' ellas es dulçe gritador,
adonada, fermosa, preçiada, cantador,
bien atal es la duenna pequenna con amor. (*st.* 1589)

    De la muger pequenna non hay comparaçión,
terrenal parayso es, e grand consolaçión,
solás et alegría, plaser et bendiçión,
mejor es en la prueba que en la salutaçión. (*st.* 1590)

    Siempre quis muger chica más que grande nin mayor,
non es desaguisado del grand mal ser foidor,
del mal tomar lo menos díselo el sabidor,
porende de las mugeres la mejor es la menor. (*st.* 1591)

    It is with a prayer to God to release him from prison
that the Archpriest opens his work. Troubadours commonly were prisoners of love, Christians were prisoners
of sin, and all members of mankind were prisoners of the
flesh, and we may guess that in his pleading Juan Ruiz
had in mind some of these people and their incarceration.
Much like Jimena, the Cid's wife, Juan Ruiz enumerates
miracles of liberation, including several mentioned by
Jimena, and begs that he be freed from his prison, know-
ing well that such liberation would be a miracle indeed.
The pattern of this prayer is a common one of the period.

    Blind beggars' ballads are seasoned with humorless
malice. In one of them the beggars are prompted to pray
aloud for the preservation of the faculty of sight of the
potential almsgivers' children.

The *serranilla,* paralleled in the passage on Doña
Endrina, is also parodied directly in the *Libro de buen
amor,* in a group of four *serranas,* and so surely must
have been a commonly employed poetic form in Spain
before the time of Juan Ruiz, who lived during the first
half of the fourteenth century. The *serranilla,* undoubtedly
from the Provençal *pastorela,* sometimes *vaqueira* or
auqueira, a short poem narrating the chance meeting and
ensuing dialogue of a gentleman and a rustic maiden, generally a shepherdess, and in which the worldly-wise gentleman usually wooes, and wins or loses, his prey, in Spain
is best exemplified in the short group of such poems in
the work of the fifteenth-century Marqués de Santillana.
Santillana, the gentleman, meets invariably lovely young
maidens. The Archpriest was wont to come upon a sturdier
specimen—and in surroundings and circumstances far
from inviting. One choice mountaineeress slings him over
her shoulder and carts him off to her abode. In the introduction to one of the *serranas* Juan Ruiz parodies a commonplace Mediaeval description, hyperbole and all, of the
ideal beauty, including one such that he himself put into
the mouth of Don Amor. There is also a hint of the story
of *Calectrix la reyna,* the ideally beautiful Amazon queen
who unashamedly propositions King Alexander in the
Libro de Alexandre:

> *De lo que contesçió al arçipreste con la serrana,*
> *et de las figuras d'ella*

Siempre ha mala manera la sierra et la altura,
si nieva o si yela, nunca da calentura;
bien ençima del puerto fasía orilla dura,
viento con grand elada, rosío con grand friura. (*st.* 980)

Como omen non siente tanto frío si corre,
corrí la cuesta ayuso, ca dis: *Quien da a la torre,*
ante dise la piedra que sale el alhorre.
Yo dixe: "So perdido si Dios non me acorre." (*st.* 981)
    Nunca desque nasçí pasé tan grand periglo
de frío; al pie del puerto falléme con vestiglo,
la más grande fantasma que vi en este siglo,
yeguarisa trefuda, talla de mal çenniglo. (*st.* 982)
    Con la coyta del frío e de la grand elada
roguél' que me quisiese ese día dar posada;
díxome que l' plasía si l' fuese bien pagada:
tóvelo a Dios en merçed, e levóme a la Tablada. (*st.* 983)
    Sus miembros e su talla non son para callar,
ca bien creed que era una grand yegua caballar;
quien con ella luchase non se podría bien fallar,
si ella non quisiese, non la podría aballar. (*st.* 984)
    En 'l Apocalypsi San Joan Evangelista
non vido tal figura nin de tan mala vista;
a grand hato daría lucha e grand conquista;
non sé de quál diablo es tal fantasma quista. (*st.* 985)
    Había la cabeza mucho grand sin guisa,
cabellos muy negros más que corneja lisa,
ojos fondos, bermejos, poco e mal devisa,
mayor es que de yegua la patada do pisa, (*st.* 986)
    las orejas mayores que de annal burrico,
el su pescuezo negro, ancho, velloso, chico,
las narises muy gordas, luengas, de zarapico,
bebería en pocos días cabdal de buhón rico. (*st.* 987)

su boca de alana, e los rostros muy gordos,
dientes anchos et luengos, asnudos e muy mordos,
las sobreçejas anchas e más negras que tordos:
los que quieran casarse aquí, non sean sordos. (*st.* 988)

Mayores que las mías tiene sus prietas barbas;
yo non vi en ella al, mas si tú en ella escarvas,
creo que fallarás de las chufetas darvas;
valdríasete más trillar en las tus parvas. (*st.* 989)

Mas en verdat si bien vi fasta la rodilla,
los huesos mucho grandes, la zanca non chiquilla,
de las cabras del fuego una grand manadilla,
sus tovillos mayores que de una annal novilla. (*st.* 990)

Más ancha que mi mano tiene la su munneca,
vellosa, pelos grandes, pero non mucho seca,
vos gorda e gangosa, a todo omen enteca,
tardía como ronca, desdonada e ueca. (*st.* 991)

El su dedo chiquillo mayor es que mi pulgar,
piensa de los mayores si te podrás pagar;
si ella algund día te quisiese espulgar,
bien sentiría tu cabeza que son biga de lagar. (*st.* 992)

Por el su garnacho tenía tetas colgadas,
dábanle a la çinta, pues que estaban dobladas,
ca estando sençillas darién so las ijadas,
a todo son de çítola andarían sin ser mostradas. (*st.* 993)

Custillas mucho grandes en su negro costado
unas tres veses contélas estando arredrado.
Dígote que non vi más, nin te será más contado,
ca mozo mesturero non es bueno para mandado. (*st.* 994)

De quanto que me dixo et de su mala talla
fise bien tres cantigas, mas non pud' bien pintalla:
las dos son chanzonetas, la otra de trotalla;
de la que te non pagares, veyla e ríe e calla. (*st.* 995)

Cantica de serrana

Cerca la Tablada
la sierra pasada
falléme con Aldara
a la madrugada. (*st.* 996)
Ençima del puerto
coydé ser muerto
de nieve e de frío
e d' ese rosío
e de grand elada. (*st.* 997)
A la deçida
di una corrida
fallé una serrana
fermosa, lozana
e bien colorada. (*st.* 998)
Dixe yo a ella:
"Homíllome, bella."
Dis: "Tú que bien corres,
"aquí non te engorres,
"anda tu jornada." (*st.* 999)
Yo l' dixe: "Frío tengo
e por eso vengo
a vos, fermosura;

quered por mesura
hoy darme posada. (*st.* 1000)
    Díxome la moza:
"Pariente, mi choza
"el que en ella posa
"conmigo desposa
"e dam' grand soldada." (*st.* 1001)
    Yo l' dixe: "De grado,
"mas soy casado
"aquí en Ferreros,
"mas de mis dineros
"darvos he, amada." (*st.* 1002)
    Dis: "Trota conmigo."
Levóme consigo
e diom' buena lumbre
como es de costumbre
de sierra nevada. (*st.* 1003)
    Diome pan de çenteno
tisnado, moreno,
e diom' vino malo
agrillo e ralo,
e carne salada. (*st.* 1004)
    Diom' queso de cabras:
"Fidalgo—dis—abras
"ese blazo et toma
"un tanto de soma
"que tengo goardada." (*st.* 1005)
    Dis: "Huesped, almuerza

"e bebe e esfuerza,
"caliéntate e paga,
"de mal non s' te faga
"fasta la tornada. (*st.* 1006)
   "Quien dones me diere
"quales yo pediere,
"habrá bien de çena
"e lechiga buena
"que no l' coste nada." (*st.* 1007)
   —"Vos, que eso desides,
"¿ por qué non pedides
"la cosa çertera?"
Ella dis: "¡Maguera!
"¿ E si m' será dada? (*st.* 1008)
   "Pues dam' una çinta
"bermeja bien tinta,
"e buena camisa
"fecha a mi guisa
"con su collarada. (*st.* 1009)
   "Et dam' buenas sartas
"de estanno e fartas,
"et dame halía
"de buena valía,
"pelleja delgada. (*st.* 1010)
   "Et dam' buena toca
"listada de cota,
"et dame zapatas
"de cuello bien altas,

"de pieza labrada. (*st.* 1011)
   "Con aquestas joyas,
"quiero que lo oyas,
"serás bien venido,
"serás mi marido
"e yo tu velada." (*st.* 1012)
   —"Serrana, sennora,
"tanto algo agora
"non tray por ventura,
"mas faré fiadura
"para la tornada." (*st.* 1013)
   Díxome la heda:
"Do non hay moneda
"non hay merchandía,
"nin hay tan buen día,
"nin cara pagada. (*st.* 1014)
   "Non hay mercadero
"bueno sin dinero,
"e yo non me pago
"del que non da algo,
"nin le dó posada. (*st.* 1015)
   "Nunca de omenaje
"pagan hostalaje;
"por dineros fase
"omen quanto plase,
"cosa es probada." (*st.* 1016)

The *Libro de Alexandre* serves as basis for parody in
several passages of the *Libro de buen amor*. There is a bit

of the *Libro de Alexandre's El mes era de mayo,* along with elements from other popular May poems, in the opening stanzas of the passage lampooning certain members of the clergy in their reaction to the spring season, *De cómo clérigos e legos e flayres e monjes e duennas e ioglares salieron a reçebir a don Amor* (stanzas 1199-1288). Ten stanzas introduce the jubilant spirit in a novel way. A sort of Franciscan medley composed of sun, Eastertide, birds, flowers, trees, men and women, followed by personified and greatly animated musical instruments, come streaming out to greet Love. The sudden transition from the animate to the inanimate is one source of humor, heightened by the fact that the *omes* and *duennas* are briefly squeezed in between the supposedly lower manifestations of life (fauna and flora in that descending order) and the inanimate musical instruments. Even more mirth-provoking is the cacaphonous mock symphony played by a great miscellany of seemingly auto-impelled musical instruments, Disney-fashion, each performing completely independently of hand or of human touch:

Día era muy santo de la Pascua mayor,
el sol era salido muy claro e de noble color,
los omes e las aves et toda noble flor
todos van resçebir cantando al Amor. (*st.* 1199)

Resçíbenlo las aves, gayos et ruysennores,
calandrias, papagayos mayores e menores,
dan cantos plasenteros e de dulçes sabores,
más alegría fasen los que son más mejores. (*st.* 1200)

Resçíbenlo los árbores con ramos et con flores
de diversas maneras, de diversos colores;

reçíbenlo los omes et duennas con amores;
con muchos instrumentos salen los atambores. (*st.* 1201)
    Allí sale gritando la guitarra morisca
de las voses aguda e de los puntos arisca,
el corpudo laúd que tiene punto a la trisca,
la guitarra latina con esos se aprisca. (*st.* 1202)
    El rabé gritador con la su alta nota,
cab' él el orabín taniendo la su rota,
el salterio con ellos más alto que la mota,
la bihuela de péndola con aquestos y sota. (*st.* 1203)
    Medio canno et arpa con el rabé morisco,
entr' ellos alegranza el galipe françisco,
la rota dis con ellos más alta que un risco,
con ella el tamborete, sin él non vale un prisco. (*st.* 1204)
    La vihuela de arco fas dulçes de bayladas,
adormiendo a veses, muy alto a las vegadas,
voses dulses, sabrosas, claras et bien pintadas,
a las gentes alegra, todas las tiene pagadas. (*st.* 1205)
    Dulçe canno entero sal con el panderete,
con sonajas de asófar fasen dulçe sonete,
los órganos y disen chanzones e motete,
la adedura albardana entre ellos se entremete. (*st.* 1206)
    Dulçema e axabeba, el finchado albogón,
çinfonía e baldosa en esta fiesta son,
el françés odreçillo con estos se compón,
la reçiancha mandurria allí fase su son. (*st.* 1207)
    Trompas e annafiles salen con atambales,
non fueron tiempo ha plasenterías tales,

tan grandes alegrías, nin atán comunales,
de juglares van llenas cuesta e eriales. (*st.* 1208)

Following this racket comes a raucous hodge-podge chorus
composed of singers and shouters of religious songs. The
performers are members of various religious orders, and
in honor of Love they move in a procession mimicking a
royal procession such as the one described in the *Libro
de Alexandre* (cf. stanzas 1376-1384), in which the whole
affair is a conglomerate of men, women, song, boys,
branches, clerics, senators, knights, and

> El pleyto de ioglares era fiera nota,
> auyé hy simfonía, arba, giga e rota,
> albogues e salterio, çítola que más trota,
> çedra e uiola que las coytas enbota. (*Alex.*, *st.* 1383)

and typical of those in fashion in Mediaeval times. Some
if not all the hyms here mentioned in burlesque were among
those commonly used in the royal processions. In one line
Juan Ruiz summarizes the effect of all the simultaneous
musical expressions of joy:

> de los grandes roídos es todo el val sonante. (*st.* 1219)

The triumphal entrance of Don Amor, with crown, sym-
bolic pennant, and throngs included, is again reminiscent
of the Alexander of the Mediaeval Spanish version of his
exploits. The *Libro de Alexandre* also furnishes the basis
for Juan Ruiz's description of Don Amor's tent (stanzas
1239 ff.), a direct parody of the description of Alexander's
tent. The *Libro de Alexandre's* author and Juan Ruiz
were, indeed, kindred spirits. Undoubtedly Juan Ruiz

learned much from the earlier poet about the technique
of the personification and animation of the inanimate, the
compression in the representation of human activity, and
methods of narration. The fact that Juan Ruiz chose the
Libro de Alexandre for parody is evidence of the thirteenth-
century book's continued popularity through at least the
first half of the fourteenth century.

Rarely did the Archpriest's boisterous laughter turn
shrill or his humor show an edge of bitterness, and, except
for some sharp barbs in the blind beggar ballads, the
nearest approach to open sarcasm in the *Libro de buen
amor* is probably to be found in the anthology favourite
entitled *Ensiemplo de la propiedat que el dinero ha,* in part
a parody on the "effects of love" listed by troubadours and
enumerated by expounders of courtly love. It is contained
in the advice that Don Amor gives the Archpriest:

Mucho fas el dinero, et mucho es de amar,
al torpe fase bueno et omen de prestar,
fase correr al cojo et al mudo fabrar,
el que non tiene manos, dineros quiere tomar. (*st.* 464)

Sea un ome nesçio et rudo labrador,
los dineros le fasen fidalgo e sabidor,
quanto más algo tiene, tanto es más de valor,
el que non ha dineros non es de sí sennor. (*st.* 465)

Si tovieres dineros, habrás consolaçión,
plaser e alegría, del papa raçión,
comprarás paraíso, ganarás salvaçión,
do son muchos dineros, es mucha bendiçión. (*st.* 466)

Yo vi en corte de Roma, do es la santidat,
que todos al dinero fasen grand homilidat,

grand honra le fasçían con grand solenidat,
todos a él se homillan como a la magestat. (*st.* 467)

    Fasié muchos priores, obispos et abades,
arzobispos, doctores, patriarcas, potestades,
a muchos clérigos nesçios dábales dinidades,
fasié de verdat mentiras, et de mentiras verdades. (*st.* 468)

    Fasía muchos clérigos e muchos ordenados,
muchos monges e monjas, religiosos sagrados,
el dinero los daba por bien examinados,
a los pobres desían que non eran letrados. (*st.* 469)

    Daba muchos juisios, mucha mala sentençia,
con muchos abogados era su mantenençia,
en tener pleytos malos et faser avenençia,
en cabo por dineros había penitençia. (*st.* 470)

    El dinero quebranta las cadenas dannosas,
tira çepos e grillos et cadenas plagosas,
el que non tiene dineros, échanle las posas,
por todo el mundo fase cosas maravillosas. (*st.* 471)

    Yo vi fer maravilla do él mucho usaba,
muchos meresçían muerte que la vida les daba,
otros eran sin culpa et luego los mataba,
muchas almas perdía, et muchas salvaba. (*st.* 472)

    Fasía perder al pobre su casa e su vinna,
sus muebles e raíçes todo los desalinna,
por todo el mundo anda su sarna e su tinna,
do el dinero juega, allí el ojo guinna. (*st.* 473)

    El fase caballeros de neçios aldeanos,
condes e ricos omes de algunos villanos,

con el dinero andan todos los omes lozanos,
quantos son en el mundo le besan hoy las manos. (*st.* 474)
　　Vi tener al dinero las mejores moradas,
altas e muy costosas, fermosas e pintadas,
castillos, eredades, et villas entorreadas,
todas al dinero sirven et suyas son compladas. (*st.* 475)
　　Comía muchos manjares de diversas naturas,
vistía los nobles pannos, doradas vestiduras,
traía joyas preçiosas en viçios et folguras,
guarnimientos estrannos, nobles cabalgaduras. (*st.* 476)
　　Yo vi a muchos monges en sus predicaçiones
denostar al dinero et a sus tentaçiones,
en cabo por dinero otorgan los perdones,
asuelven el ayuno, ansí fasen oraçiones. (*st.* 477)
　　Peroque le denuestan los monges por las plazas,
guárdanlo en covento en vasos et en tazas,
con el dinero cumplen sus menguas e sus razas,
más condesignos tienen que tordos nin picazas. (*st.* 478)
　　Como quier que los frayles et clérigos disen que aman
　　　　　　　　　　　　　　[a Dios servir,
si barruntan que el rico está para morir,
quando oyen sus dineros que comienzan a retenir,
quál de ellos lo levarán comienzan luego a rennir. (*st.* 479)
　　Monges, frayles, clérigos non toman los dineros,
bien les dan de la çeja do son sus parçioneros,
luego los toman prestos sus omes despenseros;
pues que se disen pobles, ¿qué quieren tesoreros? (*st.* 480)
　　Allí están esperando quál habrá más rico tuero;

non es muerto ya disen *Pater noster* ¡mal agüero!
como los cuervos al asno quando le desuellan el cuero:
"Cras, cras nos lo habremos, que nuestro es ya por fuero."

(st. 481)

Toda muger del mundo, et duenna de altesa,
págase del dinero et de mucha riquesa,
yo nunca vi fermosa que quisiese poblesa.
Do son muchos dineros y es mucha noblesa. (*st.* 482)

El dinero es alcalde et jues mucho loado,
éste es consejero et sotil abogado,
alguaçil et merino, bien ardit, esforzado,
de todos los ofiçios es muy apoderado. (*st.* 483)

En suma te lo digo, tómalo tú mejor,
el dinero del mundo es grand revolvedor,
sennor fase del siervo, de sennor servidor,
toda cosa del sigro se fase por su amor. (*st.* 484)

Por dineros se muda el mundo e su manera,
toda muger cobdiçiosa de algo es falaguera,
por joyas et dineros salirá de carrera,
el dar quebranta pennas, fiende dura madera. (*st.* 485)

Derrueca fuerte muro, et derriba grant torre,
a coyta et a grand priesa el mucho dar acorre.
Non a siervo captivo que el dinero non le aforre,
el que non tiene que dar, su caballo non corre. (*st.* 486)

In spite of the sarcasm, which has a general rather than
a specific aim, the Archpriest's irrepressible spirit transluces, and the selection is still typical Juan Ruiz. Animation permeates every line and produces a feeling of life.

Personification of coin and consequent lively activity of the inanimate give the impression of the modern animated cartoon. The cinematographic effect is enhanced by the constant motion deriving from the rapid passing from picture to picture, from coin's quick passage from hand to hand, and from the speed with which money works *effectively*. A large percentage of nouns, a relative lack of adjectives, vocabulary from everyday speech add to the realism. Contrast makes for humor. The wide variety of human types offers a panoramic view of society, which seems to be divided into exploiter and exploited. Busybody money reigns supreme.

Few poems in the *Libro de buen amor* missed the Archpriest's multi-barbed pen. Among those that did escape the admixture of ridicule are his *Gozos de Santa María* of the early part of the book, the *Ditado que 'l Arçipreste ofreçió a Santa María del Vado* and the two poems entitled *De la pasión de nuestro sennor Jesu Christo* of the mid part, and two *gozos*, one gloss on the *Ave María*, and the four poems entitled *Cantica de loores de Santa María*. These compositions, like the others of the *Libro de buen amor*, reflect literary styles and genres previously and currently employed by the poets who consciously followed the troubadour traditions: "Et compóselo otrosí a dar algunas lecçiones e muestra de metrificar et rimar et de trobar, con trovas et notas et rimas et decades et versos, que fis complidamente segund que esta çiençia requiere," says the Archpriest near the close of his introductory sermon. These religious pieces show the spiritual side of the Archpriest's sentiment of love and complement the worldly, giving a completion to his character and literary personality:

Del Ave María de Santa María

 Ave Maria gloriosa,
Virgen Santa preçiosa,
¡cómo eres piadosa
todavía! (*st.* 1633)
 Graçia plena, sin mansilla,
abogada,
por la tu merçed, Sennora,
fas esta maravilla
sennalada;
por la tu bondad agora
goárdame toda hora
de muerte vergonnosa,
porque loe a ti, fermosa,
noche e día. (*st.* 1634)
 Dominus tecum,
estrella resplandeçiente,
melesina de coydados,
catadura muy bella,
relusiente,
sin mansilla de pecados
por los tus gosos preçiados
te pido, virtuosa,
que me guardes, limpia rosa,
de foylía. (*st.* 1635)
 Benedicta tu,
honrada sin egualanza,
siendo Virgen conçebiste.

De los ángeles loada
en altesa,
por el fijo que pariste,
por la graçia que hobiste,
¡o bendicha fror e rosa!
tú me guarda, piadosa,
et me guía. (*st.* 1636)

   In mulieribus
escogida santa Madre,
de christianos amparanza,
de los santos bien servida;
et tu Padre
es tu fijo sin dubdanza.
¡O Virgen, mi fianza!
de gente maliçiosa,
cruel, mala, soberbiosa
me desvía. (*st.* 1637)

   Et benedictus fructus,
folgura et salvaçión
del linage humanal,
que tiraste la tristura
e perdimiento
que por nuestro esquivo mal
el diablo susio tal
con su obla engannosa
en cárçel peligrosa
ya ponía. (*st.* 1638)

Ventris tui,
santa flor non tannida,
por la tu grand santidad
tú me guarda de errar,
que en mi vida siempre siga
en bondad,
que meresca egualdad
con los santos, muy graçiosa,
en dulzor maravillosa,
¡O María! (*st.* 1639)

Cantica de loores de Santa María

Miraglos muchos fase Virgen siempre pura
agoardando los coytados
de dolor et de tristura,
el que loa tu figura,
non lo dexes olvidado,
non catando su pecado,
sálvaslo de amargura. (*st.* 1640)
Ayudas al inoçente con amor muy verdadero,
al que es tu servidor,
bien lo libras de ligero,
non le es falleçedero
tu acorro sin dudanza.
Guárdalo de mal andanza
el tu bien grande llenero. (*st.* 1641)
Reyna, Virgen, mi esfuerzo, yo so puesto en tal espanto,
por lo qual a ti bendigo

que me guardes de quebranto,
pues a ti, Sennora, canto,
tú me guarda de lisión,
de muerte et de ocasión,
por tu fijo Jesu santo. (*st.* 1642)
Yo so mucho agraviado en esta çibdad seyendo,
tu acorro et guarda fuerte
a mí libre defendiendo,
pues a ti me encomiendo,
non me seas desdennosa,
tu bondad maravillosa
loaré siempre sirviendo. (*st.* 1643)
A ti me encomiendo, Virgen Santa María,
la mi coyta tú la parte,
tú me salva e me guía,
et me guarda todavía,
piadosa Virgen Santa,
por la tu merçed que es tanta
que desir non la podría. (*st.* 1644)

Cantica de loores de Santa María
Santa Virgen escogida,
de Dios Madre muy amada,
en los çielos ensalzada,
del mundo salud e vida, (*st.* 1645)
    del mundo salud e vida,
de muerte destruimiento,
de graçia llena complida,
de coytados salvamiento,

de aqueste dolor que siento
en presión sin meresçer,
tú me denna estorçer
con el tu defendimiento. (*st.* 1646)
   Con el tu defendimiento,
non catando mi maldad
nin el mi meresçimiento,
mas la tu propia bondad,
que confieso en verdat
que so pecador errado,
de ti sea ayudado,
por la tu virginidad. (*st.* 1647)
   Por la tu virginidad,
que non ha comparaçión,
nin hobiste egualdad
en obra e entençión,
complida de bendiçión,
pero non so meresçiente,
venga a ti, Sennora, en miente
de complir mi petiçión. (*st.* 1648)
   De complir mi petiçión,
como a otros ya compliste,
de tan fuerte tentaçión
en que so coytado, triste,
pues poder has et hobiste,
tú me guarda en tu mano,
bien acorres muy de llano
al que quieres et quisiste. (*st.* 1649)

Cantica de loores de Santa María

Quiero seguir
a ti, flor de las flores,
siempre desir,
cantar de tus loores,
non me partir
de te servir,
mejor de las mejores. (*st.* 1650)

Grand fianza
he yo en ti, Sennora,
la mi esperanza
en ti es toda hora
de tribulaçión,
sin tardanza
venme librar agora. (*st.* 1651)

Virgen muy santa,
yo paso atribulado
pena atanta
con dolor atormentado
en tu esperanza
coyta atanta
que veo ¡mal pecado! (*st.* 1652)

Estrella del mar,
puerto de folgura,
de dolor complido
et de tristura,
venme librar
et conortar,

Sennora del altura. (*st.* 1653)
   Nunca falleçe
la tu merçed complida,
siempre guaresçes
de coytas et das vida,
nunca peresçe
nin entristeçe
quien a ti non olvida. (*st.* 1654)
   Sufro grand mal
sin meresçer, a tuerto,
escribo tal
porque pienso ser muerto,
mas tú me val,
que non veo al
que me saque a puerto. (*st.* 1655)

Cantica de loores de Santa María

There is a possibility of a scribal error involved in
the following selection, though similarly constructed pieces
may be found in later poetry. The first stanza is the beginning of a poem in praise of the Virgin; the remaining
stanzas, having a contrasting subject, different meter, and
different rime scheme, are another poem altogether, the
earliest known in Castilian on the theme of complaint
against Fortune, which during the early period is generally
called *ventura*, and later *fortuna*, a major theme of the
cancionero poets.

     En ti es mi esperanza,
   Virgen Santa María,

en sennor de tal valía
es razón de haber fianza. (*st.* 1656)

    Ventura astrosa,
cruel, enojosa,
captiva, mesquina,
¿por qué eres sannosa,
contra mí tan dannosa
et falsa vesina? (*st.* 1657)

    Non sé escrebir,
nin puedo desir
la coyta estranna
que me fases sofrir,
con deseo vevir
en tormenta tamanna. (*st.* 1658)

Fasta hoy todavía
mantoviste porfía
en me maltraer:
fas ya cortesía
e dame alegría,
gasajo et plaser. (*st.* 1659)

    Et si tú me tirares
coyta e pesares,
et mi grand tribulanza
en gozo tornares,
et bien ayudares,
farás buena estanza. (*st.* 1660)

    Mas si tú porfías,
et non te desvías

de mis penas cresçer,
ya las coytas mías
en muy pocos días
podrán fenesçer. (*st.* 1661)

Taking full advantage of epithet and metaphor and of certain refined prayer techniques, and choosing a light, delicate meter to create a sense of the ethereal and to match the subject of his devotion, Juan Ruiz has achieved a high level of lyricism in his poems on and to the Virgin. The interplay of second and first person, of feelings of unworthiness and confidence, of pain and joy lend an intimacy to these poems that places reader and writer in common experience.

Good humor, grace, wit, and versatility characterize most of the work of this contemporary and kindred spirit of the Italian Boccaccio (1313?-1375), and, like him, of universal appeal and so still modern. Juan Ruiz's contributions to the development of Spanish poetry are many and lasting. He is first in a long line of satiric poets, among them Quevedo and Góngora; and, although he has not yet been duly appreciated as a religious poet, his lyrics to the Virgin are among the finest of their kind.

ALFONSO XI: *Cantiga*

Em hum tiempo cogí flores
del mui nobre paraíso,
cuitado de mis amores,
e del su fremoso riso;
e sempre vivo en dolor,
e ya lo non puedo sofrir,
mais me valerá la muerte
que en el mundo vivir.
   Yo cum cuidado d' amores
vol' o vengo ora dizer,
que he d' aquesta mi senhora,
que muicho desejo aver.
En el tiempo en que solía
yo coger d' aquestas flores,
d' al cuidado nom avía
desque vi los sus amores;
e nom sé per quál ventura
me vino a defalir,
si lo fiz' el mi peccado,
si lo fizo el mal dizir.

Yo cum cuidado d' amores
vol' o vengo ora dizer,
que é d' aquesta mi senhora,
que muicho desejo aver.

No creades, mi senhora,
el mal dizer de las gentes,
ca la muerte m' es llegada
sy en elho parardes mentes;
ay, senhora, nobre rosa,
mercede vos vengo pidir,
avede de mí dolor
e no me dexedes morir.

Yo cum cuidado d' amores
vol' o veng' ora a dizer,
que he d' aquesta mi senhora,
que muicho desejo aver.

Yo cogí la flor das frores
de que tú coger solías,
cuitado de mis amores
bien sé lo que tú querías;
Dios lo pueste por tal guisa
que te lo pueda fazer,
ant' yo quería mi muerte
que te asy veja a morrer.

Yo cum cuidado d' amores
vol' o vengo ora a dizer,
que he d' aquesta mi senhora,
que muicho desejo aver.

The poem is by Alfonso XI (1312-1350). Like the miscellaneous independent poems following the *Libro de buen amor* proper, this dainty troubadouresque *cantiga* appearing in the Galician-Portuguese *Cancioneiro da Vaticana* gives us an idea of one direction Castilian poetry might have taken but for the fashion of writing lyrics in Galician-Portuguese. According to the compiler of the *cancioneiro* the *cantiga* was composed by *El Rey dom Affonso de Castella e de León que venceu el Rey de Belamarim com o poder d'allem-mar a par de Tarifa*, and so possibly was written during the last decade of Alfonso's life. As both title and refrain indicate, it belongs to the song form. It touches upon several common troubadour love themes: pleasure of love, memory of love, pain of love, love lost through slander, absence causing death, seeking of the lady's mercy.

Time and flowers together somehow make an almost irresistible combination at any time, and here the poet, setting the time-flower theme in the first line, expands it immediately to include paradise, suggestive of the timelessness of beauty, and then, by means of parallel phrasing, gives the impression of compressing paradise into his lady's smile—all in four octosyllables, half an octave. The second half of the stanza, serving as contrast to the first, expands the time theme, immediately continuing the idea of eternity in the word *siempre*, but changing the pleasures of paradise to pain *(dolor, sofrir)* that leads to a negative sort of eternity in death *(muerte)*, and *mundo* completes the contrast. As if to reinforce the impression given by the first stanza, the second repeats its structure and style. Time, flowers, the pleasure of love occupy the first half, misadventure the second, in which reason for sorrow is introduced as a new theme. In the third stanza the poet reverses the order of pleasure-sadness and alters them slightly to anxiety-hope, still retaining, however, key themes of the first stanza—death, flower, pain—as he expands on the one (slander) most recently introduced in the second, and adds that of beseeching. Flower is now singular though probably still generic in meaning *(rosa* was frequently a synonym of *flor)*. The mere single flower of the third stanza becomes superlative in the fourth and final stanza, where again appear love, pleasure, sorrow, memory, the supernatural, and death. In the constant return of the various themes and the repetition of vocabulary, and of course the cyclic refrain, the stanzas form a sort of wreath of intertwining themes, and outstanding in it the flowers. Thematic progression is achieved principally by three means: repetition in variation, gradual accretion, and intensification. The three-step progression of the flower theme illustrates well the last-mentioned: from horizontal spread in the first and second stanzas to selection in the third, and highest degree of perfection in the last. Level of perfection rises from one presumably unsurpassable in flowers of paradise to one surpassing all, flower of flowers. The surpassing quality of this flower of flowers is further intensified not only by the rhetorical device itself but also because, except for the rejected world, it is (both as flower and lady) the only tangible figure and visual image in the poem.

Periodic mood contrast and variation is one of the beauty secrets of this lyric. In each stanza one half contrasts in mood with the other half, and moods change kaleidoscopically: happiness—pain, confidence—anxiety, care—hope, indicative—subjunctive. The result of the contrast in series is a double tone or a harmonious two-voice effect, which contributes to the musicality of the song.

The quality of lightness that immediately strikes the attention of the reader has several sources: preponderance of abstract terms and of states rather than tangible matter, celestial references, artistic and emotional restraint, metric form, musicality, continual mood change, temporal rather than spatial concern, simplicity of rhetorical ornamentation.

This *cantiga* illustrates the courtly lover's religious devotion to his lady. The words and wording are so similar to those of some of the Marian poetry of the period (cf. Juan Ruiz's *Quiero seguir a ti, flor de las flores)* that only the presence of the slander theme gives a clue to the profane nature of the lyric.

Why Alfonso XI chose to write this poem in Castilian it would be difficult to say. The remaining several pieces by him in the *Cancioneiro da Vaticana* are all in Galician-Portuguese. It is fortunate that this perhaps earliest extant *cancionero* type of profane light love lyric remains to indicate the possibility of the existence of a wider early interest in Castilian courtly troubadour poetry.

POEMA DE ALFONSO ONCENO

In a history of the Spanish *romance* (ballad), a poetic form perfected in the fifteenth and early sixteenth centuries, surely many selections from the mid-fourteenth-century *Poema de Alfonso Onceno*, written or translated by Rodrigo Yáñez, would have to be numbered among the immediate antecedents of the genre. The poem as a whole reads much like a series of *romances*, sometimes rather loosely joined to contiguous material by means of rapid transitions, or deliberately inserted as semi-independent pieces in the poem. In fact, were some of the selections detached from the work and presented independently they would easily pass as true *romances* of one of the minor variant metric forms. In place of the continuous alternate assonance of the even-numbered lines that eventually predominated in the *romance*, the *Poema de Alfonso Onceno* has quatrains rimed in alternate consonance that changes from stanza to stanza. As in the *romance*, the lines are predominantly octosyllabic, though more loosely measured than in most of the known *romances* of succeeding periods. As in so many *romances* of the *cancioneros* and early *romanceros*, introductions and conclusions are lacking or are exceedingly brief, and description is achieved largely by means of simple narrative and enumerative techniques. Such characteristics can hardly be surprising, however, since they simply correspond to those of the learned poetry in vogue at the time and for a century preceding in the *mester de clerecía*. As the *romance* varies in length, in mood, in theme, so does the corresponding virtually independent excerpt from the *Poema de Alfonso Onceno*.

Prayer, cityscape, philosophic-moral proverb, lament, song of praise, Maytime reaction, scenes of courtly chivalry, ideal prince—these are some of the materials woven into the composition, as irregularly as had been the case in the style that had been prevailing in the long learned poems for a century or more. The poet was especially skillful at blending. In the following selection, for example, he moves like a cinematographer about the court on coronation day and catches the full spirit of the occasion in a series of "takes" covering important activities planned for the festivity: jousts and various games of skill in knightly pursuits, dancing, singing, playing of instruments. Pageantry and the display of fine clothes is balanced by the singing of gratitude to God for the gift of good sovereigns. The courtly sights and activities would not be complete without the element of love, and love flourishes under the influence of music and in the new warmth of Maytime:

> Por onrra e pres ganar
> ayuntó la su conpanna,
> ssu espada fue tomar
> en Ssantiago de Espanna. (*st.* 389)
> En aquel día ganó
> este rrey muy grant loor;

para Burgos se tornó
aqueste noble ssennor. (*st.* 390)
    Las Huelgas encoranaron
de pannos de gran noblesa,
por las paredes echaron
pannos de gran riquesa. (*st.* 391)
    El muy noble rrey aquel día
su corona fue tomar;
la reyna donna María
y la fiso coronar. (*st.* 392)
    Ricos omnes que llegauan,
e omnes de gran valor,
caualleros sse armauan
por mano deste ssennor; (*st.* 393)
    e físolos caualleros,
púsolos en gran altesa,
dióles plata e dineros
que valían gran riquesa. (*st.* 394)
    Nunca fue omne que viese
de tales cauallerías,
nin lengua que departiesse
de tan nobles cortesías (*st.* 395)
    qual sse fiso en uerdat
en junio, mes falaguero,
en Burgos, noble çiudat,
quando el rrey fue cauallero. (*st.* 396)
    Quien fuera aquel día
galeas viera andar

en sseco por maestría,
e caualleros justar. (*st.* 397)
    Viera otros juegos estrannos,
cantar con alegría,
e vino andar por cannos:
tomáualo quien quería. (*st.* 398)
    Vnos andauan dançando
desde el fondo fasta ençima,
e los otros bofordando,
e otros jogando esgrimma. (*st.* 399)
    Tomauan escudo e lança,
la gineta yuan jogando.
Rricas duennas fasían dança
a muy gran plaser cantando; (*st.* 400)
    e yuanles rrespondiendo
donsellas de gran altura,
el buen rrey enobleçiendo,
sennor de buena ventura. (*st.* 401)
    Cantando a gran sabor,
desían en ssu cantar:
"¡ Loado el gran Ssennor
"que tan buen rrey nos fue dar ! (*st.* 402)
    "Rey alto, de gran noblesa,
"sennor real entendido,
"Castilla cobró altesa
"el día que fue nasçido. (*st.* 403)
    "Noble escudo syn pauor,
"Dios mantenga la ssu vida;

"e cassó con mejor reyna
"que en el mundo fue nasçida. (*st.* 404)
  "Sennora non ssaben tal,
"onesta, bien pareçiente,
"e nasçió en Portogal,
"en el cabo del Poniente." (*st.* 405)
  Estas palabras desían
donsellas en ssus cantares;
los estormentos tannían
por las Huelgas los jograles. (*st.* 406)
  El laúd yuan tanniendo,
estormento falaguero,
la viuuela tanniendo,
el rabé con el salterio, (*st.* 407)
  la guitarra sserranista,
estromento con rrasón,
la exabeba morisca,
allá en medio canón, (*st.* 408)
  la gayta, que es sotil,
con que todos plaser han,
otros estromentos mill,
con la farpa de don Tristán (*st.* 409)
  que da los puntos doblados,
con que falaga el loçano
e todos los enamorados
en el tienpo del verano. (*st.* 410)
  Allí quando vienen las flores
e los árboles dan fruto,

> los leales amadores
> este tienpo preçian mucho, (*st.* 411)
>   asy commo el mes de mayo
> cuando el ruyssennor canta,
> rresponde el papagayo
> de la muy fermosa planta, (*st.* 412)
>   La calandra del otra parte,
> del muy fermoso rrosal,
> el tordo que departe
> el amor que mucho val. (*st.* 413)

The final stanzas of the selection are closely related to one of the most popular of the early *romances*, the one beginning

> Por el mes era de mayo
> cuando hace la calor,
> cuando canta la calandria
> y responde el ruiseñor ...

as well as to such selections as *El mes de mayo* of the *Libro de Alexandre.*

The prayer in the following exerpt is composed in much more orderly and elaborate fashion than the usual, and expresses genuine patriotism in place of the expected personal request. It is a combination of confession and supplication. The subjectivity of the prayer itself blends well with the detailed and picturesque lyric drama that serves as introduction:

En la su tienda yasía,
no codiçiando thesoros,
mas deseando el día
que se viese con los moros. (*st.* 1497)
 En la su cama yasiendo
con sanna del coraçón,
yasíase rreboluiendo,
commo vn brauo león; (*st.* 1498)
 e a Dios Padre pedía
que la mannana llegase;
e Dios le enbió el día,
e non quisso que tardase. (*st.* 1499)
 E el Seturno conplió
su curso, e amanesçió,
el alua luego salió,
e la lus esclaresçió. (*st.* 1500)
 Alegró el coraçón
quando el día llegó,
a Dios fiso oraçión,
de coraçón le rrogó (*st.* 1501)
 e dis: "Sennor de uerdat,
"Padre e Fijo e Spíritu Santo,
"Vn Dios, nuestra Trinidat,
"Nuestro escudo, nuestro manto, *(st.* 1502)
 "que me fesiste tú rrey,
"e me posiste en altura,
"e yo, Sennor, por tu ley,
"pongo el cuerpo en auentura, (*st.* 1503)

"contra ti so muy errado
"desde el tienpo en que nasçí,
"bien conosco mi pecado
"e el mal que merescí. (*st.* 1504)

"Dexiste que el que pecasse,
"por la boca de Jerumías,
"el que se a ti tornase,
"que tú lo rreçibirías. (*st.* 1505)

"Yo, Sennor, a ti me torno
"con muy grand deuoçión;
"a ti, Padre, Sennor bueno,
"pido merçed e perdón (*st.* 1506)

"por mí e por mi conpanna,
"que uos non dexes perder,
"e la corona de Espanna
"póngola en tu poder; (*st.* 1507)

"e ayuda a quien quisieres,
"Rey, Padre apoderado;
"de lo que, Sennor, fesieres,
"yo d' ello so muy pagado; (*st.* 1508)

"e si tienes de mí sanna
"que no escape a vida,
"mienbrat', Sennor, de Espanna,
"non sea perdida; (*st.* 1509)

"de ti sea anparada
"de Africa la destruyente,
"que la tiene amenasada
"con poderes de Oriente." (*st.* 1510)

The subjectivity of this private prayer contrasts well with the impersonal formality of an Archbishop's public prayer of consecration of arms. The Archbishop's invocation is somewhat stiffened by oratorical formula, and the inflated preamble, a gloss of the *Credo*, leaves small space for the entreaty proper. The poet again carefully prepares an appropriate introduction-background against which to place the supplication:

> En preses el rey yasía,
> misa de Santa Crus oyó,
> el arçobispo la desía,
> las armas del rrey pidió. (*st.* 1516)
>
> Sobre el altar las posieron,
> estas armas muy fermosas,
> e las armas bendixieron,
> desiendo muy nobles prosas. (*st.* 1517)
>
> de la Uirgo consagrada,
> nuestra lus e nuestro bien,
> que por el ángel fue saludada
> en el Val de Nasarén. (*st.* 1518)
>
> El arçobispo consagraua
> estas armas aquel día,
> los xristianos esforçaua,
> contra Dios Padre desía: (*st.* 1519)
>
> "Jesu Xrispto, que beniste
> "del Padre de la altura,
> "en la tierra apareçiste
> "Santo Spíritu por natura. (*st.* 1520)
>
> "Padeçiste cuyta muy fuerte

"por el mundo visitar,
"por nos padeçiste muerte
"en el Monte de Caluar. (*st.* 1521)
   "Estás a la diestra parte
"de Dios Padre Criador,
"uerdadero Dios sin arte,
"derechurero judgador. (*st.* 1522)
   "Sennor, por tu piadat,
"que naçiste sin mansiella,
"ayuda por tu bondat
"el noble rey de Castiella (*st.* 1523)
   "que posiste en altura
"e diste buen fundamento,
"tú le dar por tu mesura
"la honrra del bençimiento. (*st.* 1524)
   "Da poder a los xristianos,
"e a la tu fee muy santa,
"e destruyr los paganos,
"la santa crus adelanta." (*st.* 1525)

One of the lyric genres in which the poet of the *Poema de Alfonso Onceno* excelled is the lament in monologue. With sympathetic understanding he follows the King of Granada's emotional reaction to the loss of his most prized possession. The plight of personified Granada is the saddened king's first concern. Only after long contemplation of his beloved's fall does he become aware of his own condition, and still it is not a personal loss that he feels, but grief and distress over his powerlessness to come to her aid. The shock of the present is realistically relieved

by memory in the transfer of the afflicted one's attention
to the past and the events leading to the disaster. Realism
continues as the king still fails to see any relationship
between himself and the dire event, but first attributes defeat to an overpowering supernatural enemy force,
and then, almost comically, begins to mollify himself with
anger as he shifts the blame for defeat to an indolent
and gluttonous protector. The opening apostrophe is striking not only for the imagery itself and for the double
suffering it indicates—the pitiableness of Granada in her
present situation and the frustration felt by the king in
not being able to grieve as deeply as the sight demands—
but provides a beautiful contrast and color-texture-contour
background for the place description that consists entirely
of abstract qualities. Together the lament and its mood-
setting introduction form an excellent *romance fronterizo:*

> Este rrey quiero dexar,
> que pasó la mar salada,
> e de don Juçaf quiero fablar,
> rrey e sennor de Granada. (*st.* 1877)
>   Mal andante yua e solo,
> perdida auía la senna,
> e yua fasiendo duelo
> por los puertos de Ximena. (*st.* 1878)
>   En la Alfanbra de Granada
> entró con muy grand quebranto.
> Quebrantó la su espada,
> e començó a faser llanto. (*st.* 1879)
>   Dixo: "Coraçón de cobre,
> "¿cómmo no quiebras comigo?

"Granada la muy noble,
"oy perdiste grand albrigo, (*st.* 1880)
　"poderío e altura
"que te sienpre ennobleçió:
"mudada es tu ventura,
"la rrueda se rreboluió. (*st.* 1881)
　"La tu fama se mudó
"por que sienpre fueste honrrada,
"que te sienpre ayudó
"e te tuuo anparada. (*st.* 1882)
　"Yo tu rrey finco vençido,
"cosa non sé qué faser,
"pues el poder he perdido,
"non te puedo defender. (*st.* 1883)
　"Santiago el de Espanna,
"los mis moros me mató,
"desbarató mi conpanna,
"la mi senna quebrantó. (*st.* 1884)
　"Yo lo vi bien aquel día:
"con muchos omnes armados
"el mar seco parescía,
"e cobierto de crusados. (*st.* 1885)
　"Este rrey dixo uerdat,
"aquesto sepan sin falla,
"que Dios, rrey de piadat,
"quiso vençer la batalla. (*st.* 1886)
　"Por mostrar la su fasanna
"e el buen rrey ayudar,

"el apóstol de Espanna
"y lo quiso enbiar. (*st.* 1887)
  "Santiago glorioso
"los moros fiso morir,
"Mahomat el peresoso
"tardo non quiso benir; (*st.* 1888)
  "e quando a Meca llegó,
"echóse e adormeçió,
"o cuydo que se afogó
"con brunnuelos que comió." (*st.* 1889)

Superior to this plaint in lyric structure and effect is that of the *alcayde de Algesira*. Here the focus is constantly on the city, but both the city and its surroundings, along with the mood of the speaker, gradually change from dark and restricted to bright and expansive. The city itself determines the mood of the speaker. As the city is isolated and threatened with inundation by the miraculous flood of water loosed by the Christians' God, the *alcayde* laments in terms of *pesar, mal, mal, desanparada, perdida, mala dolençia, non, non.* He sees his city only against a background of evils. His grief swirls around the city like the heavy waters. The poet's parallel here is unique, and the more beautiful for the unobtrusiveness of the technique involved in drawing it. The parallel of isolation ends with the verses marked by the anaphora *non—non,* which links in a sort of *lexaprende* device the two halves, approximately, of the lament. The second half, in which only the word *pesar* is of the dolefully abstract nature of the key words of the first half, contains only concrete or tangible references, and these augment in size, giving Algeciras a

firm position in surroundings expanding to the limits of
the world. Again the movement suggested is like that of
a flood. Again the poet selects an unusual image, the micro-
cosmic-macrocosmic metaphor *espejo:* Algeciras for both
its geographical position and its inhabitants and their cul-
ture a mirror (-image) of Africa. In the final stanza the
espejo becomes a *flor*, the attitude is one of adoration, and
the mood one of confidence. The one abstract term, *preçio*,
stands alone in contrast with all preceding abstract terms,
like Algeciras above all earthly cities, isolated from them
by its worth as it literally was by flood waters. Needless
now to call attention to the artful mood-link between introduction and lament:

> E Dios commo es poderoso,
> que fue nado sin mansiella,
> miraclo fiso fermoso
> por el buen rrey de Castiella. (*st.* 2309)
>   E luego por este fecho
> vn diluuio allegó
> .... [*line missing*]
> toda la mar demudada cargó. (*st.* 2310)
>   Las ondas llenas benían
> de lenna para quemar,
> sierras grandes paresçían
> que venían por la mar, (*st.* 2311)
>   e en el rreal aportaua:
> mucho pessó a paganos.
> El muy noble rrey fablaua
> por esforçar los xristianos: (*st.* 2312)

"A Dios grandes graçias demos,
"nuestra fasienda bien biera,
"pues a Dios por nos auemos,
"nuestra será Algesira." (*st.* 2313)
    Grandes muelas fiso echar
toda esta rribera,
e con cadenas atar
toneles con la madera; (*st.* 2314)
    E mandóla bien çercar
noblemiente a marauilla,
que las sabras por la mar
non entrasen por la villa. (*st.* 2315)
    El alcayde esto bió,
e mudó la catadura,
en vna torre subió,
e dixo con amargura, (*st.* 2316)
    auiendo pesar e yra,
oteando a la mar:
"Algesira, Algesira,
"bínote muy grand pesar. (*st.* 2317)
    "De la çima fasta el fondo,
"mal te tienen afincada,
"e de todos los del mundo,
"mal estás desanparada. (*st.* 2318)
    "Ya dada es la sentençia,
"perdida serás ayna,
"la tu mala dolençia,
"non le salen melesina. (*st.* 2319)

"Non a físico atal
"que te pueda dar consejo;
"Africa la muy rreal,
"en ti pierde buen espejo. (*st.* 2320)
　"Bien así los africanos
"por ti auerán pesar,
"en ti cobrarán los xristianos
"todo el mundo, de mar a mar. (*st.* 2321)
　"Dios te quiera acorrer
"e te vala a esta guerra;
"si merçed ha de faser
"Dios en alguna tierra, (*st.* 2322)
　"fágalo a ti que eres flor;
"que el tu preçio alaben,
"pues la billa mejor
"es que en todo el mundo saben." (*st.* 2323)

The lament over Algeciras can be more fully appreciated
if one reads a passage that precedes it by some three-
hundred stanzas in the poem: a cityscape, the first half
of which is somewhat similar to religious poems:

　　Contarvos he vna cosa:
　cómmo ouieron castellanos
　Algesira la fermosa,
　espejo de los africanos, (*st.* 2010)
　　llaue del mar muy preçiada,
　de Espanna grant prouecho,
　e está bien asentada

en las prayas del Estrecho, (*st.* 2011)
　el alcáçar muy rreal,
fermoso commo rrobí,
torres de canto e de cal,
las mejores que yo bi, (*st.* 2012)
　Martes con sus saetas,
a buenas bien apostadas,
muy peligrosas barreras,
cartauas muy bien labradas. (*st.* 2013)
　Dos billas son de grand brío,
que están en tierra fiel,
por entre couas vn rrío,
que llaman rrío de Miel. (*st.* 2014)
　Y Ercoles la fue poblar
aquel que pobló a Seuilla,
yo non podría contar
noblesa de aquesta villa. (*st.* 2015)
Algeciras . . . , Ceuta . . . :
　E de allí se fue su vía,
allén la mar oteando,
vio Cepta cómmo yasía,
las torres bien blanqueando. (*st.* 2128)
　Todas las torres bien mira
e los puertos fue pasar,
en las playas de Algesira
su pendón fiso posar. (*st.* 2129)
　La villa vio fermosa,
el alcáçar bien labrado,

nunca fue en el mundo cosa
de que fuese más pagado. (*st*. 2130)
    Las billas bio asentadas,
sobre muy fuerte lauor,
de gentes tan bien pobradas,
que non podían mejor. (*st*, 2131)
    Ochosientos caualleros
son aquí, dan quitaçiones,
dos mill eran los arqueros,
e quatorse mill peones. (*st*. 2132)
    Algesira esplandor daba
commo estrella leuante.
Amar Beniex y estaua,
fijo de Abomelique el infante. (*st*. 2133)

Versatility was a mark of craftsmanship among the poets of the *mester de clerecía*, and was one of the assets of the author of the *Poema de Alfonso Onceno*, who was able to move with apparent ease from subject to subject and from mood to mood. Imitation of other *mester de clerecía* poems, undoubtedly including the *Libro de Alexandre*, was an important factor in the selection of both genre and theme of the digressive passages, but does not account for certain notable features of the poem, the most obvious of them being the short meter (similar to but not identical with that employed by the contemporary Sem Tob in the *Proverbios morales*), the ballad style with its narrative, dramatic, and lyric variations, and the relative lack of rhetorical showmanship—this last in spite of the fact that the poet was familiar with courtly matters and surely had access to many manuscripts representing a wide variety of learned styles. To the lyric these outstanding features lend a lightness, an even flow, and a certain unaffectedness that one normally associates with a semi-popular type of poetry, such as the ballad. The *Poema de Alfonso Onceno* is certainly one of the most important single works in the history of the creation of the *romance*.

SEM TOB DE CARRION

With the serenity and the perspective provided by emotional detachment, Juan Ruiz's contemporary the Rabbi
Sem Tob (also known as Don Santo, Don Santob or
Samtob) de Carrión views the universe, its phenomena,
and the beings that populate its earth segment. He sees
the universe as an orderly arrangement, and in it Nature
with inexorable laws, of which the wise man takes advantage and the fool makes himself the victim. Although
the title of his collection is *Proverbios morales* and the
work most certainly contains moral advice on many matters, the poet penetrates far below the surface of exemplary
behavior to discover for us and for himself that peace
and well-being come solely from living in consonance with
the universe, and that any other mode of living is simply
stupid. Stupidity and the stupid he holds in unbounded
scorn—*torpedat, torpe* (which sometimes mean or include
the meaning of wickedness, wicked) appear over and over
again in his stanzas—from which fact we may infer that
in spite of his seemingly fatalistic attitude he credited man
with the ability to determine his own destiny (free will).
His concern with the deeper meanings of morality brings

him, then, to philosophic speculation and psychological insight:

> Señor, Rey noble, alto: oy' este sermón
> que vyene dezyr Santo,   judío de Carrión, (*st.* 1)
>   comunal mente trobado,   de glosas moral mente,
> de filosofía sacado,   segunt aquí va syguiente. (*st.* 2)

and ultimately to perception of beauty. His desire to re-create the beauty he thus perceives causes him, in turn, to order and to polish his expression as one would cut and polish a jewel, until only the essential remains, and that essential in the most complexly simple form possible. Brilliance of wit thinly veiled with near-humor and slight melancholy serves well in the revealing of truth as the Rabbi sees it.

In one mood Sem Tob is comforting in his reasoning concerning the insignificance of the individual's moral deformities in comparison with God's mercy:

> Yo estando con cueyta,   por myedo de pecados
> muchos que fiz syn cuenta,   menudos e granados, (*st.* 17)
>   teníame por muerto,   mas vyno me al talante
> un conorte muy çierto,   que m' fizo byen andante: (*st.* 18)
>   ¡Omre torpe, syn seso!   Sería a Dios baldón
> la tu maldat en peso   poner con su perdón.   (*st.* 19)
>   El te fizo naçer,   bybes en merçed suya:
> ¿cómo podrá vençer   a su obra la tuya? (*st.* 20)
>   Pecar es la tu maña,   la suya, perdonar
> e alongar la saña,   los yerros oluidar. (*st.* 21)
>   Bien commo es más alto   el çielo que la tierra,

el su perdón es tanto   mayor que la tu yerra. (*st.* 22)
  Segunt el poder suyo, tanto es la obra suya
segunt el poder tuyo,   tal es la obra tuya, (*st.* 23)
  obra de omne, que nada   es, todo el su fecho
e su vyda penada   es a muy poco trecho. (*st.* 24)
  ¿Cómmo serié tan granda   com la del Criador,
que todo el mundo manda   e faz en derredor (*st.* 25)
  andar aquella rrueda   del çielo e las estrellas
que jamás nunca queda,   e sabe cuenta dellas? (*st.* 26)
  Quanto el tu estado   es ante la su gloria,
monta el tu pecado   a su misericordia. (*st.* 27)
  Sería cosa estraña,   muy fuera de natura,
la tu yerra tamaña   ser commo su mesura. (*st.* 28)
  De aquesto non temas, que seer non podría,
e non torrnes jamás   en la tu rrebeldía, (*st.* 29)
  mas te arrepentyr   e fazer oraçión,
e merçed le pedyr   con magnifestaçión (*st.* 30)
  de todo lo pasado   e partyr dello mano:
con tanto perdonado   serás bien de lyuiano. (*st.* 31)

In another mood he is encouraging in his presentation
of the quiet dignity attained by the individual in quest of
knowledge:

  En mundo tan cabdal   non a como el saber,
nin eredat nin al,   nin ningún otro aver. (*st.* 326)
  El saber es la gloria   de Dios e la su graçia;
non a tan noble joya   nin tan buena ganançia, (*st.* 327)
  nin mejor conpañón   que el libro, nin tal,
e tomar entençión   con él, más que paz val. (*st.* 328)

Quanto más fuer tomando   con el libro porfía,
tanto yrá ganando   buen saber toda vía. (*st.* 329)
    Los sabios que quería   veer, los fallará
en él, e toda vía   con ellos fablará. (*st.* 330)
    Los sabios muy granados   que omre deseava,
filósofos onrrados   que veer cobdiçiaba, (*st.* 331)
    lo que de aquellos sabyos   él cobdiçia auia,
e los sus petafios   e su sabyduría, (*st.* 332)
    ally lo fallará   en el libro sygnado,
e rrespuesta abrá   dellos por su dyctado, (*st.* 333)
    aprende nueba cosa   de muy buen saber, çierto,
e mucha buena glosa   que fyzyeron al testo. (*st.* 334)
    Si quiero, en leer   sus letras e sus versos,
más sé que non por veer   sus carrnes a sus güesos. (*st.* 335)
    La su sabiençia pura   escrybta la dexaron,
syn ninguna boltura   corporal la sumaron, (*st.* 336)
    syn buelta terrenal   de ningún alemento,
saber çelestrial,   claro entendimiento. (*st.* 337)
    Por esto solo quier   tod' omre de cordura
a los sabios veer,   non por la su fygura. (*st.* 338)
    Por ende tal amigo   non a como el libro:
pora los sabios digo,   que con torpes non me libro. (*st.* 339)

In still another ne gently urges the righteous man to bear
willingly the cost of his righteousness, and thereby to enjoy
its rewards:

Non sabe la persona
torpe que se baldona

por las priesas del mundo
que nos da amenudo; (*st.* 34)
   non sabe que la manera
del mundo ésta era:
tener syenpre viçiosos
a los onbres astrosos, (*st.* 35)
   e ser d' él guerreados
los omnes onrrados.
Alça los ojos, acata:
verás en la mar alta (*st.* 36)
   e sobre las sus cuestas
andan cosas muertas,
e yazen çafondadas
en él piedras presçiadas, (*st.* 37)
   e el peso así
avaga otrosí
la más llena balança,
e la más vazya alça; (*st.* 38)
   e en el çielo estrellas,
e sabe cuenta d' ellas
non escoresçen vna
sy non el sol e la luna. (*st.* 39)

Antithesis, and its frequent paradoxes and perspectives, exemplified in this toiling of the righteous and leisure of the worthless, preoccupies him again and again in the *Proverbios morales:*

En sueño vna fermosa   besaua vna vegada,
estando muy medrosa   de los de su posada: (*st.* 32)

fallé boca sabrosa,   saliua muy tenprada;
non vi tan dulçe cosa,   mas agra a la dexada. (*st.* 33)

Quiero dezyr del mundo   e de las sus maneras,
e cómmo de él dubdo   palabras muy çerteras, (*st.* 70)
que non sé tomar tiento   nin fazer pleytesía,
de acuerdos más de çiento   me torno cada día. (*st.* 71)

Lo que vno denuesta,   veo a otro loallo;
lo que éste apuesta,   veo a otro afeallo. (*st.* 72)

La vara que menguada   la diz el conprador,
esta mesma sobrada   la diz el vendedor. (*st.* 73)

El que lança la lança   semejal' vaguarosa,
pero al que alcança   semejal' presurosa. (*st.* 74)

Farían dos amigos   çinta de vn anillo
en que dos enemigos   non metrién vn dedillo. (*st.* 75)

Con lo que Lope gana,   Rodrigo enpobresçe;
con lo que Sancho sana,   Domingo adoleçe. (*st.* 76)

Quien a fazer senblante   de su vezino tyene
ojo, syn catar ante   lo que a él conuiene, (*st.* 77)
en muy grant yerro puede   caher muy de rrafez,
que vna cosa piede   la sal, otra la pez. (*st.* 78)

Por lo que éste faze   cosa, otro la dexa;
con lo que a mí plaze   mucho, otro se quexa. (*st.* 79)

El sol la sal atiesta   e la pez enblandesçe,
la mexilla faz prieta,   el lienço enblanquesçe; (*st.* 80)
e él es eso mesmo   asy en su altura
quando faz frío cuemo   quando faze calura. (*st.* 81)

Buenos nomres sabemos   al fablar afellar.
¡Quántos males podemos   afellar al callar! (*st.* 607)

El fablar es clareza,   el callar, escureza;
el fablar es franqueza,   el callar, escaseza; (*st.* 608)
    el fablar, ligereza,   e el callar, pereza.
El fablar es rriqueza,   e el callar, pobreza; (*st.* 609)
    el callar, torpedat,   e el fablar, saber;
el callar, çeguedat,   el el fablar, vista aver. (*st.* 610)
    Cuerpo es el callar,   e el fablar, su alma;
omne es el fablar,   e el callar, su cama. (*st.* 611)
    El callar es dormir,   el fablar, despertar;
el callar exprimir,   el fablar, leuantar. (*st.* 612)
    El callar es tardada,   el fablar ayna;
el fablar es espada   e el callar su vayna. (*st.* 613)
    Talega es el callar,   e el algo que yaze
en ella es el fablar,   e prouecho non faze (*st.* 614)
    en quanto ençerrado   en ella estudiere:
non será más honrrado   por eillo cuyo fuere. (*st.* 615)
    El callar es ninguno,   que non meresçe nonbre,
e el fablar es alguno: por él es omne honbre. (*st.* 616)
    Figura el fablar   al callar e asy
non sabe el callar   de otri nin de sy. (*st.* 617)
    El fablar sabe byen   el callar rrazonar,
que mal guisado tyen   de lo gualardonar. (*st.* 618)

    Las bestias an afán   e mal por non fablar,
e los omres lo an   lo más por non callar. (*st.* 578)

He is a man of his own time in his quest of the golden
mean, usually termed *mesura* and occasionally *medida* in
Mediaeval vocabulary, and a precursor of Jorge Manrique
in his treatment of time:

Toda buena costomre   a çertera medida,
que si la pasa omre,   su bondat es perdida. (*st.* 112)
 Tal es vn dedo fuera   de la rraya signada
como si lueñe fuera   dende vna jornada. (*st.* 113)
 Cueydando que auía   menos el omre loco
en lo que se perdía   por mucho que por poco, (*st.* 114)
 quando por poco estoruo,   perdió lo que buscava,
del gran pesar que ovo   nunca se conortava. (*st.* 115)
 Non sab' que por cobrirse   del ojo cumple tanto
vn lienço com' si fuese   muro de cal e canto. (*st.* 116)
 Tanto sé lo que yaze   allende del destajo,
quanto sé lo que s' faze   el de allende de Tajo. (*st.* 117)
 Lo que suyo non era,   tanto son dos pasadas
lueñe d' él com' si fuera   dende vynte jornadas: (*st.* 118)
 tan lueñe está yer   como el año pasado.
A quien a de seer   de feridas guardado, (*st.* 119)
 tanto val vn escudo   entr' él e la saeta
como que todo el mundo   entr' él a ella meta, (*st.* 120)
 que pues non le firió,   tal es vn dedo çerca
d' él como la que dio   allende de la çerca. (*st.* 121)
 El día de yer tanto   alcançar non podriemos,
nin más nin menos, quanto   oy mil años fariemos. (*st.* 122)
 Non por mucho andar   alcançan lo pasado,
ni s' pierde por quedar   lo que non es llegado. (*st.* 123)

The poet temporarily loses in his race with time:

 Las mis canas teñílas,   non por las aborresçer,
nin por desdezyrlas,   nin mançebo paresçer, (*st.* 45)

mas con miedo sobejo   de omes que buscarían
en mí seso de viejo   e non lo fallarían. (*st.* 46)

but finds a means of vanquishing it:

De peligro e mengua   sy quieres seer quito,
guárdate de tu lengua,   e más de tu escribto. (*st.* 456)
De vna fabla, conquista   puede naçer, d' y muerte,
e de vna sola vista   creçe gran amor fuerte. (*st.* 457)
Pero lo que fablares,   sy escribto non es,
sy por tu pro fallares,   negarlu as después. (*st.* 458)
Negar lo que se dize,   a vezes a lugar,
mas sy escrybto yaze,   non se puede negar. (*st.* 459)
La palabra a pueca   sazón es olvidada,
e la escritura fynca   para syenpre guardada; (*st.* 460)
e la rrazón que puesta   non yaze en escryto,
tal es commo saeta   que non llega al fyto. (*st.* 461)
Los vnos de vna guisa   dizen, los otros de otra;
nunca de su pesquisa   vyene çierta obra: (*st.* 462)
de los qu' y estobieron,   pocos se acordarán
de cómo lo oyeron,   e non conçertarán. (*st.* 463)

as others before him had done (see selection on books,
above). Time is not alone in its disregard of man. Material
surroundings are fully as insensitive to human ills. In view
of a growing tendency among poets of the period to anthro-
pomorphize, the following selection on the impassivity of
natural surroundings is significant, and equally so the
poet's insistence on man's assuming full responsibility for
his own acts:

Del mundo mal dezymos,   e en él otro mal
non ha synon nos mismos,   nin vestigclos nin al. (*st.* 650)
El mundo non tyen ojo,   nin entyende fazer
a vn omne enojo   e a otro plazer. (*st.* 651)
Razónal' cada vno   segunt la su fazyenda,
él non ha con ninguno   amistad nin contyenda, (*st.* 652)
nin se paga nin se ensaña,   nin ama nin desama,
nin ha ninguna maña,   nin rresponde nin llama. (*st.* 653)
El es vno todavía   quanto es denostado,
atal commo el día,   que es muncho loado. (*st.* 654)
El viçioso rrazónal'   bien, tenlo por amigo;
el cuytado baldónal',   tienlo por enemigo. (*st.* 655)
Non le fallan ningunt   canbio los sabidores:
los canbios son segunt   los sus rreçebidores. (*st.* 656)
La espera del çielo   lo faze que no s' mesçe,
porque amor nin çelo   de cosa non le cresçe. (*st.* 657)
So vn çielo todavía   ençerrados yazemos,
fazemos noche e día   e nos al non sabemos. (*st.* 658)
A esta lueñe tierra,   mundo posymos nonbre:
sy verdat es o mentira,   d' él más non sabe omne. (*st.* 659)

The closing lines foreshadow Calderón's *La vida es sueño*. Indeed, the passage as a whole contains the lesson Segismundo must learn if he will change himself to man from beast.

The poet's recognition of the total indifference of both Nature and fellow-human toward the man of worth would seem to place Sem Tob among the pessimists:

Esfuerço en dos cosas   non puede omre tomar,
tanto son de dubdosas: el mundo e la mar. (*st.* 417)
　　Su bien non es seguro,   tan çiertos son sus camios,
nin es su plazer puro,   con sus malos rresabios: (*st.* 418)
　　torrna syn detenençia   la mar mansa muy brava,
e el mundo espreçia   oy al que ayer onrraua. (*st.* 419)
　　Porende el gran estadu   al omre de saber
　　faze bevyr cuytado   e tristeza auer. (*st.* 420)

but the resultant sadness is offset immediately by the ploce-
reinforced emphasis on the masterfulness of the man of
determination buffeted though he is by care:

El omre que es omre   syenpre bieve cueytado,
sy rryco o sy pobre   non le mengua cuydado. (*st.* 421)

It is man's ability to survive his disasters—*faze bevyr,
syenpre bieve*—that really counts. This particular selection
illustrates well Sem Tob's skill in finding the apt expression, in reducing universal nature synecdochally to one
syllable (*mar*) and in emphasizing in that one syllable
infinite oscillation as well as opposing extremes of motion.
In these stanzas, typically though less directly than is his
wont, he voices his preoccupation with the stress and the
paradox of ever-present antithetical forces: the constancy
of inconstancy, the unchangeableness of change, the in-
evitability of bitter after sweet, the containing of meek-
ness and fierceness in the same essence, the springing of
today's scorn and yesterday's honor from the same source.
Later he finds that man desires change, demands it almost,
and so explains, perhaps, an important principle of art—
and of progress:

> De más que es natura   del omre enojarse
> de lo que mucho tura   e conelio quexarse. (*st.* 473)
> Por tal de mudar cosa   nueba de cada día,
> por poco la fermosa   por fea camyiaría. (*st.* 474)

In his aphoristic and sometimes lyric manner Sem Tob can compress a whole poem into two lines and at the same time give us a lesson on perspective, such as that "beauty is in the eye of the beholder:"

> Plaz al ojo del lobo   con el polvo del ganado. (*st.* 164)

or consolation in the thought of the limitation of time's power:

> Quando la rrosa seca   e en su tienpo sale,
> el agua d' ella finca   rosada, que más vale. (*st.* 5)

or warning on the length of the liar's tongue:

> Non a cosa más larga   que lengua de mintroso,
> nin çima más amarga   a comienço sabroso. (*st.* 350)

The tone of the whole work is grave. Even the humor that sometimes shows through—often in the form of irony contained in paradox—is usually laden with seriousness, since in the poet's apraisal of existence balance between opposing forces is near absolute. An excellent illustration of Sem Tob's subtle humor is found in the example of the scissors, which presents well his thesis of matter's disinterestedness in man's existence and man's attempts to interfere with matter's functions, his observation concern-

ing the illusory nature of the submission of the inanimate
to the will of the animate, and also his lesson on the value
of brotherly love. The humor is achieved in part through
the gradual anthropomorphization of the scissors, in part
through unadornment of the truth, in part through the
measured and even pace corresponding to the inexorable-
ness of Nature's law, in part through the juxtaposition
of man's will and Nature's law and the view of man mas-
tered by his own creation and literally caught in his own
vise, but mostly through exposure of the foolishness of
attempting to disregard the laws of Nature (human will
versus the laws of physics):

Quien buena ermandat   aprender la quisyese,
e buena amizdat   vsar sabor obiese, (*st.* 514)
    syenpre meter debía   mientes en las tygeras,
e d' ellas aprendería   muchas buenas maneras, (*st.* 515)
    que quando meto mientes,   cosas tan derecheras
non fallo entre las gentes   commo son las tyseras: (*st.* 516)
    Parten al que las parte,   e non por se vengar,
synon con gran talante   que an de se legar. (*st.* 517)
    Como en rrío quedo,   el que s' metyó entre ellas
entró, e el su dedo   metió entre dos muelas. (*st.* 518)
    Quien mal rreçibió d' ellas,   él mesmo se lo busca,
que de su grado d' ellas   non buscarién mal nunca. (*st.* 519)
    Desque de entr' ellas sal,   con tanto son pagadas,
que nunca fazen mal   en quanto son juntadas. (*st.* 520)
    Yazen boca con boca   e manos sobre manos:
tan semejados nonca   non vy yo dos ermanos. (*st.* 521)
    Tan gran amor obieron,   leal e verdadero,

que amas se çiñeron   con vn solo çintero. (*st.* 522)
     Por el d' estar en vno,   syenpre amas a dos,
e fazer de dos vno,   fazen de vno dos. *(st.* 523)

Nature's mill-wheel persistence in her own way is seen as such, and not as the whim of the Fortune so dear to poets of the following century.

Unemotionally the poet contemplates natural phenomena to discover their essence, to become aware once again of the immutability of change, to learn to conduct himself in accord with his surroundings:

     Por eso a menudo   el omne entendido
a los canbios del mundo   está bien perçebido. (*st.* 638)

to be at one with the divine will:

     La merçed de Dios sola   es la fiuzia çierta:
otra ninguna, ¿dóla   en mundo que non mienta? (*st.* 643)
     De lo que a Dios plaze,   nos pesar non tomemos:
bien es quanto El faze   e nos no llo entendemos. (*st.* 644)
     Al omne más le dio,   e de mejor mercado,
de lo que entendió   que l' era más forçado. (*st.* 645)
     De lo que más prouecha,   de aquello más auemos:
pro del agua muecha   e del ayre tenemos; (*st.* 646)
     e syn fuego omne vida   vn punto non avría,
e syn fierro guarida   jamás non fallaría. (*st.* 647)

In his artistic imitation of homely style Sem Tob not only takes advantage of numerous rhetorical devices of his time in order to achieve the compression, concision, and apt phrasing that immediately individualize his style, but develops an original variation of the *mester de clerecía*. In adapting the current major poetic form to gnomic expression Sem Tob keeps his work relatively (though not entirely) free from dependency on narrative techniques, limits rather strictly the number of stanzas to be devoted to any one subject, dispenses almost entirely with modulation between sequences but makes abundant use of enjambment within a sequence, reduces the *cuaderna vía* quatrain to a couplet but retains the sense of quatrain by sharpening the caesura with riming of first hemistichs independently of the end-rime so that each stanza contains internal mono-rime different from and in addition to verse-end monorime, and consequently greatly alters the rhythmic effect of the Alexandrine, giving it on the one hand a short-interval regularity, and on the other, as offset, free-flow.

The *Proverbios morales* is not a collection of miscellaneous maxims. It is the orderly expression of Sem Tob's philosophic thought and poetic feeling. Mood is as clearly discernible as moral in spite of the poet's steadfastly calm attitude towards the vicissitudes of life and his imperturbability in accepting the seeming contradictions in universal being.

POEMA DE JOSE

In his account of the experiences of the Biblical figure of Joseph, son of Jacob, the anonymous author of the fourteenth-century *Poema de José* seldom strays for long into lyricism, so intent he is on telling his tale faithfully. For this reason it is pleasant to come unexpectedly upon a momentary burst of light and color and the sight of silkiness and precious stones in a description of Joseph, in which we see not the person but rather his effect.

The *cuaderna vía*, though it has lost some of its rigidity of measure, still serves the learned poet well, and his knowledge of the favourite poetic devices of the *mester de clerecía* is evident particularly in his use of hyperbaton, synthetic and synonymic parallelism, and contrast, in the enumerative effect of his measured statements, and in his dependence on narrative for purposes of description:

A pocos de días a la su tierra llegaron.

Yusuf luego fue suelto, en el río lo vaçiaron,

de púlpura e de seda muy bien lo aguisaron,

de piedras preçiosas muy bien lo agastonaron. (*st.* 58)

Cuando por la billa entró, las gentes se maravellaban,

el día era nublo e él bien lo aclaraba,
maguer que era oscuro, él bien lo blanqueaba,
por doquier que pasaba él todo lo alombraba. (*st.* 59)
    Deçían las gentes ad aquel mercadero
se era aquél ángel u hombre santurero;
dijo: "Anda mí es cativo leal e verdadero;
"querríalo vender, si l' fallase mercadero." (*st.* 60)

PERO LOPEZ DE AYALA

One of the finest examples of the *mester de clerecía* is certainly the *Rimado de palacio* by Pero López de Ayala (1332-1407), whose outstanding political career led to his attaining the chancellorship of Castile in 1398 and fitted him especially well for handling the sort of material on which he builds his poem. The work contains more than 1600 strophes, most of them in *cuaderna vía*. It was composed near the end of the century, and is the last known *mester de clerecía* poem in which the *cuaderna vía* was employed. Particular note should be given to the circumstances under which at least most of the composition was done: *Este libro fiço el honrrado caballero Pero López de Ayala estando preso e llámase El libro de palaçio.*

Contrition and religious faith are the predominating sentiments in the opening strophes of the *Rimado de palacio*. Contrition opens the way for the introduction of the theme of the Ten Commandments, all of which the poet declares he has broken. Like the Commandments, each of the seven deadly sins is treated individually and in each the poet confesses that he has indulged. Next come the seven Works of Mercy, which the poet states he has often left undone, and after them come the five senses, which he blames for their share of causing sinners' plight. Enumeration of the seven Works of the Holy Ghost *(las siete obras espirituales)* then gives him an opportunity to display corresponding sins of omission:

> Entre los mis pecados e mis muy grandes males,
> confesaré, Sennor, obras espirituales,
> que son siete por cuenta, aquí porné yo quáles,
> que non las conplir omne son pecados mortales. (*st.* 174)

With this list the compendium of Christian doctrine is completed, and the poet is free to turn his attention to other matters: plight of the Church in its schismatic condition, corruption in governmental, commercial, and professional affairs. The lengthy list of complaints brings him again to a consideration of abstract qualities: *justiçia, perdón, franquesa, del escaso, tenprança, humildat, fortitudo,* and *maliçia.* In a nineteen-stanza *Rogaria* he then prays to God for protection from sin and harm, and for forgiveness for his many errors, for which he feels that punishment is just. Contrition still is both theme and mood, and the appeal is for mercy and compassion for his weakness, and for strength to bear tribulation, instead of special favor of the moment. López de Ayala follows in a general way the earlier prayer pattern of the *Poema de Mío Cid,* of Berceo's works, and of the *Libro de buen amor,* but is concerned with deeper thought, manifests greater subjectivity, and composes with more unity and coherence. Enumeration of appropriate example to remind God of his past mercies now has lost its monotony and has become an effective ornament that gives relief from the concentration on the sinner-poet in his personal relationship with God.

The Biblical references, moreover, are slightly expanded by means of the rhetorical device of *amplificatio,* so that the reader is given an opportunity to ponder over the thought and to appreciate the image and its significance. Alternation between impersonal third person and personal first person has the effect of bringing universal man and specific individual together into one conscious being at once in consonance and in contradiction with the will of God. Words denoting somber thought and painful feeling fill the prayer to convey the moral message to the reader and make him wish to share the guilt and the punishment:

Sennor, tú nos defiende e nos guarda de ocasión;
asás fasemos yerros, de que pedimos perdón.
Si todo lo pensases, ¿quál sería aquel varón
que pueda sofrir las penas que meresçe con rasón? (*st.* 384)

Espeçialmente te ruego ¡o Sennor! humilmente
que en las mis tribulaçiones me fagas por paçiente,
verdadera paçiençia, verdadera me uenga miente,
ca tus dulçes castigos son enplasto al doliente. (*st.* 385)

Contra ti fui fallido, e en todo muy errado,
non ha punto en el día que yo pasé sin pecado,
en faser a ti enojo era todo mi cuydado,
mas la tu mano muy luenga çedo me ovo alcançado. (*st.* 386)

Como muy justo jues enbías el tu castigo,
sobre aquel que tú más amas e le tienes por amigo,
aquel que tú nunca vesitas cuéntolo por enemigo,
por ende yo, sennor, tengo que prouaste bien comigo.
                                        (*st.* 387)
En muchas mannas penas los que quieres castigar,

a los unos atormentas que te sepan confesar,
como fesiste al çiego, que non fue por el pecar
nin su padre nin su madre, mas tu gloria demostrar.

(*st.* 388)

Por probar su paçiençia al santo Job atormentaste,
liçençia de le dar penas a Satanás otorgaste,
e desque en él viste buena fe e le prouaste,
sobre el tu miserycordia muy ayna le tornaste. (*st.* 389)

Porque non soberueçiese Sant Pablo en las visiones,
resçibió muchos tormentos e muchas persecuçiones,
e sufrió en la su vida de la carne aguisones,
mas con la su fortalesa vençió las tribulaçiones. (*st.* 390)

A otro, Sennor, persigues, porque lo ves perdido,
en vanidat del mundo e pecados muy metido,
e porque, Sennor, non vaya al fuego ençendido,
aquel que tú vesitas non le pones en oluido. (*st.* 391)

Otros tú castigas por sienpre su pecado,
así como en Egipto, aquel pueblo porfiado,
desque lo açotaste y fue por ti llagado,
aquí e en el otro mundo fincó así condenado. (*st.* 392)

Una sennal avemos que podamos entender,
a quien les tú açotas por los tú bien faser,
aquéstos son, Sennor, los que a tu plaser
emiendan las sus vidas, non se quieren perder. (*st.* 393)

Al que en este mundo el bien nunca le fal,
nin pie le entropieça, nin nunca siente más mal,
non es buena salut, ésta es grave sennal,
Sennor, de tal ventura tú me guarda e tú me val. (*st.* 394)

Tu siervo so, Sennor, pobre criasón;
cunple la tu voluntad, asy como es rasón,
e si por mis pecados yo he d' auer tribulaçión,
sea en este mundo, e en el otro saluaçión. (*st.* 395)

 Por siempre te acuerda, non te olvides, Sennor,
que ayas piedat del flaco pecador,
que a ti, Sennor, conosçe, que fueste el formador,
que somos flaca masa, llena de mucho error. (*st.* 396)

 Agradéscote, Sennor, que quisiste castigar
este siervo tan malo, e aquí lo vesytar,
en ti es toda mi fiusia syn otro ningunt dudar;
acórreme, Sennor, que pueda bien acabar. (*st.* 397)

 Por la tu piedat grant tienpo me esperaste,
pecando de cada día, los mis yerros non cataste,
por la tu miserycordia muy manso me açotaste;
e ti espero merçed, pues aquí non me olvidaste. (*st.* 398)

 E qualquier cosa, Sennor, que tú esperes de mí,
lo tengo por mejor, e yo así lo entendí;
fas de mí lo que quisieres, todo tienpo e aquí;
si pasé persecuçiones, bien te lo meresçí. (*st.* 399)

 Non sé, Sennor, otra arma que tome en tal sasón,
con que yo me defienda de aquesta tribulaçión,
sinon lágrimas de sangre de todo mi coraçón,
e a ti devotamente faser sienpre oraçión. (*st.* 400)

 Pongo por abogada a tu madre Santa María,
aquélla que del mundo fue acorro e lus del día,
a quien sienpre me encomiendo e llamo todavía,
que por mí te ofresca aquesta petiçión mía. (*st.* 401)

De te faser oraçión, sienpre seré aperçebido,
con devoto coraçón e con todo vmil gemido,
e tengo grant esperança que seré yo oydo,
pues lo pido a Sennor sabidor e sofrido. (*st.* 402)

One of his greatest errors, he feels, is having served earthly masters when he should have been serving God. This thought he expresses as introduction to the *Fechos del palaçio:*

Grant tiempo de mi vida pasé mal despendiendo,
a sennores terrenales con grant cura syruiendo,
agora ya lo veo e lo vo entendiendo,
que quien y más trabaja más yrá perdiendo. (*st.* 422)

The long satire that follows is one of the best known portions of the poem. As he sees the situation, incompetence, indifference, and corruption, particularly bribery, have infected every individual at court, from the most insignificant doorman to the king himself (though the king is not included in the specific charge of bribery), and the lawyers thrive on fleecing the honest and trusting man who wishes merely to collect overdue wages earned in service to his country. The satire is cast in narrative rather than lyric form, and we follow the innocent subject as he becomes the victim of extortion at each effort, unsuccessful, to claim the wages due him. Even the reader feels frustrated before the end of the tedious repetition of exhausting and impoverishing effort as the poor man is shunted from one callously unconcerned individual to another, including the king himself. The monotonous style deliberately chosen for the passage contributes much to the mood of irritation engendered by the incidents themselves, each almost identical to the next. López de Ayala thus expands on one detail of a theme previously employed by Juan Ruiz in the selection *De la propiedat qu' el dinero ha*, but what Juan Ruiz saw as grim comedy and accepted as part of human living, López de Ayala sees as tragedy and moral decay, though he maintains, as did Juan Ruiz, strict impersonality in his satire, except for reference to the king.

In a more benevolent and reflective mood Ayala offers *Consejo para toda persona*, in which the passages on the themes of peace and death, in spite of their didacticism and a certain prolixity, bring to the reader the sensations of peace and melancholy and, if not an acceptance, at least an awareness, of the inevitable:

Eso mesmo te digo, por te bien consejar,
que en ti mesmo fagas la pas sienpre morar;
Dios te ayudará e te fará cobrar
este mundo e el otro, e te puede salvar. (*st.* 535)

Por mucho que ayunes e fagas oraçión,
y oygas muchas misas e muy luengo sermón,
e des muchas limosnas e a pobres raçión,
si pas en ti no ouieres, estarás en ocasión. (*st.* 536)

Ca si non perdonas al que te fallesçió,
e te dura rencor contra el que a ti erró,
la pas e caridat en ti ya fallesçió,
e quien sin ella ayuna, a tanto se perdió. (*st.* 537)

Dises el *Pater noster* e pides al Sennor:
"Sennor, tú perdona a mí muy pecador,
"asy como yo perdono a quien me fiso error,"
e por este dicho solo será tu judgador. (*st.* 538)

Non matara Caym a Abel, su hermano,
si touiera con pas el su coraçón sano,
nin Absalón fisiera la guerra tan en vano,
e contra David, su padre, non tendiera la mano. (*st.* 539)

Si en sí pas ouiera Judas aquel traydor,
nunca él pensara de vender al Sennor;
non puede el diablo ser nunca morador
en casa que ay pas, concordia e buen amor. (*st.* 540)

Quien este mundo ama e sigue su carrera,
acresçienta por çierto lenna en su foguera,
por mucho plaser que ha, mucho pesar espera,
e con mala vianda cobra mucha dentera. (*st.* 552)

Bien sabes tú por çierto, e non deues dudar,
ca la muerte non sabe a ninguno perdonar,
a grandes e pequennos todos quiere matar,
e todos en común por ella han de pasar. (*st.* 553)

Esta mata los moços, los mançebos loçanos,
los viejos e los fuertes, nunca los dexa sanos,
nin perdona los humildes, nin sobervios nin ufanos,
nin los pobres escapan, nin los ricos han manos. (*st.* 554)

Pues el que esto espera, ¿ por qué ensoberueçe?
¿ A qué enquiere riquesas? o ¿ por qué orgulleçe?
¿ Qué le cunplen las onrras a quien así podresçe?
ca todo en vna ora espantosa fallesçe. (*st.* 555)

Así como la sonbra nuestra vida se va,
que nunca más torna, nin de vos curará;
lo que aquí fasemos, allá se paresçerá,
o bien o mal qual fuere, tal galardón aurá. (*st.* 556)

Cuydo estar seguro a beuir luengamente,
ordeno mi fasienda muy solepnemente,
con mucha vanagloria, e non me viene miente
que antes que amanesca so muerto o doliente. (*st.* 557)

Desta vana fasanna cuenta nuestro Sennor
en el su Evangelio, por nos guardar de error,
de un rico que auía del mundo grant amor,
e non auía de muerte resçelo nin pauor. (*st.* 558)

Desía él asy: "Este anno que será,
"yo auré mucho vino, lo nuevo que verná,
"e mucho trigo e çeuada, e non me caberá
"en estos mis çilleros, si otro cobro non ha. (*st.* 559)

"Mis casas son pequennas, e non podrán caber
"estos vinos e panes que tengo de coger;
"mas he pensado al que quiero yo faser
"otras cosas más grandes, para tan grant auer." (*st.* 560)

Pensando en tal gloria vana e perigrosa,
oyera vna vos fuerte e muy espantosa:
"Mesquino, sey çierto que non te valdrá cosa,
"que esta noche non mueras muerte muy rebatosa." (*st.* 561)

Non está bien seguro el que así ha de caer,
nin deue ser alegre el que tanto ha de temer;
e por tanto, amigos, queramos nos doler,
non ayamos grant mal por tan poco plaser. (*st.* 562)

Oluidemos riquesas, non nos fagan çegar,
nin queramos thesoros tan fuertes allegar,
para bien las cobdiçie quien las quiere cobrar,
para partir a pobres e la suma saluar. (*st.* 563)

More abstract and less emotional than Juan Ruiz's account of death, López de Ayala's sermonet appeals to reason. In place of incessant activity of personified beings typical of some of the earlier works on the subject, López de Ayala creates a mood of calmness and, through merism (*st.* 553-554) and appropriate vocabulary, of expansion that foreshadows the serenity of a Jorge Manrique. He offers simple facts and advice, gently leading to a practical prescription for salvation. Death is about to become the agent of peace. The light and quiet melancholy that pervades the piece, the grave tone, the intangibility of inevitable death accentuate the lyric feeling that predominates in the selection in spite of the intruding narrative.

Lyric poetry as an independent genre and consciously composed as such in Castilian began to flourish widely in the fifteenth century, when it was collected and copied into *cancioneros,* that is, books in manuscript (or, by the end of the century, in print) containing, often along with poems in the *mester de clerecía* mode, strictly lyric or near-lyric heterogeneous compositions by various poets or, occasionally, by a single poet. The lyric compositions are usually short or relatively so and are independent of each other though at times a group of poems may be written on the same subject or be one of several "answers" *(respuestas)* of identical pattern in response to a "question" *(pregunta)* whose metric pattern and subject development constituted a model to be followed in each of the answers. Although the first known Castilian *cancionero,* the *Cancionero de Baena,* dates from the mid-fifteenth century, the idea for such a collection seems to have been evolving throughout the history of Spanish poetry. There were, of course, the various thirteenth-century (and later) Galician-Portuguese *cancioneiros* to serve as early models. All the long *mester*

de clerecía poems in Castilian that contain separable lyric
passages are in varying degree essentially of the nature of
the *cancioneros,* the fundamental difference being that the
lyric passages of the *mester de clerecía* are merely separable but not separate from the surrounding material, with
which they are attached by some sort of nexus, however
simple. In the *cancioneros* the prose rubric roughly corres-
ponds to the *mester de clerecía* nexus. The rubric, often
rather lengthy, normally acts as introduction to the poem
and gives any information necessary for the proper understanding of the subject treated or tells what prompted the
poet to compose his verses. Some poems, particularly the
short ones, were not infrequently left altogether without
a rubric or were given the barest of titles, the latter often
indicating nothing more than the type of poem presented,
such as *song, ditty, prayer.* It should be remarked—and the
fact emphasized—that writing of the older type of long
poem was by no means abandoned and poems in the *mester
de clerecía* can occasionally be found in the *cancioneros.*
The anonymous *Decir a las siete virtudes,* included in the
Cancionero de Baena, is a good example of the genre as it
had developed from the *mester de clerecía* and appeared
in the early fifteenth century. The growing tendency,
already evident in such works as the *Libro de buen amor*
and the *Proverbios morales,* to gather similar pieces together in one collection is particularly notable in the
Rimado de palacio.

In almost precisely the middle of his lengthy didactico-
satiric poem Ayala inserts what amounts to a little *cancionero* (stanzas 704-868), lyric in subject matter and expression, and varied in metric form and in genre. Explanatory
material, which serves as nexus-rubric, fuses with the main
part of the poem by means of the *cuaderna vía,* while the

individual poems (with two exceptions) are immediately distinguishable as separate entities by their differentiating metric forms. Verse forms include the *alejandrino* in its final stage of development (*i.e.*, transitional between *alejandrino* and octosyllable), the octosyllable at a transitional stage (between the primitive stiff form and the final flexible form), and the *verso de arte mayor*, a highly flexible verse popular in the fifteenth century but just beginning to appear at the end of the fourteenth. Strophe varies likewise, and includes the *cuaderna vía*, certain types of the *canción*, the *zéjel*, and the *copla de arte menor* and *copla de arte mayor*. In style as well as in form this little collection is transitional, sharing equally Mediaeval and pre-Renaissance traits.

The little *cancionero* recounts a sequence of emotional experiences and the poet's reactions to them: imprisonment (probably literal though possibly figurative also) with its tribulations and consequent testing of his patience (which calls up the example of Job), liberation and the joy and thanksgiving resulting from it, joy cut short and turned to sorrow and worry over the precarious schismatic situation of the Church, penitence following upon feelings of unworthiness, consolation in his devotion to Saint Mary and in his own learning and creative writing. Cut off as he is from all human succor, the poet is driven in upon himself, upon his religious faith as a passive sustaining force, and upon his own creative powers as an active defensive-offensive means of combatting the static pressure of his isolation and imprisonment. The order of the poems of this little *cancionero* follows the emotion cycle perfectly: emotion of disillusionment and frustration and fear and perhaps claustrophobia rises gradually to a point of near-frantic struggle for hope, expends its violence partly through

psychological effort and partly through physical means,
and, giving way to faith, subsides gradually, bringing the
poet to a state of passiveness and melancholy and peace of
mind, so that he is finally able to view his situation with
some objectivity and endure it with patience, and eventually
to return to hope.

Mediaeval poets commonly made laudatory remarks
about their own artistry, and expressed their intention to
use their talents for the benefit of God or of the Virgin
Mary. With like intent López de Ayala devoutly turns his
efforts to praise:

> Con buena entinçión segunt que Dios sabe,
> trabajo en faser estas tales cosas,
> pues otra sçiençia ninguna non cabe
> en mi cabeça, conpongo mis prosas
> loando aquella que es pura llaue
> de el parayso e flores e rosas:
> ésta es la Virgen a quien dixo *"Ave"*
> Gabriel, con otras palabras fermosas. (*st.* 826)

At the same time, and in a more intensely subjective mood
than we might expect to find in his day, and with a less
Mediaeval attitude, he confesses melancholically that as a
poet he derives solace from the practice of his art:

> Quando enojado e flaco me siento,
> tomo grant espaçio mi tienpo pasar
> en faser rimos, sy quier fasta çiento,
> ca tiran de mí enojo e pesar,
> pues pasa mi vida así como viento

oy si non cras sin más y tardar,
por me consolar éste es fundamento,
non es perder tienpo en oçio e vagar. (*st.* 827)

It was deep tribulation both physical and spiritual that caused him to seek the solace of creative lyric-writing and of religious devotion:

Non puedo alongar ya más el mi sermón,
ca estó tribulado en cuerpo e en coraçón,
e muy mucho enojado con aquesta mi prisión,
e quería tornar a Dios mi coraçón. (*st.* 704)

Quando aquí escriuía, estoue muy quexado,
de muchas grandes penas e de mucho cuydado,
con muy grandes gimidos a Dios era tornado,
rogarle que quisyere acorrer al cuytado. (*st.* 705)

E fise estonçe así por me más consolar,
pidiendo a Dios merçed, que me quisiese librar,
que quisiese valerme, sy me más oluidar,
disiendo asy aqueste mi cantar: (*st.* 706)

Cantar

Sennor, si tú has dada
tu sentençia contra mí,
por merçed te pido aquí
que me sea revocada. (st. 707)

Tú, Sennor, tienes judgado por tu alta prouidençia,
que emendando el pecado se mude la tu sentençia:
por ende con penitençia e con voluntad quebrantada,
he mi vida ordenada, por conplir lo que fallí:

Sennor, si tú has dada
tu sentençia contra mí,
por merçed te pido aquí
que me sea reuocada. (st. 708)

Con tu ayuda, Sennor, e de la Sennora mía,
podré yo muy pecador emendarme todavía,
e tu seruiçio será en cobrar esta vegada
vna oveja muy errada, que en el yermo me perdí.

Sennor, si tú has dada
tu sentençia contra mí,
por merçed te pido aquí
que me sea revocada. (st. 709)

Non sea yo desechado de la tu merçed muy grande,
e a sieruo tan errado con sanna non le demande,
e con cruesa non ande por juysio la tu spada,
e séame otorgada piedat sy fallesçí.

Sennor, si tú has dada
tu sentençia contra mí,
por merçed te pido aquí
que me sea reuocada. (st. 710)

Prayer turned to song (with refrain) here repeats in light
form the essence of the earlier *Rogaria,* but the near-
hopelessness and the harshness of the poet's situation can
be felt, and give special poignancy to the song. Note the
eight-plus-eight-syllable lines in which each hemistich
takes part in the rime, and that the full stanzas repeat
the rimes of the song refrain: *abba;cdcddaab,* etc.

The poet's own art brings him a measure of relief and confidence, and moves him to prolong the lyric mood he has created for himself:

Después deste cantar, finqué más spaçiado,
teniendo en Dios mi juisio de ser por él librado,
e por estar más firme, fise otro deytado,
a Dios me confesando, como sieruo culpado. (*st.* 711)

Deytado

Non entres en juisio con el tu siervo, Sennor,
ca yo so tu vençido e conosco mi error;
muestra tu piedat e tu bendito amor,
amansa la tu sanna e non paresca aquí,
e pueda en mi vida a ty dar loor
de los bienes e graçias que de ty resçebí. (*st.* 712)
Mucho pequé, Sennor, e contra ti erré,
los tus dies mandamientos muy poco los guardé,
con los çinco sentidos de todo mal obré,
obras de piedat muchas veses fally;
Sennor, merçed demando, pues creo la tu fee,
que aya yo perdón del mal que meresçy. (*st.* 713)
Gravemente pequé en otros muchos males,
en los siete pecados, que se nonbran mortales,
que si tú piadoso agora non me vales,
todos podrán desir que con rasón cay,
que yo veo mis culpas e mis yerros atales
que de otro pecador a tantos non ley. (*st.* 714)
De todas mis maldades fago mi confisión;

tú por la tu graçia dame la contriçión
que pueda en mis días conplir satisfacçión
de las menguas e yerros en que yo fallesçí,
e loaré el tu nombre sienpre toda sasón,
en cuya ley adoro después que yo nasçí. (*st.* 715)

Sufro, Sennor, tristura e penas cada día;
pero, Sennor, non sufro tanto como deuía,
mas he resçelo, Sennor, que por flaquesa mía
non lo pueda sofrir, por esto entendy
pedir a ti, Sennor, sy tu merçed sería
que non fuese la pena más luenga que sofrí. (*st.* 716)

De muchos enemigos, Sennor, soy perseguido,
contra el cuerpo e el alma de todo es mal traydo,
viuo vida penada, triste, aborresçido,
e si tú non me consuelas e ¿qué será de mí?
Acórreme, Sennor, e sea defendido,
por la tu santa graçia, non me pierda así. (*st.* 717)

De cada día fago a ti los mis clamores
con lloros e gemidos, sospiros e tremores,
ca tú solo, Dios, eres salud de pecadores,
cuyo acorro espero, e al non entendí.
Sennor mío, amansa mis llagas e dolores,
e vean enemigos a qué Sennor seruí. (*st.* 718)

Torna, Sennor, a mí tu fas, e toma mi oraçión,
non dexes que falesca en la tribulaçión,
la vos e mi gemido ayas toda sasón
porque todos entiendan que tu graçia sentí,

ca en la tu esperança tengo mi coraçón
sienpre noches e días, en al non comedí. (*st.* 719)
    A ti alço mis manos e muestro mi cuidado
que me libres, Sennor, non pase tan cuytado,
ca si me tú non vales fincaré oluidado,
e a ti loor non es que digan que perdí,
pues a tan alto Sennor yo so acomendado
con quien yo me fasta agora de todos defendí. (*st.* 720)
    Los días me fallesçen, el mal se me acreçienta,
non ha mal nin perigros qu' el mi coraçón non sienta;
Sennor, tú me defiende, non muera en tormenta,
e me pueda loar que con tu poder vençí
a los mis enemigos, e su pensar les mienta,
non digan que de acorro menguado pereçí. (*st.* 721)
    Grant tienpo ha que como mi pan con amargura,
nunca de mí se parten enojos e tristura;
Sennor, tú me ayuda e toma de mí cura,
e sea en penitençia el mal que padesçí,
e me libra de cuytas e cárcel e tristura,
e entienda que me vales después que a ti gemí. (*st.* 722)
    Sennor, si viuiere, por sienpre contaré
tus grandes maravillas e a ti loaré;
e si yo aquí muero, todo lo callaré,
nin podría desir nada de lo que vi:
por tu bondat lo fas, que yo sienpre erré,
de bienes que me diste poco te agradesçí. (*st.* 723)

    Sennora, tú me val, Virgen Santa María,
a quien sienpre me encomiendo de noche e de día,

e sey mi ayudadora e abogada mía,
e al tu Fijo bendito por mí ruega e di:
"Dame aqueste sieruo que me llama cada día,
"ca las sus oraçiones con lágrimas oy." (*st.* 724)

The first four stanzas of this *zéjel* in *alejandrinos* fuse in miniature a confession, a prayer, and a compendium of Christian doctrine, and by means of this miniature the *deytado* directly and quickly reflects the early part of the *Rimado de palacio* and so is blended with it. What follows this introduction is a convincing picture of the poet's torment. Strikingly he opens the body of the composition with the word *Sufro*, theme of the poem. In gradual crescendo he moves from *tristura* and *penas* through *soy perseguido contra el cuerpo e el alma, triste, aborresçido,* to a state of dramatic anguish shown in *clamores, lloros, gemidos, sospiros, tremores,* and from an almost benumbing paroxism that suddenly blots out the present, he turns to the suffering of the past (stanza 722), to the future for a moment, and then concludes with a slight bit of confession that completes a frame begun in the opening lines. As a sort of epilogue the poet calls on the Virgin to plead his cause. In this poem López de Ayala displays his skill in the use of the device of *amplificatio* and demonstrates his ability both to build and to sustain a mood.

The nexus-rubric following the *deytado* explains the next selection thus:

Acordándome sienpre de la sennora mía,
la su Madre, noble Virgen Santa María,
físele otra cantiga que quisiere mi vía
sienpre aderesçar, segunt menester auía. (*st.* 725)

Asás era quexado quando fis el cantar,
segunt son las palabras lo podedes notar,
disiendo: *"Aue Maria"*, la quise saludar
en estos pocos versos que d' ella fuy rimar. (*st.* 726)

The *cantiga* (or *cantar*) is an artfully complex gloss on the
Ave Maria, but one in which the text is not allowed to
protrude and in which no phrase of the text is limited to
a single gloss, or gloss to a specific length. A swirl effect
is produced in place of the rectilinear sequence of the usual
gloss, such as that by Juan Ruiz on the same text. The
last stanzas contain some elaboration on details of the text.
The poet almost—but not quite!—forgets himself and his
circumstances in writing this song, which reflects one of
the few pleasant moods of the doleful poet. Here López de
Ayala demonstrates well his ability to adapt the *cuaderna
vía* to song, as Berceo had done with the hymn:

Cantiga

Dios te salue, presçiosa Reyna de gran valía,
esfuerço e conorte de quien en ti se fía,
a ti viene tu sieruo ofreçerte este día
vna pequenna prosa, e dis: *Aue Maria*. (st. 727)

María, muy graçiosa, tu nonbre es loado,
así te llamó el ángel que a ti fue enbiado,
quando te saludara e te traxo recabdo
que fijo de Dios e omne en ti serié encarnado. (*st.* 728)

Graçia de Dios es contigo, e fue aquella sasón,
maguer ouiste espanto en el tu coraçón,

con mucha humildança e firme devoçión
dixiste: "Dios lo cunpla segunt el tu sermón". (*st.* 729)
 Llena de Spíritu Santo fueste, sennora mía,
e fincaste prennada del Saluador Mexía,
Virgen sienpre e donsella, que a tal porto conplía
el nasçimiento santo de quien esto fasía. (*st.* 730)
 El sennor Dios que crió el cielo e la mar
te quiso de tal don e tal graçia dotar
que tú fueses la Madre del que venía saluar
el humanal linage que fiso Adám pecar. (*st.* 731)
 Contigo trinidat allí fue ayuntada,
la corte çelestial en ty fiso morada,
Madre de Dios, Sposa, Fija, fueste llamada,
así eras de los santos antes profetisada. (*st.* 732)
 Vendicha tú, la Madre que a Dios conçebiste,
vendicha la muger que tal Fijo pariste,
vendicha la donçella que nunca corronpiste,
vendicha e loada que tal Fijo nos diste. (*st.* 733)
 Tú eres abogada de nos los pecadores,
a ti llaman los tristes e los que sienten dolores,
tú amansas cuidados, enojos e temores,
los que están en perigro a ti fasen clamores. (*st.* 734)
 En las mugeres todas tú fueste scogida
sola, Sennora mía, por quien ouieron vida
los que yasían en pena e en cuyta dolorida
en los bajos abismos por la culpa deuidos. (*st.* 735)
 Bendito es el que ayudas e en ti tiene sperança,
a los que así se te acomiendan acorres syn dudança,

por ti llegan al puerto de toda buen andança;
sennora, tú me vale en esta grant tribulança. (*st.* 736)
　　Fruto del tu vientre el mundo redimió;
lo que el primero omne por su culpa perdió
por él fue todo saluo que nos tal fruto dio;
sienpre sea bendicho, e así lo digo yo. (*st.* 737)
　　Jesús, nonbre muy santo, deuemos adorar,
fincando los ynojos lo deuemos nonbrar;
las virtudes del çielo a éste suelen loar,
delante él deuemos la tierra nos besar. (*st.* 738)
　　Santa María, Santa Virgen muy gloriosa,
de las flores tú flor e de las rosas rosa,
resçive estos versos, sennora piadosa,
del tu sieruo que padesçe pena muy perigrosa. (*st.* 739)
　　Ruega por mí, sennora, mucho lo he menester,
con la tu graçiosa ayuda non me quiera falleçer,
pues viuo muy penado bien me puedes acorrer,
ca toda mi fiusia en ti la fui poner. (*st.* 740)
　　Si de aquí tú me libras, sienpre te loaré,
las tus casas muy santas yo las vesitaré,
Monserrat e Guadalupe, e allí te seruiré,
alçando a ti las manos, muchas graçias te daré. (*st.* 741)

Another explanation follows, with its mention of comfort gained from lyric-writing:

Después que estas saludes aquí fuy escriuir,
e de la Virgen muy santa que sienpre amé seruir,
tomé en mí conorte, e fuy de mí partir

grant parte del enojo que me fasía morir. (*st.* 742)

Puse mi esfuerço e todo mi cuydado
en Dios e en su merçed, ca fuy luego acordado
del verso del profecta que dise al cuytado:
"Dexa en Dios tus quexas; él te porná recabdo." (*st.* 743)

Otrosí prometí luego mi romería
a la ymagen blanca de la Virgen María
que estaba en Toledo e que allí me ofreçía
con mis joyas e donas, segunt que yo deuía. (*st.* 744)

Fise dende luego vn pequenno cantar
e aquí lo escreuí por non lo olvidar:
quiera por su merçed ella me ayudar,
ca todo su esfuerço en ella fuy dexar. (*st.* 745)

The *cantar* so introduced is short and light in its *copla
de arte menor* form, but is weighted with the poet's cares.
It is the poet, not the Virgin, who is the real subject of the
poem, though poem and Virgin together fortify the poet
against the harshness of his imprisonment:

Cantar

Quando me veo quexado,
a ti fago mis clamores,
luego so conortado
de todos grandes dolores;
en ti son los mis amores
e serán con sperança
que me tires tribulança
e te sirva muy más ledo. (*st.* 746)
Sienpre oue devoçión

en la tu noble figura
a quien fago oraçión
quando yo siento tristura;
de mí quieras auer cura
pues spero perdonança
por ti, e en oluidança
non me dexes yaser quedo. (*st.* 747)
    Si tomaste contra mí
por los mis pecados sanna,
Sennora, te pido aquí
que non sea ya tamanna,
e a la mi cuyta estranna
acorre con alegrança
non muera en desesperança
e en tormento tan asedo. (*st.* 748)
    Sennora mía, muy franca,
por ti cuydo ir muy çedo
seruir tu imagen blanca
de la eglesia de Toledo. (*st.* 749)

The nexus-rubric that connects this *cantar* with the next one probably contains no exaggeration:

Esta cantiga me fiso mayor esfuerço tener
en esta Virgen muy santa, que tiene el poder
de valer a tal tormento qual yo yba padesçer
en la prisión tan dura que omne non podría creer. (*st.* 750)
    Yo estaua ençerrado en vna casa escura,
trabado de vna cadena asás grande e dura,

mi conorte era todo adorar la su figura,
ca nunca fallé christiano que de mí ouiese cura. (*st.* 751)
    Acordándome del mundo e de la su malandança,
e cómo es movediso e anda sienpre en balança,
tenía que no era estranno pasar yo tribulança,
dexé pensar en ello e puse en Dios mi sperança. (*st.* 752)
    Pero que non podía el mundo así del todo oluidar,
como si yo yasía en tan estrecho logar
oluidado de plaser e cansado de pesar,
fise luego deste fecho aqueste breue cantar. (*st.* 753)

The *cantar* that follows this introduction could pass as a troubadour love lyric. The light line and stanza *(copla de arte menor)*, the *lexaprende*, the emphasis on *tristura*, the contrast *tristura-grant cuidado* and *plaser-alegría*, the abandonment and the anger, the strange land, forgetfulness, dark prison, constant pain, sad heart are all from the lover's lament, but in this case the meaning is literal:

> *Tristura e grant cuidado*
> *son comigo todavía,*
> *pues plaser e alegría*
> *así m' an desanparado. (st.* 754)
>   Así m' an desanparado
> sin los nunca mereçer,
> ca sienpre amé plaser,
> de alegría muy pagado,
> e agora por mi pecado
> contra mí tomaron sanna,
> en esta tierra estranna

me dejaron oluidado.

La tristura e grant cuydado
son comigo todavía,
pues plaser e alegría
así m' an desanparado. (st. 755)

Dexáronme oluidado
en vna prisión escura,
de cuydado e tristura
me fallaron muy penado,
pues me vieron apartado,
nunca se parten de mí,
desde entonçe fasta aquí
dellos ando acompannado.

La tristura e grant cuydado
son comigo todavía,
pues plaser e alegría
asy m' an desanparado. (st. 756)

Dellos ando aconpannado
en mi triste coraçón,
sienpre e en toda sasón
lo tiene muy bien guardado,
e veo que a su grado
de mí non se partirán,
e comigo morarán
en cuanto fuere cuytado.

La tristura e grant cuydado
son comigo todavía,
pues plaser e alegría
asy m' an desanparado. (st. 757)

The tempered, undramatic sadness, like that of the Galician or Portuguese *saudade*, the grammatically passive position of the poet, the abstract quality of all nouns and adjectives except *tierra* and *prisión*, the unobtrusive nature of the verbs, together provide a sweet aftermath to the almost frenzied emotion of the *deytado*. The handling of the verbs with their subjects and objects is of special interest. In the active construction the poet is only twice the subject of a verb; otherwise he is either object or passive subject. Verb subjects denoting a positive mood are pleasure and happiness, and those denoting a negative one are sadness and care. The verbs are often dependent on an adjectival past participle to complete their meaning or are intransitive or denote mental rather than physical action, and consequently lack some of the force normally expected of a verb. This special selection and treatment of verbs contributes to the subjectivity and the delicate emotional charm of the poem.

With the composing of this song complete serenity returns to the poet, who compares his lot with that of Job:

Después d' esto, acordé dexar así de pensar
en el mundo, e torné a otra rasón cuydar,
de lo qu' el santo Job desía por nos conortar,
sus palabras virtuosas quales yo podré contar. (*st.* 758)

Si bienes resçebimos muy grandes del Sennor,
rasón es que soportemos al, si viniere peor,
ca bienes tribulaçiones sienpre son al pecador:
Dios lo parte como él quiere, conuiene ser sofridor *(st.* 759)

e tomar en paçiençia las penas que nos dará,
e darle por ello graçias, e él por su merced querrá

acorrer a las cuytas con el grant poder que ha,
ca sienpre así lo fase e lo fiso e lo fará. (*st.* 760)

E torné luego a faser a Dios mi petiçión
e pedirle por merçed desta tribulaçión
que me libre e me guarde e me dé consolaçión,
e fise yo luego esta pobre oraçión: (*st.* 761)

The *Oración* that follows (stanzas 762-774) is a neatly constructed theme-with-variations composition the body of which consists of the expected examples of liberation, one per stanza. The final appeal (stanza 774) is to Saint Mary to plead his case for him. López de Ayala follows the standard Mediaeval prayer pattern, but now in utmost perfection.

Little by little the poet's anguish has been assuaged and his hope renewed:

El día que acabé este cantar faser,
tomé en mí esfuerço, conorte e plaser:
Dios me acorrerá al mi grant menester,
pues toda mi esperança en él yba poner. (*st.* 775)

In his new confidence he ceases dwelling on past and present tribulations, he looks upward and to the future, and makes a promise, and the promise inspires him to compose a new song:

Cantar

Sennora, por quanto supe
tus acorros, en ti espero,
e a tu casa en Guadalupe
prometo de ser romero. (st. 780)

Tú muy dulçe melesina fueste sienpre a cuytados,
e acorriste muy ayna a los tus encomendados,
por ende en mis cuidados e mi prisión tan dura,
vesitar la tu figura fue mi talante primero.

> *Sennora, por quanto supe*
> *tus acorros, en ti spero,*
> *e a tu casa en Guadalupe*
> *prometo de ser romero. (st.* 781)

En mis cuytas todavía sienpre te llamo, Sennora,
¡o dulçe abogada mía!, e por ende te adora
el mi coraçón agora en esta muy grant tristura,
por él cuydo auer folgura e conorte verdadero.

> *Sennora, por quanto supe*
> *tus acorros, en ti spero,*
> *e a tu casa en Guadalupe*
> *prometo de ser romero. (st.* 782)

Tú que eres la estrella que guardas a los errados,
amansa mi querella, e perdón de mis pecados
tú me gana, e oluidados sean por la tu mesura,
e me lleua aquel altura do es el plaser entero.

> *Sennora, por quanto supe*
> *tus acorros, en ti spero,*
> *e a tu casa en Guadalupe*
> *prometo de ser romero. (st.* 783)

Release from prison does come to him, but thanksgiving is not followed by joy: a new sadness falls upon the

poet for the schism in the Church. The schism becomes
the topic of his longest *deytado*. The poem, which is written
entirely in *coplas de arte mayor*, begins with a sustained
metaphor:

> La naue de sant Pedro pasa grande tormenta,
> e non cura ninguno de la ir a acorrer;
> de mill e tresientos e ocho con setenta
> asy la veo fuerte padesçer,
> e quien lo puede non quiere valer,
> e asy está en punto de ser anegada
> sy Dios non acorre aquesta vegada
> por su misericordia, segunt suele faser. (*st.* 794)
> Veo grandes ondas e ola espantosa,
> el piélago grande, el mastel fendido,
> seguro non falla el puerto de posa,
> el su gouernalle está enflaqueçido
> de los marineros e puesto en oluido,
> las áncoras fuertes non le tienen prouecho,
> sus tablas por fuerça quebradas de fecho,
> acorro de cabres paresçe perdido. (*st.* 795)

the meaning of which is then explained in detail.

A series of *cantares* to Saint Mary, in *coplas de arte
menor*, and a *deytado* in *cuaderna vía* bring the *cancionero*
to a close. One of the *cantares* is unusual for its refreshing
imagery:

> *Sennora, estrella lusiente*
> *que a todo el mundo guía,*

guía a este tu seruiente
que su alma en ti fía. (st. 830)

A canela bien oliente
eres sennora conparada,
de la tierra del Oriente
es olor muy apreçiada.
A ti fas clamor la gente
en sus cuytas todavía,
quien por pecador se siente
llamando: "¡Santa María!"

Sennora, estrella lusiente
que a todo el mundo guía,
guía a este tu seruiente
que su alma en ti fía. (st. 831)

Al cedro en la altura
te conpara Salomón,
eguala tu fermosura
al ciprés del monte Sión;
palma fresca en verdura,
fermosa e de grant valía,
oliua la Escriptura
te llama, Sennora mía.

Sennora, estrella lusiente
que a todo el mundo guía,
guía a este tu seruiente
que su alma en ti fía. (st. 832)

De la mar eres estrella,
del çielo puerta lunbrosa,

después del parto donsella,
de Dios Padre fija, esposa.
Tú amansaste la querella
que por Eua a nos uenía,
e el mal que fiso ella
por ti ouo mejoría.
  Sennora, estrella lusiente
  que todo el mundo guía,
  guía a este tu seruiente
  que su alma en ti fía. (st. 833)

The melancholy poet moves back to the didactic, re-counting at great length the trials of Job, with whom he feels close kinship, since with Job's life his ran a close parallel. Other moral lessons follow, and some of them are embellished with examples from the Old Testament. Although most of the verses of these sections are rather prosaic, some of them contain lyric expressions, but these are sporadic.

DIEGO HURTADO DE MENDOZA: *Cossante*

Diego Hurtado de Mendoza (d. 1404), contemporary of López de Ayala and father of Iñigo López de Mendoza, Marqués de Santillana, was one of the early poets who followed closely the Galician-Portuguese *cancioneiro* tradition in writing poetry in Castilian. He was attracted particularly to the song and dance elements characteristic of types based on popular poetic expression, and is best known for his lilting *Cossante:*

A aquel árbol que mueve la foxa
algo se le antoxa.

Aquel árbol del bel mirar
façe de manyera flores quiere dar:
algo se le antoxa.

Aquel árbol del bel veyer
façe de manyera quiere floreçer:
algo se le antoxa.

Façe de manyera flores quiere dar;
ya se demuestra, salidlas mirar:
algo se le antoxa.

Façe de manyera quiere floreçer;
ya se demuestra, salidlas a ver:
algo se le antoxa.

Ya se demuestra, salidlas mirar,
vengan las damas las fructas cortar:
algo se le antoxa.

Seemingly simple, the poem is relatively complex. Although the basic technique is theme-with-variations, variation is reduced to the barest minimum, whereas repetition and parallelism are at a maximum. An exceedingly tight interweaving of stylistic devices subtly yet strongly suggests choral dancing. The repetition of marked rhythmic beat is accentuated not only by regular and frequent repetition of the refrain but also by the interlocking anaphora involving whole phrases (a-ab-ab-bc-bc-cd), by the regular double alternation of the rime (paroxytonic introductory verse and refrain as against oxytonic body-verses; oxytonic body-couplets consonating alternately in -*ar* and -*er*), and by the synonymy and the near-epiphora in the intertwined *mirar-ver* endings. This chain-like structure contains both image and motion of dancers in circular or semi-circular formation in which the participants take turns in pantomiming solo parts. The use of anaphora parallels exactly a progression of involvement in the poem: *a* draws our eyes to the tree and its over-all beauty; *b* follows each succeeding *a* immediately to narrow the scope of our perception to the abstract detail of the *algo* that approaches the concrete but never quite achieves it in the concept wavering between the tangible fulfillment *flower (flores)* and the pure intangible inceptive action of *flowering (floreçer);* midway in the poem *a*, the object observed, is replaced by *c*, the observer, and intertwines with *b*, which has now replaced *a* in the relative position of the stanza, and in so doing has been triply emphasized—first by immediate repetition of itself, second by gaining first-line position in the stanza, and third by serving as the constant in the body of the poem and so joining securely *a* and *c*, observed and observer.

Spring's call here is basically equivalent to that of the May poem of the *Libro de Alexandre,* but what a world of refinement in but a century of time! In the earlier poem the human activity engendered by the season sprawls about, and the reader is expected to have the desire to participate in the rollicking. There is no central figure. Reactions to springtime are physical and emotional, elemental, uninhibited, reduced almost to animal level. In the *cossante* attention is directed to one figure, the burgeoning tree (sometimes interpreted symbolically as the tree of love), and feeling is concentrated in a single reaction, delicate and purely aesthetic. The reader is invited to share vicariously in the extasy of birth-giving. There is a gentle balance between human perceptive appreciation and a phenomenon of nature—and one recalls immediately the almond blossom of Calderón's *La vida es sueño.* Progress in lyric technique is evident in this complete reversal of focus. Accumulation and amassing of materials is no longer necessary. Against the earlier compression of a broad scene into a given small space, as in Berceo's introduction to the *Milagros de Nuestra Señora,* we here find elaboration on a single detail. The poet is able to sum up poignantly in one detail the whole feeling of springtime, to catch the thrill of witnessing for a single instant the stage at which life and new beauty are on the verge of coming into being, to stay that fleeting moment.

This *cossante* appears, appropriately and by strange coincidence, at the precise moment when Castilian lyric poetry is on the verge of achieving independent existence. With amazing exactness it describes the state of that poetry at that specific moment: *face de manyera flores quiere dar.*

BIBLIOGRAPHY

Texts of the selections presented are based on the following editions (in each case the first listed edition is the one most closely followed and from which line or stanza numbering is taken):

Poema de Mío Cid

Cantares del Cid Campeador, conocidos con el nombre de Poema del Cid, ed. Florencio Janer in *Poetas castellanos anteriores al siglo XV* (Madrid, 1864) *(Biblioteca de Autores Españoles,* vol. 57); *Poema de Mío Cid,* ed. Ramón Menéndez Pidal (Madrid, 1923) *(Clásicos Castellanos,* vol. 24)

Razón de amor

Ramón Menéndez Pidal, "Razón de amor con los denuestos del agua y el vino," *Revue Hispanique,* XIII (1905), pp. 602-618; G. H. London, "The *Razón de amor* and the *Denuestos del agua y el vino,*" *Romance Philology,* XIX (1965), pp. 28-47.

Gonzalo de Berceo

Poesías de Gonzalo de Berceo, ed. Florencio Janer, *op. cit.; Milagros de Nuestra Señora,* ed. A. G. Solalinde

(Madrid, 1922) *(Clásicos Castellanos,* vol. 44)

El libro de Alexandre

> *El libro de Alexandre,* ed. Florencio Janer, *op. cit.;*
> *El libro de Alexandre,* ed. Raymond S. Willis, Jr.
> (Princeton and Paris, 1934).

Poema de Fernán González

> *Lehendas del Conde Don Fernando de Castylla, cono-*
> *cidas con el nombre de Poema del Conde Fernán Gon-*
> *zález,* ed. Florencio Janer, *op. cit.; Poema de Fernán*
> *Gonçalez,* ed. C. Carroll Marden (Baltimore, 1904).

Historia Troyana

> *Historia Troyana en prosa y verso, texto de hacia 1270,*
> publicada por R. Menéndez Pidal con la cooperación
> de E. Varón Vallejo (Madrid, 1934) *(Revista de Filo-*
> *logía Española,* Anejo XVIII).

Juan Ruiz, Arcipreste de Hita

> *Libro de Cantares de Joan Roiz, Arçipreste de Fita,*
> ed. Florencio Janer, *op. cit.; Libro de buen amor,* ed.
> Julio Cejador y Frauca, 2 vols. (Madrid, 1913) *(Clá-*
> *sicos Castellanos,* vols. 14 and 17).

Alfonso XI: Cantiga

> Selection No. 209, beginning *Em hum tiempo cogi*
> *flores,* in the *Cancioneiro portuguez da Vaticana,* ed·
> Theophilo Braga (Lisboa, 1878), p. 42.

Poema de Alfonso Onceno

> *Poema de Alfonso Onceno, Rey de Castilla y de León,*
> ed. Florencio Janer, *op. cit.; El poema de Alfonso XI,*
> ed. Yo Ten Cate (Madrid, 1956) *(Revista de Filología*
> *Española,* Anejo LXV).

Sem Tob de Carrión
Santob de Carrión: *Proverbios morales,* ed. Ig. González Llubera, Cambridge, 1947).

Poema de José
Poema de José ed. Florencio Janer, *op. cit.*

Pero López de Ayala
Rimado de Palacio, ed. Florencio Janer, *op. cit.;* Poesías del Canciller Pero López de Ayala, ed. Albert F. Kuersteiner, vol. I (New York, 1920).

Diego Hurtado de Mendoza: Cossante
Selection without title, ed. José Amador de los Ríos, *Historia crítica de la literatura española,* vol. V (Madrid, 1864), pp. 293-294.

Other works quoted or specifically mentioned include:

Andreas Capellanus, *The Art of Courtly Love,* trans. John J. Parry (New York, 1959, second printing 1964) [trans. of *De arte honeste amandi*].

Chaytor, H. J., *The Troubadours* (Cambridge, 1912)

Green, Otis H., *Spain and the Western Tradition: The Castilian Mind in Literature from* El Cid *to Calderón,* vol. I (Madison, 1963).

Santillana, Marqués de (Iñigo López de Mendoza), *Letter of the Marquis of Santillana to Don Peter, Constable of Portugal,* ed. Antonio R. Pastor and Edgar Prestage (Oxford, 1927).

The International Encyclopaedic Dictionary (Press Publishing Co., Chicago, 1901).

Webster's New International Dictionary of the English Language, second edition (Springfield, 1935)

Highly recommended as a reference work is:

Encyclopedia of Poetry and Poetics, ed. Alex Preminger, Frank J. Warnke, and O. B. Hardison, Jr. (Princeton, 1965).

GLOSSARY OF LITERARY TERMS

accentual meter: verse measure system based on the number of predetermined stress beats per line and the pattern of their distribution. The most common patterns (rhythmic units) are: trochee (óo), iamb (oó), dactyl (óoo), amphibrach (oóo), anapest (ooó).

agudo: oxytone or oxytonic.

alba: dawn song recounting the parting of lovers at dawn.

alejandrino: a bipartite line of seven-plus-seven syllables. See: Spanish count.

allegory: the literary (narrative, poetic, dramatic) representation of an abstract idea (moral, philosophic, etc.) as incarnated or otherwise informed or figured, or of the interaction of two or more such ideas.

alliteration: repetition of the same sound or sounds in two or more words standing near each other.

allusion: indirect or passing mention or reference to something assumed to be too well known to need further identification or explanation. The reader is expected to supply amplification with additional facts as needed to complete the thought suggested by the allusion.

a lo divino: an expression describing a work or type of work that has been turned from profane to religious purpose either through minor modifications (such as change of names, epithets, etc.) or through close imitation of style and subject matter. *A lo profano* is the expression denoting the contrary.

amphibrach: See: accentual meter.

amplificatio(n): the enlarging on a subject, usually by the addition of details, especially for the purposes of explanation or rhetorical effect. Dilation.

anadiplosis: the repetition of all or part of the last line of one stanza in the first line of the next. The repetition may also affect clauses regardless of meter. Called by the troubadours *lexaprende, lexaprén,* or *dexaprende.*

anapest: See: accentual meter.

anaphora: repetition of a word or expression at the beginning of two or more successive clauses, lines, or stanzas.

annominatio: a form of alliteration in which a whole word is repeated.

antanaclasis: repetition of a word with change of sense or in resuming the thread of discourse.

antepenult: the syllable preceding the penult.

anthropomorphism, anthropomorphization: the attribution of human form or traits to non-human beings or objects.

anticlimax: progression of ideas or words in descending order of importance in meaning to give the effect of belittling or of lessening of importance of the subject under consideration.

antithesis: vivid contrast achieved by means of the

conspicuous placing of words or passages of opposite meaning.

antithetic(al) parallelism: See: parallelism.

aphorism: a concise statement of a universal truth.

apocope: the omission of the final letter(s) or syllable of a word.

apologue: a moral allegory, usually in the form of an animal story.

apostrophe: words usually breaking the thread of discourse and addressed to a person present or to an absent, dead, or personified being as if it were a present and living person.

arte mayor: See: *verso de arte mayor, copla de arte mayor.*

assonance: in Spanish, the riming of vowels only, that is, of the last stressed vowel and the last vowel (or stressed vowel of a diphthong) of one line with the corresponding vowels of another, without regard for other vowels or for consonants.

asyndeton: omission of conjunctions or certain other particles in a series of parallel words, phrases, or clauses, especially for rhetorical effect.

auqueira: See: *serranilla.*

caesura: a pause midway in a line of poetry, specifically a predetermined metric pause coinciding with a rhetorical pause, usually at or near the middle of the line (called *medial* caesura as opposed to *initial* or *terminal* caesura).

canción de vela: vigil song.

cancioneiro: the Portuguese or Galician-Portuguese equivalent of the Spanish *cancionero.*

cancionero: a book containing an assortment of poems written either by various poets or by a single poet.

cantar: a song, or words for a song.

cantiga or cántiga: a song, or words for a song.

cantiga de amigo: a plaint (usually Galician-Portuguese) sung by a maiden in lamenting the absence of her lover.

catalogue verse: verse containing lists of persons, places, things, or ideas which have a common denominator such as heroism, learning, a special quality or property.

chiasmus: reversal of the order of terms in one of two corresponding phrases or clauses that would be parallel except for the inversion.

circumlocution: a roundabout statement substituted for a simple one. Periphrasis.

climactic parallelism: See: parallelism.

climax: the highest point of importance or force in the ascending progression of ideas expressed in a series of words, phrases, clauses, recorded events, etc.

cobla continuada: a monorimed stanza.

común, in the expression *arte común:* the use of a new set of rimes in each stanza of a poem.

consonance: in Spanish, the riming of both vowels and consonants from the stressed vowel to and including the final sound—not to be confused with the English term denoting the riming of consonants only in words in which the vowels in rime position differ.

contrast: juxtaposition of sounds, words, ideas, etc. having opposite effects or meanings, in order to give emphasis or startling effect.

copla: stanza.

copla de arte mayor: a stanza (usually an octave divided into two equal parts the lines of which rime in alternate (ABAB) or enclosing (ABBA) pattern) composed of *versos de arte mayor.*

copla de arte menor: a stanza corresponding to the *copla de arte mayor* in pattern, but written in octosyllabic, or shorter, verse.

correlative verse: verse containing a list of words of the same part of speech, usually nouns or verbs, followed by a verse containing a list of words of a different part of speech but corresponding vertically to the list in the preceding line.

cossante: a type of poem the technique for the composition of which is based on the techniques of popular song and dance.

couplet: two consecutive monorimed lines, or a stanza composed of two such lines.

cuaderna vía: monorimed quatrains composed of *alejandrino* verse.

cumulative parallelism: See: parallelism.

dactyl: See: accentual meter.

debate: a poetic argument between two persons or, more often, between two personified beings.

derivatio: paronym.

dexaprende: lexaprén.

deytado: a poem (apparently a generic term).

dieresis: the distribution into separate syllables of the vowels that normally form a diphthong or triphthong. Note: vowels of a diphthong formed from a Latin single vowel *(ie* from *e, ue* from *o)* cannot be so divided.

dirge: a lamentation, often a song, for the dead. It

may include eulogy of the deceased, consolatory remarks for the mourners, prayer, and other appropriately solemn forms.

doublet: a pair (of synonyms, epithets, etc.).

drut: Old Provençal term denoting the troubadour's position (accepted lover) in the fourth and final stage in the service of love (see quotation from Chaytor in chapter on *Razón de amor*).

elision: the suppression of a final vowel of a word before an initial vowel of the following word.

encadenado: repetition of the final word of one line as the initial word of the next.

endecha: a dirge or lament, usually written in short verse having a single assonance in alternating lines.

enjamb(e)ment: run-on, that is, the continuing in one line or hemistich an unfinished phrase or clause ending the preceding line or hemistich.

entendedor: Old Provençal term denoting the troubadour's position (recognized suitor) in the third of four stages in the service of love (see quotation from Chaytor in the chapter on *Razón de amor*).

enumeration: a form of synecdoche consisting of a listing of related objects, qualities, events, personages, etc., usually to give an idea of an entirety.

envelope stanza: a stanza beginning and ending with the same word, phrase, or line.

epic: a poem, usually lengthy, recounting the heroic deeds of a popular national personage.

epigram: a brief poem consisting of a witty expression of an observation or thought.

epilogue: a short passage, often one of address to the

reader or patron, appended to the main body of a work as a sort of second and sometimes only loosely related conclusion.

epiphonema: An exclamatory sentence or climactic statement placed at the end of a passage or poem.

epiphora: the ending of two or more successive lines (or clauses or sentences) with the same word(s).

epithet: a descriptive word or phrase, often of metaphorical character, designating a special quality peculiar to a specific person, or sometimes to a thing, to whose name it may be attached or whose name it may replace.

esdrújulo: proparoxytone or proparoxytonic.

exclamation: an emphatic utterance expressing sudden strong emotion.

fable: a story (often of animals personified) intended to teach a moral.

fegnedor: Old Provençal term denoting the troubadour's position (of aspirant) in the first of four stages in the service of love (see quotation from Chaytor in chapter on *Razón de amor*).

fin' amors: idealized love (of the troubadours) as opposed to *fol' amors*, lust.

fol' amors: concupiscence, in the troubadours' treatment of the love theme.

gloss: amplification of a text. Usually one line of the text becomes the theme of one stanza, in proper succession, and is repeated verbatim in that stanza, most often appearing as its final line.

gnome: a brief, condensed, and usually sharp or witty statement of a universal truth.

gozo: a lyric poem relating usually a series of joys of

Saint Mary (annunciation, conception, adoration by the Magi, etc.) or similar subject.

grave: paroxytone or paroxytonic.

hemistich: half (or approximately half) a line having mid-caesura.

heptasyllable: a line of seven syllables or their equivalent. See Spanish count.

hiatus: in Spanish verse, the counting separately of contiguous vowels of separate words, so that in the count a new syllable begins with the initial vowel of the second word.

hyperbaton: transposition of the normal (prose) word order of a phrase or clause.

hyperbole: an obvious and great exaggeration, employed for emphasis or for pure embellishment.

hypotyposis: vivid description, especially of unrealistic or imagined things.

hypozeuxis: the use of successive complete clauses in parallel construction.

iamb: See: accentual meter.

image: a literary figuration.

imagery: literary figurations (images) used for the sake of clarity, mood building, directing of the imagination, embellishment, and similar purposes.

irony: a type of humor, or sometimes of pathos, involving a parallel, usually two meanings—one superficial and one parallel underlying true meaning—that superficially are or may seem to be opposites. Expression contrary to meaning. Occurrence of the logical but unexpected.

laisse: a term used in connection with epic and certain types of popular verse of the *mester de juglaría;* it denotes strophic division characterized by irregularity of length and by monorime in assonance. A new *laisse* is indicated by change in assonance.

lexaprén, lexaprende, or *lexa-prende:* a form of anadiplosis in which all or part of the last line of a stanza is repeated in the first line of the next. The words repeated may be given in the same or another order.

litotes: understatement, usually a statement in the negative denoting in reality the opposite, affirmative, concept.

llano: synonym of *grave,* that is, paroxytone or paroxytonic.

lyric: see discussion in first chapter.

maestría mayor, in the expression *arte de maestría mayor:* repetition of the rimes of the first stanza in each of the following stanzas of the poem.

maestría menor, in the expression *arte de maestría menor:* synonymous with the term *media maestría* and denoting riming that involves the repetition of at least one rime (but not all—see *maestría mayor)* of the first stanza in each stanza throughout the poem.

mansobre: thought to be alternation (or other scheme) of rimes closely related through the root of the riming word; *derivatio* employed in sets of words in rime position (Old Provençal *rims derivatius).*

maxim: a brief succinct statement usually concerning moral behaviour or containing a statement of universal truth.

merism: a form of synecdoche in which a totality is expressed by the mention of contrasting parts.

mester de clerecía: see first chapter.

mester de juglaría: see first chapter.

metabasis: transition from subject to subject.

metaphor: the naming of one object or idea in place of another with which it has some trait in common.

metastasis: change of subject, especially sudden transition.

metonymy: the use of one word for another to which it is closely related, such as cause for effect or effect for cause, possessor for possession, place for its product.

minstrel: a late Mediaeval popular entertainer *(juglar)* who recited compositions of the *mester de juglaría* type.

modulation: art of transition from one subject or mood to another, especially of transition without a break in the continuity of the thought.

monologue: a speech uttered by one person.

monorime: identical end-rime throughout a stanza, *laisse,* or poem.

nexus: a short passage that serves primarily to link smoothly two longer passages, one preceding and one following. *Cf.* modulation.

octave: an eight-line stanza.

octosyllable: a line having eight syllables or their equivalent, Spanish count (which see).

onomatopoeia: the use of words whose sound suggests their meaning.

oxytone: a word having the main stress on the last syllable.

palilogy: the immediate and conspicuous repetition of a word or phrase.

palinode: a retraction or recantation, in Mediaeval poetry often concerning wordly love.

paradox: a seeming contradiction or self-contradiction.

paragoge: the addition of a vowel or a syllable at the end of a word.

parallelism: equivalence of construction of two or more consecutive lines, phrases, clauses, or passages. Verse parallelism has been divided into the following types: 1) *synonymic* or *synonymous,* in which the second line repeats the thought of the first, 2) *antithetical,* in which the second line states a contrast to the first, 3) *synthetic* or *cumulative,* in which the second line completes, supplements, or continues the thought stated in the first, and may be one of a series of such lines, and 4) *climactic,* in which the second line continues and augments the thought begun in the first, and may be one of a series of such lines.

paraphrase: a restatement of a text by way of variation on it, often in the form of amplification.

pareado: couplet.

parody: a comic imitation of a literary work or convention, sometimes for the purpose of ridicule, sometimes for sheer entertainment.

paronymy: use of words having the same root. Also called polyptoton, paregmenon, *derivatio.*

paroxytone: a word whose principle stress falls on the penult.

pastorela: See: *serranilla.*

penult: the next-to-the-last syllable of a word.

periphrasis: an indirect and roundabout expression used in place of a direct and shorter one. Circumlocution.

personification: the representation of an object, an idea, or a non-human being as a person.

plaint: a complaint or a lament, usually in the form of a song or a lyric poem.

ploce: the reiteration of a word for the purpose of intensifying its meaning.

polysyndeton: the repetition of conjunctions or certain other particles connecting or introducing words, phrases, or clauses of a series.

precador: Old Provençal term denoting the troubadour's position (as suppliant) in the second of four stages in the service of love (see quotation from Chaytor in chapter on *Razón de amor*).

pregunta: a question propounded in a poem and calling for an answer in the form of a *respuesta*.

proparoxytone: a word whose inner stress falls on the antepenult.

prosopopoeia: the representation of an absent or dead person as present and living; sometimes personification.

psychomorphism: the attribution of human mental and emotional processes to non-human beings and objects.

quatrain: a stanza having four lines.

refrain: a stanza, regularly shorter than those of the body of the poem, containing the theme of the poem and repeated at set intervals, most commonly after each stanza, of the poem. The meter of the refrain is not necessarily the same as that of the body of the poem.

respuesta: an answer to a *pregunta*. The *respuesta* must be of the same length and follow exactly the same metric form as the *pregunta* and, if possible, even repeat the *pregunta's* rimes and their order. Frequently more than one poet writes a *respuesta* to a single *pregunta*.

rhetorical question: a question propounded not to be

answered directly but to emphasize an idea or to cause the reader to ponder over the subject of the question.

rhythmic unit: a cluster of two or more syllables having a given stress pattern and commonly used as the basis of measure in accentual meter (which see).

rime, rhyme: the correspondence of sound in the final syllable(s) of two or more words. The rime begins normally with the last stressed vowel, and may involve vowels only or both vowels and consonants (see *assonance* and *consonance*).

romance: a ballad written usually in octosyllabic verse and riming in a single assonance throughout but in the even-numbered lines only. Occasionally a *romance* is written in another meter and/or may have another type and pattern of rime, such as the couplet in consonance.

romance fronterizo: a historical or pseudo-historical *romance* describing frontier warfare between Christians and Moors.

rubric: a title or identification preceding a poem, and any explanation that may either follow or replace the title.

romancero: a collection of *romances,* or *romances* collectively.

satire: a poem or other literary work of attack on human vice or folly, the latter sometimes broadly interpreted. Ridicule of a literary work or convention, usually in the form of parody.

senhal: a pseudonym by which the troubadour lover refers to his lady in order to hide her identity and so to protect her reputation.

series: a succession of like elements (usually words, but sometimes phrases or clauses) in parallel construction.

sermonet: a miniature sermon or a sermon-like passage.

serranilla: a short poem narrating the chance meeting and ensuing dialogue of a gentleman and a shepherdess or any rustic maiden, and in which the worldly-wise gentleman usually wooes, and wins or loses, his intended victim. In Provençal poetry the form was usually called *pastorela,* or, if the maiden was tending animals other than sheep (such as cows or geese) the name sometimes changed accordingly, as, for example, *vaqueira, auqueira.*

simile: an explanatory comparison of one thing to another that it resembles in some respect. A simile begins with an introductory word such as *like* or *as.*

Spanish count: Spanish syllable-count verse is measured by the number of syllables per line, the syllables being counted to *one* (and *only,* one) *beyond* the last stressed syllable whether such posttonic syllable is present or not, that is, oxytones and proparoxytones are counted as if they were paroxytones. In early poetry hiatus and dieresis were common; in later poetry (mid-fifteenth century and after) these were largely avoided and were gradually replaced by frequent synaloepha and not infrequent synaeresis.

stanza: a group of two or more successive lines arranged in predetermined pattern (including rime scheme) forming a unit within a poem.

strophe: a stanza or a *laisse.*

syllabic meter: verse measure determined by the number of syllables per line (see Spanish count). The most commonly used verses so measured are: tetrasyllable, pentasyllable, hexasyllable, heptasyllable, octosyllable, enneasyllable, decasyllable, hendecasyllable, dodecasyllable, tridecasyllable, tetradecasyllable, having, respectivey, 4, 5, 6, 7, 8, 9, 10, 11, 12, 13 and 14 syllables. The Spanish terms are, respectively, *tetrasílabo, pentasílabo, hexa-*

sílabo, heptasílabo, octosílabo (or *arte real, pie de romance*), *eneasílabo* (or *nonisílabo, novesílabo*), *decasílabo, endeca-sílabo, dodecasílabo, tredecasílabo* (or *tredesílabo*), *tetra-decasílabo.*

synaeresis: the forming of a diphthong or triphthong from consecutive vowels that normally belong to separate syllables within a word.

syn(a)esthesia: the appeal to one sense by stimulation of another, *e.g.,* a sweet cry.

synaloepha: the joining together and counting as if they were in one syllable contiguous vowels of separate words.

synecdoche: a figure of speech in which a part re-presents or suggests the whole, or the whole the part.

synonymic parallelism: See: parallelism.

synonymous parallelism: See: parallelism.

synonomy: the use of synonyms for explication, em-phasis, amplification, or embellishment.

synthetic parallelism: See: parallelism.

trochee: See: accentual meter.

troubadour: late Mediaeval poet the major theme of whose compositions was generally courtly love. The most famous were from Provence, in southern France.

vaqueira: See: *serranilla.*

verso de arte mayor: a type of line, popular in the late fourteenth century and throughout the fifteenth, in which the measure is determined more by stress beat than by syllable count. The rhythm is amphibrachic, and the line is divided into two hemistichs having the time-measure of six syllables each, though first and last syllables of the hemistich are often actually missing.

zéjel: in its simplest form, a poem composed of stanzas riming *aaab, cccb, dddb,* and so on, the *b* rime remaining constant throughout the poem. Loosely, any poem in which this pattern forms the basis of the metric structure and is clearly discernible in it.

zeugma: the use of one word to govern or modify two or more words in the same sentence.